A Woman's Wealth

MASCOT BOOKS

www.mascotbooks.com

A Woman's Wealth: Wisdom for Building Personal and Financial Security

For more information, please contact:
Mascot Books, an imprint of Amplify Publishing Group
620 Herndon Parkway, Suite 220
Herndon, VA 20170
info@mascotbooks.com

Library of Congress Control Number: 2024919447

CPSIA Code: PRV0924A

ISBN-13: 978-1-63755-872-0

Printed in the United States

This book is dedicated to us: the women who persevered to share knowledge with other women wanting to build financial independence and security. Meeting in homes, restaurants, phone calls, and Zoom meetings, we got it done—*despite* everything else we had going on in our lives. It seems a woman's work is never finished, and the days run long, but the passion to share our stories and life experiences with others made it all possible.

We also thank the significant others who shared this endeavor. You were there for us as we skipped family meals and events here and there so we could put in the hours writing. We are grateful to you. A special callout to Mascot Books for working with us over several years to bring our work to the public.

A Woman's Wealth

Wisdom for Building Personal and Financial Security

WOMEN ON MONEY COLLECTIVE

CONTENTS

INTRODUCTION

SHARED WISDOM FROM WOMEN ON MONEY

Kathleen Tedesco
MBA, financial planner

This book came about because a group of friends in varying professional disciplines wanted to help other women achieve financial security, for themselves and for the ones they love. Frustrated with the gaps in understanding and practicality we often see slowing women's progress in achieving their goals, we began speaking publicly—in seminars, and even on local television—about money for women. We want to break the "money silence"—that is, the reluctance of many women to discuss financial subjects with their significant others. We want to make this necessary topic safe to discuss in dealing with life decisions.

Too often, financial decisions are an exercise in relationship dysfunction. Healthy, balanced relationships, in our view, should allow partners to engage with each other on almost any subject—including money. For single people, financial decisions need to be made with honesty and purpose. There may be no one to catch you if you fall.

Almost any decision or transaction you enter into is protected or regulated by our system of law. Our most intimate relationship, marriage, is of course protected and governed by statutory and case law. Going into a marriage, or coming out of one—through divorce, or the death of a spouse—presents financial challenges, as well as the joy or sorrow of sharing one's life with another. Financing a household and children takes a practical approach, as does long-term wealth-building.

In writing this book, the authors recognize that you may feel unprepared for what you feel is your current priority in ordering your life. We are writing with this thought in mind—to allow you to board the bus from any stop, and start moving forward to your desired destination.

In an effort to have a more impactful discussion—one that will allow you to move forward within a sixty- to ninety-day time period—we will structure this book as if we are sharing insights into a new diet plan. Week by week, month by month, you choose which goals to set. We offer "recipes" for a process to accomplish those goals.

Each of the women in this authors' circle decided to contribute because of some person or event that inspired her earlier in life. We will each share these revelation moments as we lay out a starting foundation for you in the various money-related spheres we address. There is a reason we are all here having this conversation. We want you to feel more certain of your financial success and security. We want you to assert your role in your personal finances. This behavior will benefit you and protect your children and your family.

Since we will be sharing insights, and what I will call "Aha!" moments, I will tell you one of mine. In my twenties, I was hired into my first corporate job. I was earning a much higher salary, but I was still making the transition from a small business that I owned with a partner. I had no retirement savings—a fact brought to my attention by the CPA I hired to do my tax filing. He explained how I could invest in an IRA—individual retirement account—to lower my tax bill and start the process of accumulating long-term savings.

I headed off to a securities brokerage to open an account. At that time, rules governing brokers were less stringent; so I found myself, in my naïveté, steered into a perfectly unsuitable investment. The broker of the day quote-unquote "sold" me, a woman with no savings or securities, warrants on a junk bond. I discovered my error within a day or so and got mad at myself, and at him for placing me into a very risky investment. Really mad.

So, I did some research. I marched back into the brokerage office to demand that the same broker sell my junk bond warrants. I chose not to close the IRA; instead, I told him to use the proceeds to buy me shares of the then recent public stock offering of a major software company. My experiences with investments progressed after that, and I added to the account each year, or I made a 401(k) plan contribution.

The lesson learned, for me, was to always do my own homework and make my own decisions. I now find trusted professionals to counsel me when there is something I really don't know. I was proud of myself for standing my ground and not slinking away, embarrassed at my mistake. The outcome was significant as I started down the path of becoming an investor, rather than a woman looking for a lower tax bill.

In this book, we will assume you want to start wherever you may be in life—whether you are a beginner, or have some years of experience or professional experts to guide you. Whatever the starting point, we will help you set your goals. You will then decide upon the strategies to begin getting there. Follow the week-by-week program to do this after consulting the relevant subject chapter for your needs. You will find the trajectory that makes sense for you.

Too often, women trust others without fully examining the facts of the situation. This book will help you verify your choices and put you on a solid foundation for realizing your initiatives in personal finance—whether these involve planning for marriage or divorce, buying or selling property, or building assets for retirement. The authors of this book address money in all of its aspects, including credit, estate planning, family law, investments, mortgages, savings, starting a business, Social Security, and taxes. Additionally, we discuss how to negotiate and draft contracts to protect your interests for any matters involving money with significant others.

Above all, don't just stand where you are. If you are stuck—for lack of confidence or knowledge—and unable to progress, then know you have resources to turn to. Women are in your community in a variety of professions to mentor and guide you. We, as authors, were each mentored by others and chose to give back to help other women by writing this book.

If you have comments to share with us, please send them to us via our publisher, Mascot Books.

San Rafael, California
September 2022

CHAPTER ONE

RUNNING A BUSINESS WHILE OVERCOMING RACIAL AND GENDER BIAS

Letitia Hanke

Entrepreneur and CEO of Alternative Roofing Solutions, Inc., DBA ARS Roofing and Gutters; founder of The LIME Foundation

"When you think of quitting, remember why you started." –John Di Lemme

I am the chief executive officer of a roofing and construction company employing twenty-three people year-round in northern California. Owning my own business enabled me to build security and income that supported me and my son. I am also the founder and president of a nonprofit foundation that I created to advocate for underserved communities. Our three programs are designed to serve our seniors, veterans, and at-risk youth to address adversities that they face—such as bullying, racism, and low self-esteem. I am writing this chapter to tell my story and what I have learned over the years.

When I was five years old, my parents moved my brother and me from Berkeley, California, to a small town in Lake County called Middletown, California. Anybody who is familiar with Lake County knows that Black Americans are few there. The public school that we attended was pretty much an all-white school. In the entire school, grades K-12, with approximately eight hundred kids, there were only about seven Black students.

There were kids that had literally never seen a Black person before. At times, they were brutal to me: They would spit on me, pull my hair, call me "nappy headed," or find some way to body-shame or "color"-shame me. They called me "blacky," "darky," and "Hershey bar" (although I do love me some Hershey bar); but they would also call me "ugly," or "dumb nigger." I was told I would never amount to anything because I was Black.

Teachers saw this cruelty, but they looked the other way and ignored it. They saw kids push me to the ground and steal my lunch or punch me in the stomach because I was on the see-saw before them; yet they never reported it. This torture started when I was five and lasted until I was nine. I started believing that I was ugly and dumb, and I hated that I was different. Many times, I wondered, "Why do they hate me?"

To add to the bullying, I was sexually molested by a family member in the summer of 1983 when I was seven years old. I didn't know what to do; who to talk to; who to tell. My parents had just spent their life savings to move us to the country for a better life. Little did they know, my life had become so much worse.

I was a deeply depressed and confused little girl. *How do I tell my father, a Pentecostal minister, about my sexual abuse? How do I tell my mother that her little girl is being spit on at school because of the color of my skin?*

I ended up doing the only thing I could do: hide. At lunch, I found a place behind a big oak tree where I could hide and kids wouldn't find me. I could eat my lunch in peace and listen to music on my Walkman. It was my heaven.

One day, when I was eight years old, my music teacher came to me and asked me if I would like to learn how to play the trumpet.

"Why not?" I said.

She told me to come to her classroom at lunch. Every day, she put a trumpet in my hands and taught me how to play. It was a way for me to get away from those bullies and channel all that loneliness and sadness into expressing myself through music.

I played that trumpet every day. I learned how to read music. I started playing with the elementary band. By the time I was nine years old, I was put in the high school band, and things changed for me. I made friends with my high-school bandmates, and luckily many came to my rescue when those bullies would come at me.

I began believing in myself. My confidence level rose, and I started excelling in school and making more friends. Although my self-esteem had been boosted, kids continued to attempt to break me down. They would tease me about my "big lips," especially when I played the trumpet. My lips were so big that they would spill over the sides of the trumpet mouthpiece. It was just something else they could bully me about. I gave up on the trumpet; I took up piano and drums instead.

Throughout elementary and high school, I continued with my music. Music made me come alive; it gave me an outlet and let me escape to a calm place.

I graduated from high school a year early, mainly because I couldn't wait to get away. I was anxious to get out into the world. My bullies said I would never amount to anything, but I wanted to prove them wrong.

After graduating from high school at seventeen, I went straight to college. I was accepted to the University of California at Berkeley and California State University at Sonoma, but I ended up going to Sonoma State University in Rohnert Park because it was more of a small-town school. I decided that I wanted to become a rock star, so my major was Music in the Recording and Performing Arts, with Communications as my minor.

My freshman year, I set myself up to go to school full-time and work part-time on campus. I met a woman on campus who recommended a vocal jazz class that she was taking. I was three credits short for my class schedule, so I said, "Why not?"

After a few public performances in my vocal jazz class, several bands asked me to sing with them at local gigs. I had the time of my life going to gigs on the weekend and writing music in the recording studio. I was going to school full-time, working three jobs, and gigging on the weekends.

In 1996—my junior year—I realized that I really wasn't having the typical college life because I was working so much. I wanted to be able to have more time to gig and write music, so I made the decision to find a single well-paying job. That's when I started my first roofing company job.

I worked for a roofing company for about a year and a half as the receptionist—answering phones, filing, and such . . . until I caught the office manager embezzling from the boss.

I didn't know what to do. They had been best friends for thirty years. In the end, I did what any other person would probably do: I made sure the boss knew the truth. I spoke to the accountant, and she relayed my evidence to the boss. The boss fired his friend as the office manager. Instead of hiring another office manager, he came to me. He asked if I felt that I could do the office manager's job.

I said, "Why not?" He offered me the position, and I accepted it. I knew I could do the job. I just needed to believe in myself.

Over the course of eight years, I was promoted from receptionist to office manager, and then to management. My boss decided that he wanted to retire. He asked me to buy his company. But I wasn't a roofer; how was I supposed to own a roofing company without knowing how to roof? So, for four years, my boss trained me, and I learned roofing so I could get my own contractor's license.

Unfortunately, I had to steer my own course away from him when it became clear that he had intentions for me that I did not share. He began to make sexual gestures towards me. I remember working late nights in the office and seeing him looking at racy magazines in his office across from mine. One day, he came over to me and showed me a lingerie magazine.

"You would look really good in this," he said. It was a photo of a Black lady in a red lace teddy. I laughed it off and buried my head back in my work.

A few months later, he came to me and said, straight-up, "You know, I just want to let you know that I'm highly attracted to you. I know you would never do anything because I'm your boss and everything, but I just wanted you to know that."

Naturally, I was stunned and uncomfortable. "You're right . . . I would never do anything," I replied.

He didn't harass me again after that, but I couldn't trust that he would back off for good. I didn't wait to find out.

In 2004, I passed the Contractors State License Board. I started my own roofing company. This was my chance to show that I would amount to something.

But owning a roofing construction company as a Black woman came with many challenges. The industry was not very accepting of me, and I found myself doing what I had learned to do when I was up against a challenge: I hid. So, for many years as the CEO of my own company, I would sign my name "L.R. Hanke" instead of "Letitia Hanke" so no one would know that I was female. I wore jeans and boots with polo shirts or flannels to blend in with the guys.

I remember my first networking event. It was a construction networking dinner with about fifty people. Most of them were men, and the few women in the room were their wives or the office managers of the companies. I was the only female CEO there, but I was willing to give it a shot and see if I could connect with some contractors.

I walked up to the bar to get my drink. There were three contractors standing at the bar, drinking beer. One of the contractor's asked, "Hey, you work for ARS Roofing, huh?" He looked down at my polo shirt with my logo on it.

"Yes. I'm actually the CEO," I replied.

He snickered. "Ha! From the kitchen to the rooftop, huh?"

His other contractor buddies laughed.

Now, what do you think my response was? I know some of you would have had a lot to say, probably with many expletives; but in that moment of "hiding" . . . I chuckled.

Needless to say, I never went to that meeting again.

I found myself having to overcome fears dating from my childhood. It wasn't until years later that I finally broke out of my former self—the scared child.

I was able to break free, ironically, because of an unpleasant encounter with two prospective clients.

Our initial conversation on the phone was positive. The couple said they were quite interested in hiring my roofing company. I offered to bring roofing samples and the contract to their home so we could finalize the deal.

Upon my arrival at their home, the wife opened the door, gasped, and took a step back.

It startled me for a moment, but then I stuck out my hand. "Hello! I'm Letitia. Nice to meet you in person."

She reluctantly shook my hand. Her husband appeared at the door, and I immediately stuck my hand out to shake his.

"Roy. It's so nice to finally meet you," I said.

Roy looked down at my hand, back up at my face, down at my hand again, and walked away.

At that point, I really wasn't sure what to do. Eleanor invited me into their kitchen. Roy had disappeared into their family room area. I proceeded anyway.

"Which roof did you decide on?" I asked Eleanor.

Eleanor immediately got antsy. "Actually, we've decided not to do the roof this year, but we appreciate that you came out."

This didn't make any sense at all. As of two days earlier, they were ready to sign. Attempting to salvage the deal, I said, "I understand. Well, I brought the sample boards that you requested. Would you like to look at the roofing colors and make a note for when you're ready?"

"Let's just do that on your way out," she said.

She stood up, and I gathered my items and made my way toward the door. Roy came back in.

"I just want to let you know that we have an alarm system in our house, and if anyone tries to break in, it's going to go off really loudly," Roy said.

Silence.

I replied with a smile. "Thank you very much for that information. You both have a nice day."

I got in my car, drove around the corner, pulled over, and bawled my eyes out. Their blatant racism took me back to those days of being called "blacky" and "n-word." I couldn't stop crying for over half an hour.

I resolved to never feel that way again. I wasn't going to give up. I made the biggest decision of my life that day: *I wasn't going to hide anymore.*

I drove back to my office, told my staff about what happened, and put the client's proposal through a shredder. I didn't want or need to do business with people like that.

I decided to rebuild my branding image around me: a capable Black woman with a skilled roofing crew. Within weeks, I completely revamped my business and myself. I got out of those jeans and flannels and started dressing like the CEO that I was. I put my full name on everything: "Letitia Hanke." I posted my photo on all of my marketing tools to ensure that everyone would know that I'm Black and I'm female.

This move catapulted my business. In a couple short years, my company increased in value from 2 million dollars to 3.4 million dollars. This success ignited my passion for giving back to others, especially those who have suffered as I have.

YOUR TIME TO CHECK IN

So, you have decided you want a business—one that you will create and run. What will drive you to persist when the going gets tough? How can you scale your operations and navigate any headwinds you encounter? Make a list of your responses. This is the start of your ninety-day plan.

If you have a business already, what goals did you previously consider unattainable? How can you push yourself to another milestone? Make a list. Identify what you can do in ninety days, accomplish your goal, and roll to the next.

KEEP THE SPARK GROWING

Not satisfied with just running my roofing and construction company, I started my nonprofit, The LIME Foundation, in 2015. "LIME" is my son Emil's name spelled backwards. When he was seven years old, kids started calling him names and bullying him for being multiracial. They called him "Lime" instead of his name, "Emil."

I sat him down and told him, for the first time, about the bullying that I had endured. I explained to him that he must be strong and never let those bullies get him down. He took those words to heart; he's the most resilient kid I know.

Now, I spend most of my time with my nonprofit helping young people overcome their struggles in life. I help them find a way to express themselves and to find their light through music, creativity, and performing arts.

My other program, The Nextgen Trades Academy, offers education and training in the construction trades to help disadvantaged and minority youth get into a lucrative career. Our young people are going through so much, and sometimes they just need a few words of encouragement to turn their lives around.

So, when you enter this world of business entrepreneurship, it's important for you to know that your story is an important part of your success and the success of others. Your story is what will help you persevere through whatever is thrown at you—and there will be stuff thrown at you; just know that now. Continue to dig deep and just keep on keeping on, but most of all: "When you think of quitting, remember why you started."

NINETY-DAY WRAP-UP

- Write a list of self-defeating thoughts or attitudes that you want to overcome.
- Write a list of your business milestones, one by one, for each ninety-day period.
- Identify obstacles.
- Find your mentors who can help you on the path.
- Don't let go. Persist.
- Be proud of who you are, the company you create, and your employees.
- Celebrate your milestones.
- Stay with your intentions. Build on them.
- Pray to your higher power for peace and guidance.
- Share your story.

CHAPTER TWO

IT'S YOUR MONEY—TAKE CONTROL

Kathleen Tedesco
MBA, financial planner

In taking charge of your finances to accomplish another goal—something you really want to do you—you first need to take stock of where you are. Assess. Judge where you are in life, in dollars and cents; and judge where you are in the continuum of where you want to be ten or twenty years from now.

Usually, people who read this chapter do not start from ground zero in their planning. They read with a specific goal in mind—something yet to accomplish. Others are seeking help in clearing the clutter to get the goal done.

Before I begin my topic, let me share something about what drives me. I became a professional financial planner in my industry as a passion, as well as a livelihood. Early in my working career, I saw friends and family face life crises, with sometimes disastrous results. My own parents lived the proverbial "paycheck to paycheck" life, never having enough left over each month to pay all of the bills and house and feed a family of six. I vowed never in my adult life to return to that way of living.

Two marriages and one child later, I can say that I probably landed on my feet better than most after a divorce transition. But my success was hard-won. It evolved as I drew my boundaries on my goals and my spending. While married, I sometimes found myself unable to negotiate the very intimate topic of money with my partners. Money was a taboo topic; asking questions about money inevitably resulted in a disagreement, with my spouses imposing their will on mine.

Over time, this imbalance did not work for me. My accommodating personality finally snapped when the father of my child chose his "wants" over my child's needs. My younger self tended to cave in the face of obstinance; but finally, I had had enough.

Over time, I acquired skills and trained in mediation techniques to negotiate confrontation more effectively. My goal now is to achieve compromises more skillfully. Through my seminars and public talks, I seek to help other women get on a steady course to financial success to protect themselves, their children, and others they care about.

So, let's get clarity on where to start with financial planning. I suggest a ninety-day boot camp approach to overcome your tendencies to procrastinate.

First, know what you have. Dig through the clutter if you must, assemble your documents, and create a balance sheet and cash flow statement for your household.

Let's talk about clutter. It can be mental or physical, but either way, it impedes your ability to focus on achieving positive outcomes in the months and years ahead.

Financial clutter can be the "stuff" of accumulated small purchases, or it can be the outcome of big decisions with consequences.

Discussions about how to manage the financial clutter or the outcomes can cause friction with our significant others.

While anything can be negotiated, often money decisions are not. As in my own experience, women in relationships often cede control over this necessary resource to their significant other. Women who are single shoulder more responsibility in this respect, as the outcomes are theirs alone.

In this game of sums, you will need to find motivation to keep striving for the better numbers that will fund your life transitions and goals. So as the conversation begins, and begins deep, what are your goals? What are your values? What is really the priority for you and your family, or for you alone? What things in life really gratify and motivate you? Where are the roadblocks that prevent you from achieving more of this realization?

Wherever you are in your choices for moving toward your goal, you need to take stock to formulate the right set of actions for moving forward. For this, I will refer you to the addendums in the back of this book to inventory what you have and what you spend.

As you inventory, you will begin to see the disconnects or gaps in your knowledge that will need to be bridged. You will see what conversations you will need to have to obtain missing information and other information that affects your financial security, as well as that of your family and children.

Life evolves, as we know, in an incremental fashion—day-to-day. Whatever action you take as the result of reading this book will set you on a trajectory to get to where you want to be. You should have expectations of when you need to see result. Using my sixty- to ninety-day work plan format, you can create momentum that, if carried through, can make a difference.

Perhaps you opened the mail today and saw one too many bills. Perhaps you realized, after reviewing your bank statements, that paying off your student loan could take years, and would necessitate hard decisions about how to align goals with your everyday obligations. Or maybe you are fortunate to have cash piling up in a bank account, but are not sure how to shepherd these assets to buy a home or to start an investment program.

Sometimes, the impetus is a life change, like marriage, death, or divorce.

Whatever the trigger, you are here, on this page, wanting to assess your situation. Knowing where you are will allow you to steer yourself towards where you want to be. For sixty to ninety days, you will take week-by-week actions to put the key in the ignition and start driving down the road. This is a road trip, with many twists and turns along the way and unforeseen events. If you are married, or in a committed relationship, involve your partner. You will be sharing the driving and the discovery of your resolve.

I often think about how single-minded and focused my most successful clients have been. Saving for the future often means giving up something in the immediacy of today, and taking satisfaction in another form. Getting your heart aligned with your head comes more naturally if you have a spiritual or value-based approach to life.

Money is not an abstract concept. Money is a resource that allows us a standard of living. Before you use it on "wants," rather than needs—or on status, rather than pragmatism—ask yourself: What really motivates you? What would really make you happy?

Often the answer that I hear is that money buys the freedom of time with family. Time is the most precious resource any of us can own. Some people also say that money buys security and freedom from want.

Whatever your motive may be, use it to motivate yourself on the path to incremental realization of your goal.

So, what are you about? What keeps you up at night? What goal, if left unaccomplished, would become a deep regret later in life? The answers to these questions will help lead you on the path you have chosen.

CASE STUDY: WHY WOMEN NEED TO OWN THEIR FINANCIAL LIVES

Years ago, a friend of mine on the West Coast called me suddenly and blurted out the unexpected words, "My husband has died."

I recall with regret that I said to her, "Is this a joke? He is forty-two."

I was stunned. I did not believe a man so young could just suddenly die.

She explained that her husband had a bad cold, and that it became pneumonia. He died that day, at home, alone, after refusing to see a doctor. She returned from work, accompanied by her two-year-old daughter, and found his lifeless body on the floor with an arm outstretched to a phone—presumably, to call for help.

When I received her call, I was in New York City working on my finance degree. My dear friend, who had served as my maid of honor at my wedding just a year before, lived in southern California. (I will call her "Candy" for the remainder of this story.) She was ten years younger than her husband. She was uninformed about financial matters; and clearly, she was distraught. I asked how I could help.

I flew out the next day to help and discovered, within the first thirty minutes in her home, that we had quite a bit to do.

Her husband's name was the only one on the title for their bank accounts, the family home, and even his car. The funeral parlor and cemetery wanted advance payment for the final arrangements, and Candy couldn't even write a check on the accounts to make this happen. The only account she controlled was a household spending account fed by her own small paycheck—a paltry sum, deposited monthly.

This situation served as a fast lesson for me in what not to do in a marriage. Women incur a lot of risk by delegating financial matters to their husbands.

I reflected and asked, "What about life insurance? Surely, that will help in this situation."

We called his employer's office to report his death, and learned that the husband, who we will call "Don," had never updated his policy to benefit his wife. His still-living mother was still the beneficiary.

Thankfully, a second policy existed—privately owned, and purchased by the husband, naming his wife and child as the beneficiaries. We called the insurance company. Under normal circumstances, it would have taken days or weeks to get any payout, as there was a process of filing the death certificate.

Luckily, the agent was a friend of the family and was able to get a settlement the day before the funeral. We could bury Don without passing the hat around to family and friends to cover the expense.

The payoff provided by the second life insurance policy turned out to be a godsend that kept her afloat for the ensuing six months. She could pay bills, keep the house, and maintain a normal life until she could wrest back control of the family assets.

California is a community property statc. I wrongly assumed that it would be a simple matter to transfer the title for Don's bank holdings and 401(k) balance to Candy, considering that they were married. This was not to be. We learned that because the wife was not named as a "payable on death" beneficiary, all these holdings were subject to a six-month probate process in this state. This meant Candy would have to retain an attorney and file a motion that the assets be awarded to her if no other beneficiary, such as her mother-in-law, was already named.

Since we were not sure the insurance company could come through so quickly, we continued to move forward on trying to access accounts. I put Candy in my rental car, and we drove to see a lawyer at a firm widely advertised on television—one that seemed to invite the average Joe or Jill to come in with their troubles.

In the process of settling the estate, we also uncovered liabilities. Don had spent a sizable sum of money on himself for a trip abroad with a friend, and the credit card bills remained to be paid. Thankfully, the life insurance covered this debt, too. The wife was able to sell the husband's car months later, once the title was given to her in the probate process. Surprisingly, the mother-in-law did not cede control of any payouts provided by the employer life insurance, though her son had left a two-year-old child fatherless.

LESSONS TO BE LEARNED FROM THIS STORY

- Participate in all decisions about family finances.
- Verify all beneficiary choices on all accounts.
- Be adequately insured to cover emergencies and to protect those you love.
- Pay attention to account titling. Actual account and asset titling can override wills and trusts, so these choices are important.
- Assume a fiduciary responsibility to your spouse, and hold your spouse accountable for the same. Neither of you should jeopardize your family's security with reckless spending or behavior. Do your due diligence on financial choices that could create instability in the event of a disaster.
- Do not assume that if you drop the ball, your relatives will help.
- Be informed about estate planning. Especially discuss and plan for every eventuality if you have children.

BACK TO BASICS

Taking stock of where you are at begins with a couple of spreadsheets. Appendixes for these are found in the back of this booklet.

We will start by creating a personal financial statement. You can use this for your own information, as well as with lenders, should you ever need to seek financing for your home. You will total all current assets and long-term assets, and subtract all current and long-term liabilities. The result will provide your net worth.

If you are married, you may wish to create a joint personal

financial statement. Keep in mind that you and your spouse may each have separate assets as well as marital assets. The statutes and case law prevailing in each state will dictate the relative classification of your assets. You may or may not wish to distinguish separate and community property in tallying your personal financial statement.

THE BUDGET

First, let's figure out your monthly spend rate, which will show how you currently use money. With that info, you can begin to see how to free up cash and divert some of this spending into savings. Eventually, those savings can fund your short-term and long-term goals.

Using the spreadsheet provided at the end of this chapter, or creating one of your own, enter your spending by category, then by line item. If you are testing whether and by how much you can reduce spending for various categories, use a second column to log pro forma (revised) expenditures against the actual expenditures entered in the first column.

If you prefer not to track monthly expenses for routine purchases like gas and food, consider doing it once or twice a year to establish your baseline. You can make adjustments for unusual months by budgeting forward. Do not forget to save ahead for Thanksgiving and other important family holidays.

If you have no clue what you spend on food or gasoline, start keeping track a month prior to this exercise. Use the "grandma" method—that is, cash in envelopes or a cookie jar and kept receipts for any money spent. The receipts go back in the jar. At the end of the month, add the cash outlays to those made using your debit card. Don't resort to using a credit card unless you can pay off the balance monthly. The sum totals will tell you what you have spent on groceries and separately on meals out.

This exercise can be important for any level of wealth. Money is a precious resource and should be used with intention, and not blithely. While money may be in abundant supply during working years, part of your monthly cash flow should be treated as seed capital for investments to sustain cash flow during the lean years.

Living with intention also means designating some of your cash to fund your children's goals, upgrade your house, retire, and give to charity. For couples with minor children, saving behavior may be driven by a quality-of-life goal. Parents may wish to allow for one spouse to parent full-time at home.

Now that you have your monthly budget, look it over to see where most of your money goes. For most people living in urban areas of the US, the top expense is housing, followed by transportation, healthcare, and food. The order of these expenses varies greatly depending on age, number of people in the household, and whether an employer is paying the cost of health insurance.

Now for the hard part. It's time for the hard—but necessary—conversation with a spouse or significant other about how to optimize your budget to achieve a goal. For instance, if you wish to save 20 percent of incoming cash for an eventual house purchase or upgrade, you need to make sure your other expenses stay within their predicted ranges. The total cannot exceed 100 percent.

Be realistic. There will be month-to-month fluctuations in any expense category. However, emergencies should be paid out of cash reserves, not cash flow. For this reason, it's important to create savings buckets.

Money is a touchy subject as it touches every aspect of our lives. If you find yourself going off the rails in a discussion about family finances, think about reducing the stress of the conversation.

Budget a window of time—a standing appointment—for this conversation, rather than springing it on someone. It could be set as a standing appointment for noon on the second and fourth Saturdays of the month, for example.

Learn some mediation techniques. Many books exist on this subject, and I personally found mediation techniques invaluable when working with my teen daughter, who is now an adult. Become an active listener during the conversation, and observe the conversation give-and-take. Acknowledge what you are hearing by rephrasing what the person has just said in a neutral tone, rather than reacting from the gut when you disagree. If a statement was made in anger, you can rephrase in a neutral tone. You can ask the person what outcome they want from the conversation. Try to find the common ground to work through the difficulties of compromise.

With my teen daughter, the conversation might start about doing dishes, migrate to the level of her cash allowance, and then result in a blowup about a "go or no-go" decision for an expense.

Using mediation techniques, I would start the conversation each time with a statement: "What I hear you saying is that you do not enjoy doing dishes."

She would then respond.

"So is the issue the timing, or the task of doing them at all?" I might ask.

She would respond.

"So how will the dishes get done, if no one wants to do them?" I might ask, seeking common ground. "Do you have a solution to propose?"

If she asks for a bigger allowance to do her share, I might then ask her how this would play out with other uses of money she wants or desires.

By this point, we are actually conversing, not arguing.

If you find yourself losing your cool, you can also take a "rain check" in a conversation and reschedule with the person if necessary. You might say, "I see that this topic is not a good fit for you (or me) right now. Let's reschedule the conversation to a time you and I can talk in a less stressed way. Can I suggest tomorrow at 9:00 a.m.?" You have just moved on to finding common ground by seeking agreement on a time to converse.

Always use neutral vocabulary in these exchanges. Avoid using insults, charged terms, or swear words. Don't use the phrase "You always . . ." or "You never . . ." Do not push buttons when seeking compromise.

"Here's the deal: we call the shots when you're young, you call the shots when we're old, and everything in between is a non-stop battle for control."

BUILDING THE FOUNDATION

Now you have built the budget, and it's worthy of a test drive. See if it moves you closer to your goals and expected outcomes. Schedule a conversation with your significant other to decide on goals for freed-up cash. In other words, how does the extra cash get allocated to goals, and how are your goals prioritized?

Let's say you have chosen a goal to eliminate credit card balances. You will need to determine a length of time for achieving this goal, and a realistic schedule for paying down balances. You and your significant other should get very focused about how to make this happen given your monthly income. What expenses need to be reduced or eliminated to make the debt reduction goal happen?

No one gets to be the "adult child" in this conversation. If you really want success, and not a false start, both you and your partner need to own the process and outcome together.

Alternatively, how can you as a couple bring in more revenue to finance this objective? Perhaps the solution is another job or type of employment; or perhaps it is a temporary side gig. Perhaps it is financed using your other investment assets more wisely, to generate the extra income needed.

Or, say you and your partner want to improve your home, but would need a home equity loan to do so. Perhaps a higher credit score could reduce your cost to take out the loan. How much of your own savings could be used to finance the improvement?

Treat this decision as you would any investment decision. Before committing cash to finance it, judge the creditworthiness of your house and neighborhood. In many areas of the country, for instance, home values generally trend upwards in good times, and go flat in economic downturns. If values for homes are trending down, you need to think again about whether and when to invest further. If your aim is to eventually sell, then judge the probability of profit after taxes and real estate commissions.

Say that in this "go or no-go" context, you and your significant other decide it's a "go"—that is, you judge the probability of making a profit on the house sale to be good. You consider this an investment in long-term wealth creation. You can create a spreadsheet, or use an online calculator, to evaluate how fast you can put together your own money or take out a loan to make your down payment. A list of useful URLs for online calculators follows at the end of this chapter. It is always safer to make decisions about investment outcomes using math as a guide, rather than emotions.

VALUES-DRIVEN CHOICES

Whether you are in a position in life where you are already comfortable, or climbing the ladder to get there, make your money decisions with intention. That is, make deliberate decisions that support your life priorities—or spiritual values—and the rest usually falls into place.

For instance, as a single person, perhaps you establish a financial goal to purchase a home—the sooner, the better. Having a clear goal will allow you to make some sacrifices to attain it.

If you are a partner in a couple and you are building toward security for your family, then your first goal may not be the purchase of a house, but rather, steady employment and life insurance. Your financial plan would identify how to best progress from your starting blocks to build from week to week, month to month, and year to year.

Many clients I counsel want to support their churches and community, too. For them, even modest contributions toward a greater good bring a feeling of contribution and self-fulfillment. Making room in your budget for spiritual or community gifts is fine, as long as they are a budgeted part of your financial road map.

Of course, as you navigate life, you will hopefully be accumulating more assets—some for your personal use, some for building working capital, and others for long-term investments. Some of the money to be allocated may come from an inheritance. Once you have your financial foundation in place, it becomes easier to take the next steps toward intentionally and prudently managing your wealth. If you are married, don't forget to consider the implications of separate and community property. If you feel a postnuptial agreement may be in order, check with a family law attorney.

Consider estate planning so that your hard-earned assets don't get hit with probate fees upon your death, or the death of a spouse. Probate fees can consume a significant chunk of an estate. Preparing a trust can avoid this problem. A will alone does not suffice, especially if you own a home, because assets left under a will are still subject to probate in the courts.

LIFE-CHANGING WEALTH

Almost everyone aspires to build enough wealth for a comfortable life. But some of us will attain wealth on a larger scale in our lifetime—due to diligence, or good fortune, or both. To sustain this good fortune, financial planning is extremely important.

Have clarity about your goals, or you may become careless in your choices of people and professionals who can help you accomplish your wishes. If you have set your values, align yourself with people who share them. Do not rely on blind faith in strangers with great resumes. Carefully vet anyone you work with on money matters and investments.

The most prudent approach is to diversify and to avoid risky investment, unless you can stick to a defined limit and no more of your investable assets. Keep it small. As they say, "don't risk the store"—that is, don't allow one bad bet to undermine or bury your nest egg.

Once your financial plan is set, stay the course. Do the yearly reality checks to see if you are still on target, or if it is time for a recalibration or reboot.

In legal circles, there is a concept known as the "prudent man theory." This concept emerged from case law in court decisions involving management of financial assets: "What would a prudent man (or woman) do, when managing wealth?"

This question can inspire a long discourse. Suffice it to say here that when managing financial assets meant to sustain a couple or a surviving spouse and family over many years, you—as the manager—have a fiduciary responsibility to make sound decisions. Having conversations with not one, but several competent professionals can clarify the best course for investing money so that it grows; produces income; and does not risk high volatility, or even total loss.

If an investment sounds too good to be true, it probably is. Learn to read prospectuses and fine print, and avoid any long-term lock-in of your investments when you are deferring income.

When deciding with an investment counselor how to invest, remember that liquidity risk—that is, the risk of not having access to your money when you need it—can be just as important as the risk of market downturns.

Other forms of risk include inflation and interest rate risk, which can lower bond valuations. A well-structured bond portfolio allows a laddering of maturities to allow the owner to reinvest into new bonds at new interest rates and total maturities as the old bonds come due. Dividend-paying stocks usually pay once a quarter (four times yearly). Mutual funds may pay income every month, or not at all. The whole idea is to keep the income coming as often as possible to supplement your other sources of income in retirement. If you count on appreciation alone, and hold growth stocks, you may find yourself paying high taxes on capital gains when it is time to sell shares.

CHOICES OF INVESTMENTS

When deciding on investments, judge where you are in your knowledge about markets and available investable resources. Anyone just starting with investments should seriously consider staying with certificates of deposit, mutual funds, and ETFs for a while to establish a solid foundation before adding other investments. Educate yourself about the spectrum for risk and determine where you belong for risk tolerance.

The average standard deviation of a fund relative to the S&P 500 index of the stock market is generally shown by a beta statistic. I know this vocabulary introduces technical jargon, but it is important to understand that a small capitalization fund can exhibit larger valuation swings than, for instance, a large capitalization fund. These swings can affect values greatly, and for that reason, small cap funds or stocks may deserve a smaller percentage of a portfolio than large capitalization stocks.

Your appetite for risk can be measured on a risk-tolerance questionnaire and will tell you and your advisor how much standard deviation you can handle before you fold your cards and walk. You can diagnose your own risk tolerance as conservative, moderate, or aggressive using a variety of tools online, or a simple quiz. Ask your advisor for one.

With regards to choosing a portfolio mix of suitable investments, many online planning tools will present you with a pie chart with slices indicating the relative weights suggested for large cap, mid cap, and small cap stocks, bonds, and international holdings. These proportions vary with risk tolerance, but you can also add other considerations beyond what is presented. Factor in your own personal need for liquidity, and your age. Older people, for instance, usually want to dial down their risk, as they have less ability to make up for losses once retired. See samples for pie charts for allocation by age and risk tolerance at the back of this chapter.

Investment risk comes in various forms, including risk of capital loss, risk of taxation, risk of needing the capital back within the proposed time horizon, risk of inflation, and risk of volatility; as well as credit risk—referring to bond ratings or the ability of a company to pay promised dividends and interest. Use of a mutual fund or ETF may help temper these risks with diversification.

Investment real estate is not an asset usually shown on these allocation pie charts, but it can be a great long-term diversifier. Investment real estate has its own risk parameters, including liquidity and valuation risk. Any real estate investment should be considered to be relatively illiquid, as it is not as easy to sell real property as it is to sell a virtual asset, like a stock. Investment real estate can provide an important source of income for retirement; but like any investment, it merits further analysis. Such a decision should be evaluated as carefully as any major business decision, with spreadsheet analysis and tax and legal consultations. Identify sources of risk, such as tenant failures to pay and added legal costs, and decide whether these are risks you can afford to carry.

ASK QUESTIONS

Don't be afraid to sharpen your pencils, do some analysis, and mark up the spreadsheets. Ask questions of the experts with whom you have chosen to work. Get to know yourself and your deepest concerns, as well as your dearest wishes for a fulfilled life that aligns with your values. Work with your significant other to get on the same page and to make money an okay topic to discuss as needed without discomfort.

CHANGING COURSE

A lot of people who I see for professional guidance got to me the hard way. Something happened in their lives to throw them off course, and they wanted to steer the car back onto the right road; or somewhere along the journey, they realized they would run out of gas before they got to their destination. Recalibration is necessary, and it can be painful.

Sometimes there is a pattern that needs to be broken, and the break with the past must be made hand-in-hand with a significant other. It may be time to set up once-a-week or once-a-month "money dates" to review finances. This is also a good time to talk about the one-and-done financial decisions, as well as bigger decisions about long-term goals.

Other times, a life event has intervened. One spouse has taken ill, and now it's time for the other partner to take stock of how this situation will change their expected outcomes. Or, the recalibration may come about because of a recent death, or an imminent divorce—a life built for two must now accommodate two living separately.

The important thing is to own your financial life—that is, don't delegate the decisions to anyone. You may participate in them, as spouses do in a marriage; but ceding financial control and authority will always introduce instability. This is not a healthy, balanced situation. Many books have been written on this topic, so I will not digress too much here. If a spouse wants security for themself, as well as for their children, it's important to participate in the economic decisions that underpin the security of the household and the economic structure of the family.

Take heart. Many times, when faced with difficult transitions, I have thought of my grandmother. As a fourteen-year-old girl in 1918, she passed herself off as someone older to make the long and difficult journey from Europe to the United States. She took a job as a nanny with a family who spoke her language. Always frugal, she managed to save money until she met her husband. They married, and they were able to buy a home. While they had many good times later in life, the early years became difficult during the Great Depression.

My grandmother taught me the value of saving in preparation for the rainy days that could come anytime. She also taught me how to stretch a dollar when the situation warrants.

In my own life, I have seen others rebuild from ashes through grit, determination, and optimism. You may find that you make your best decisions when you reach deep inside and ask what stuff you are really made of—what you would do to make the people you care for proud.

If you don't have one or more people you trust, look for mentors with whom to discuss money matters. Get good advice from people who know you and your situation. Don't overly rely on popular advice published by strangers. Sometimes it helps to build a team of professionals if your money matters are large. Online forums can help, but they are no substitute for real human relationships with people that really know you.

People with modest means may need to build a support group, which can include like-minded friends or neighbors. Together, you can encourage each other to create goals and to keep going. Being in a group can offer you some power, as well, like the power to bring in an expert speaker to delve into things you all wish to know but weren't ready to ask one-on-one.

Interestingly, I have found via YouTube that there is now a new movement of people embracing frugality to reach their goals of retiring younger. They describe their shared thought processes and approach with the acronym "FIRE"—Financial Independence and Early Retirement. A lot of people are podcasting on things that my grandmother shared with me many years ago. These conversations may or may not resonate with you, but they are empowering if you want to learn how to create the bridges from here to there. Your "there" will be wherever you really want to head.

Your progress in this journey will vary based on your income, spending, investment, and time. Oh, and yes: taxation matters. This is even more reason to review any plans with your tax professional.

MAPPING LIFE TRANSITIONS

Draw your road map to success with a timeline. Establish how many years it will take to meet your first, second, and third goals. Think about how much money you can save or invest for each goal, and how to free up the cash from your daily spending needs to do so.

These decisions must precede any choice about risk tolerance. If you decide to head down the road of riskier investments because you think the growth will lower the capital needed to meet your goal, first remember that you must factor in expectations for the next slice of time ahead of you—economic performance, performance of markets, and direction of interest rates.

If you absolutely *must* have a certain sum by the end of three years, for instance, you would not want to incur risk that would jeopardize this outcome. With any projection, allow for margins of error or standard deviation in returns. For instance, you might set an arbitrary standard of 5 to 10 percent plus or minus your target and save even more, just in case.

Look at spreadsheet results with the help of a professional. The longer the time projection, the more likely you will want to test assumptions or discount eventual returns of capital for the time value of money. I am referring to net present value and future value analysis. Once you decide on the rate of inflation or interest rate to use, the algorithms built into financial planning software adjust automatically. The idea is to save enough money for a future expense that you can pay it, despite an increase in inflation. This invaluable analysis will also tell you what level of investment risk you may need to accept to grow your money within the time available.

BUILDING WEALTH

Looking at your personal finance ratios may also help. For instance, compute these ratios for yourself, and see how they compare to budget spending for your area or zip code. Find this information on websites like www.numbeo.com or www.city-data.com.

THE 50-20-30 RULE

Many planners recommend that no more than 50 percent of your cash inflows should be going to cover essentials like food, housing, and repayment of long-term educational debt. Twenty percent should be allocated to your future needs, such as purchase of a home or retirement. The remaining 30 percent should be allocated to lifestyle choices, including subscriptions, memberships, vacations, and private schools for children. Check how you compare in your housing costs relative to income for your area, at www.numbeo.com/cost-of-living/in/(name of your town).

THE 28-36 RULE

Lenders use this ratio to judge whether more than 28 percent of your gross monthly income is covering house-related expenses inclusive of mortgage principal, interest, property taxes, and insurance costs. The total debt payments made, inclusive of consumer debt, should not exceed 36 percent of your income.

SAVINGS GOALS

Your savings ratio is equal to the amount you save annually, divided by the amount you earn annually. How much of your gross annual income are you investing into long-term savings accounts? How much equity are you adding to your real estate annually?

Do not equate equity with your mortgage payments; only a portion of mortgage payments pays down the actual principal, to create additional equity. You could add your savings and your equity accumulation to determine what portion of your income is actually powering you to your annual goal.

SAVINGS PROGRESS

If your goal is to save one million dollars for retirement, what progress are you making annually toward this goal? To judge, you will need to look at not only your annual set-asides, but also the growth you are realizing to fuel your progress. Your chosen risk allocation for investments will affect how much growth you experience in the money set aside, over the number of years you have established to reach your goal. Among the online tools you may wish to consider for judging this are the portfolio reviews offered by Morningstar.com, a subscription service, allowing measures for variability in returns as well as general long-term trends for your funds and other holdings.

EMERGENCY SAVINGS

Aim to have three months' income saved in a cash savings account to avoid ever resorting to credit cards to cover emergencies. If putting aside this money is a scramble, consider this exercise a wake-up call to reduce spending in a big way. Getting the equivalent of three months' income saved for those unpredictable emergencies can get you on track to achieve other goals. If the day jobs don't permit you to save, despite your best efforts, consider some side jobs or projects to bring in the cash and get the emergency account funded. Be creative and work at this as a family, so that everyone shares the knowledge and gratification of achieving this measure of financial freedom.

Starting an investment program while you are young allows you to build your base with the power of compounding. Starting later in life might mean scrambling to save ever bigger sums each year to finance a nearer-term retirement.

QUICK EXERCISE

Take two minutes and tally up how to divert ten to twenty dollars of your daily spending into savings. What ten- to twenty-dollar items can you live without? What monthly expense can you eliminate?

Examples:

- Commuting one or two days a week using a bicycle or public transportation
- Avoiding dry cleaning charges
- Doing your own manicures and pedicures
- Cutting cable television
- Reducing cell phone use
- Making your own lunches
- Replacing paid movie subscriptions with DVD checkouts from the local library
- Transferring car insurance to a pay-by-the-mile subscription formula—cheaper for low-mileage drivers
- Putting children in public school, rather than private school, and using a tutor to address any educational gaps

A combination of these savings can be aggregated to get you closer to your goals.

Many dividend-paying stock companies allow incremental purchase of their shares through Compuserve.com and other transfer agent firms. The dividends can be used to buy additional shares. Having an extra three to five hundred dollars per month from daily savings would enable you to buy shares every month in a steadily earning stock, which could help fund your retirement, a child's college savings, or a dream vacation.

Which of these goals can you accomplish in ninety days? Set your sights on doing those first.

At the end of the ninety days, start a new rolling set of goals to get you nearer to an ultimate savings goal for a stated purpose—whether the goal is long-term, such as funding retirement; or short-term, such as replacing a roof, buying a new car, or taking a vacation.

Long-term goals benefit from plans for long-term investments. When managing retirement accounts, think about risk tolerance over the long-haul. That is, unless you are already retired and reliant on income distributions, in which case you should think more about historic rates of growth for individual assets than the performance in any one quarter. Focus on putting more money aside, rather than on picking that one stock or fund that will push you into early retirement. There is too much risk that the latter approach will fail you, as timing the market remains more art than science.

Starting when you are young gives you some help from the power of compounding. Over a twenty-year period, for instance, a 3 percent annual return can compound to a total return on principal of 80.6 percent over the twenty years. Use the 50-30-20 rule in budgeting to be able to free up 20 percent of incoming salaries and income into your long-term savings goals.

CASE STUDY: HOW NOT TO BUY A HOUSE

Real estate is probably the most significant asset anyone can own. For most people, getting the down payment together is a long process—unless you are blessed with cheaper housing stock in areas away from the nation's urban coasts. A home in Nashville, TN, for instance, can cost $200,000 for three bedrooms; in the San Francisco Bay area, the same house might market for $850,000. The down payment for the house in Nashville might be as little as $40,000, while the house in the Bay Area might require $170,000 down or more.

For this reason, it may be tempting to shortcut the process of getting together a down payment by pooling resources with friends and/or family. The hard decisions that factor into this approach center on how to share title, and how to document expectations of eventual repayment or buyout.

For one set of friends who bought a house together, the transaction proved disastrous, eventually ending the friendships built over many years. Some, if not all, of the problems could have been avoided if the friends had first created a legal agreement articulating the terms of their engagement.

The saga began when one friend, who we will call "Harry," inherited some money from a grandmother. He was sharing housing outside of San Francisco with another friend, who we will call "Tim." Since Tim was handy and knew carpentry, the two began shopping for an extreme fixer-upper to buy and eventually flip for sale. They found one and shared the title on the purchase. With one friend supplying the down, the other supplying the labor, the two transformed the house from a burnt-out shell left from a house fire to a comfortable four-bedroom, two-bath in a vibrant neighborhood. Since neither friend had any credit history, the parents of the carpenter, Tim, co-signed on the loan. The plan then was to take the parents off title once the two stakeholders made enough payments to create credit history.

Nine months later, they were able to buy out the parents. Both friends were making the payments. Then Harry moved out, and Tim stayed, still making the payments.

Five years later, Harry moved back in with a girlfriend and wanted to borrow money against the house to take back his share of equity. Harry and his girlfriend became husband and wife, and wanted to stay in the house as part of the deal. The loan was obtained, and both friends were named as responsible owners.

But the proceeds of the loan only benefited one owner. The carpenter, Tim, thought to have a note attached to the loan in which Harry agreed to continue to make payments. But when Harry defaulted, Tim had to assume the payments or risk losing his credit score—and, possibly, the house.

Tim decided to buy out the couple because he no longer had any interest in sharing the house, but it took a mediator and many consultations with an attorney to finally get the deal that pushed the marriage partners to leave.

Tim was left alone in the house. He held the sole title, but he also had paid off the loan *and* another $20,000 over what appraisers felt the house was really worth.

LESSONS LEARNED FROM THIS STORY

- Approach investing in any asset in a business-like matter. Just as a business might have articles of incorporation, friends in a real estate venture should have a legal agreement that governs the promises, expectations, and eventual buyout terms for their venture.
- Stick to deadlines and exit plans. While the house deal started out as a flip, the actual exit was delayed, tying up capital for a long period of time. In this case, it was a ten-year investment.
- Use an attorney when sharing real estate ventures with friends, family, or other investors. The attorney can clarify how title ownership disputes get resolved before they become a problem.
- Manage your credit. A desire to shortcut the accumulation of a down payment led the friends in this story to borrow from parents. Luckily the two friends were responsible

enough to pay back the parents within the time agreed, preserving the parents' credit scores as well as helping the two friends establish their own.

- Real estate investments can lead to attachment. The ground under one's feet is important. Sharing ownership with someone else may spark rivalries or disagreements where none existed before.

PLANNING FOR DOWNSIZING OR RELOCATION

People who start charting their plans may find that it makes sense to change cities or states in order to achieve their goals within a shorter time frame. In some states, these transitions are becoming the norm. California, for instance, has been losing residents to other states for more than fifteen years. Ignoring the influx of foreign nationals and immigrants, the state lost more domestic residents than any other state in the continental US between 1990 and 2010. Leading destination states have been Florida, Texas, North Carolina, Georgia, and Arizona.[1]

A young couple wanting to buy a home, but unable to muster the $100,000 down payment necessary in one state, may consider the chance to relocate for work and buy easily elsewhere for much less down. Aging-in-place may not be an option in an expensive city, where the value of the residence far exceeds the value of investment assets. A move across state lines, or to a less expensive locale, can create many options for an enhanced quality of life.

Using financial planning, people can judge which scenario may optimize the outcome given the time available and the money spent. If you are doing your own analysis, don't forget to factor in switching costs—that is, the expense necessary to actually re-stage your life elsewhere. These might include the real estate agent fee to sell your home, or the actual cost to move your furniture. They may also include an expected drop in income, if moving from a high-wage area to a lower-wage area.

There are two websites that I find very useful in making these comparisons. One is www.numbeo.com, as I have mentioned before. The other is www.city-data.com, which can provide invaluable information on the actual expenses by spending category you may incur living in any one community.

Here is a sample ledger to get you started on your analysis. You will find other considerations to factor in. Don't hesitate to sit down with a good financial planner in your community to assess how your expectations compare to the situations that actually play out.

PUSHING THE RESET BUTTON AFTER A CATASTROPHIC EVENT

Recently, people around the world coped with widespread unemployment and shelter-in-place orders resulting from an outbreak of the COVID-19 virus. Businesses shut down, employees were furloughed, and the US and global economies reeled as people stayed home to stay safe. At the start of 2020, few people had foreseen this crisis, which within months saw more than one million people in the US alone affected by a potentially fatal illness. Many people and small businesses had little cash reserved, and despite government subsidies, they had problems paying for the basics of life or staying afloat long enough to reopen. The problems that ensued are still with us.

In any crisis, there are lessons to be learned. Whether the crisis you experience is a pandemic or something more personal, such as a death in the family, you will never regret being prepared.

Having cash reserves and savings will give you peace of mind and the ability to cope until the next set of goals comes into focus. Just as you are pushing the reset button for this ninety-day plan, you will work on stabilizing the new set of circumstances and reviewing what you can do in the ensuing ninety days to stay on course towards your goal, or to work toward your new goals.

As a financial advisor, I have sometimes been shocked upon discovery of how little a well-dressed, well-spoken client actually had in the bank at the end of the day. I have also wondered how my older client with the tattered wallet actually found his way to building riches and peace of mind through his frugality—when he passed, he left his wealth to more than a dozen friends who will always remember him.

In times of trouble, reflect on what you can learn and make resolutions for the future. Like my immigrant grandmother many years ago, do not assume someone will bail you out if things go wrong. Keep some cash in savings just in case, and build up your reserves using the tips that I have shared.

WHERE DO YOU WANT TO ACTUALLY LIVE, NOW OR IN THE FUTURE?

As a financial planner, I cannot hide from myself. When I applied my knowledge to my own situation, I began to plan for a relocation of my practice to another state. I realized that a lower-cost state could free up capital and allow me to balance my budgets with my desires for experiences and quality of life. This capital could be used, in part, to further my investments; but also to play a little more after hours, and do the things I love. The daily pressure to cover the living expenses associated with keeping a house, a car, and some livestock would diminish in a lower-cost area. I would have more time for friends and family, and to participate in the community. I played the game of sums—which I described in the introduction to this chapter—and decided to make the change.

I formulated a plan and vetted it with the people around me who are experienced in credit, mortgages, real estate, and my profession. Together, we found a new path and a new geography. Over the months of investigation and visits to properties out of state, I found my new home, and my new life. Luckily, I am often able to work with my clients virtually; and post-COVID-19, this may be a new norm.

Financial planning doesn't have to be a joyless grind to make ends meet. Using these tools can clear doubt and open new windows of opportunity. You will hopefully find a new focus on what is important to you and your family.

Suggested Asset Allocations

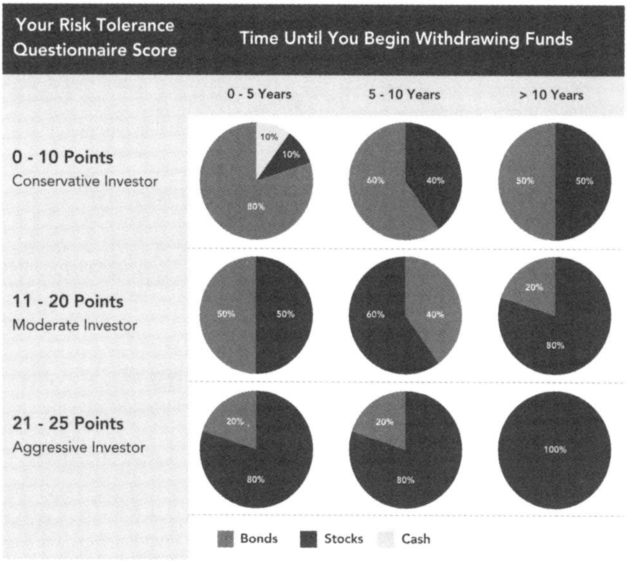

Annual Income Payment Amounts										
Source	Tax Treatment	Year of Retirement	Years 1-2	Years 3-4	Years 5-10	Years 10-15	Years 15-20	Years 20-25	Years 25-30	Years 30-35
Social Security (combined)										
IRA Income, combined										
Annuity (1), NQ										
Annuity (2), Q										
Other, i.e. yield from investments										
Farm Income										
Rental Property Income										
Salary (ies)										
Pension (s)										
Totals	$		$	$	$	$	$	$	$	$
Less Living Expenses	$		$	$	$	$	$	$	$	$
Surplus/Deficit	$		$	$	$	$	$	$	$	$

RECOMMENDED ONLINE CALCULATORS

- Bankrate: bankrate.com/calculators
- Numbeo: numbeo.com
- NerdWallet: nerdwallet.com/article/insurance/insurance-calculators
- AARP: aarp.org/retirement/retirement-calculatorcalculator.net/retirement-calculator.html

CHAPTER THREE

WOMEN AND CREDIT

Kathryn Davis

The financial climate for women today is at once terrifying and better than it's ever been. Women and men have the same legal rights to own property; get a credit card in their name; and vote for the legislators that will make decisions about the financial futures of all Americans—but we know the world didn't always look this way.

In fact, it wasn't until 1968 that the Department of Housing and Urban Development (HUD) made it a violation of the federal Fair Housing Law to deny a pregnant woman a mortgage because she was on maternity leave. This law forbids discrimination in real estate transactions including mortgage lending on the basis of race, color, national origin, religion, sex, disability, or familial status. In 1968, however, this assumed the pregnant women was cosigning with her husband; it would be another six years until the federal government would put in place the Equal Credit Opportunity Act (ECOA), which stated that lenders could not deny credit on the basis of gender, race, marital status, national origin, or religion. Prior to 1974, a woman could not get any credit on her own!

Despite the equal access to financial information and credit products today, more than twenty-six million Americans remain "credit invisible." They have no credit history with any of the three main credit reporting agencies in this country. Over half of all credit users have a low—or "subprime"—credit score. One in three has a FICO credit score lower than 620, making them unable to get credit cards, mortgages, and loans with reasonable terms and interest rates.

According to a report by Suparna Bhaskaran titled "Pinklining," the financial sector takes advantage of less-than-desirable economic conditions experienced by some women.[1] For example, during the peak of the subprime lending boom, women were 30 to 46 percent more likely to get a subprime loan with unfavorable terms than men. Nearly 60 percent of payday loan customers are women. These loans have an average annual interest rate of 400 percent.

Sometimes referred to as "survival spending" loans, certain financial products trap women in a cycle of debt. When they can't keep up with high payments, out-of-control interest rates, and fees, their credit scores suffer.

While women have access to more financial products than they have at any other point in history, they also shoulder more debt and higher monthly payments. The wage gap has something to do with this. Women currently make around $0.76 per $1.00 that men earn within the same job position. Due to the fact that men receive higher payments in the workforce, they tend to have more money to spend, which typically results in men making larger, more significant purchases like cars, homes, or various luxury items . . . and having the ability to pay for them.

But don't worry if you find yourself in a less-than-ideal financial situation. There's never been a better time to turn things around. You also don't have to be wealthy to avail yourself of better credit. In fact, women of all different socioeconomic backgrounds who have healthy credit scores have been able to access low-cost loans, low-interest credit cards, the best lease terms for vehicles, and better mortgage rate options.

So where do you start? Generally, good credit is as a result of using credit wisely—which means when you use credit, you ideally should pay it off immediately, or in a reasonable amount of time. It's important to understand, however, that many people—men *and* women—who don't have any credit at all or who have bad credit aren't in their current situation because they went on one shopping spree after another. Divorce, death, and illness are just a few of the top and most common reasons that people may find themselves in financial trouble. While the circumstances that led to bad credit or a lack of knowledge about credit may be out of your control, it's possible to change your circumstances.

WHAT CAN WOMEN DO TO TAKE CARE OF THEIR CREDIT SCORES?

Credit doesn't discriminate, and it doesn't come naturally for anyone. Operating from a base of certainty requires the desire to learn. Even if you don't have much money, you can change this part of your financial reality over time if you are curious, willing to learn, and ready to change long-held false beliefs about money and credit.

This is precisely the right time to pause and ask yourself, how does personal financial success *look*? How does it *feel*? Take the time to consider how you want to live. Think about what your life would be like if your financial situation were different.

It would be helpful if you had a personal vision for your future. When you understand where you are going, and you are motivated to get there, you'll also have the will, determination, and stamina to complete the hard work of reaching your financial goals.

Maybe you are already in a downward spiral of debt and financial hardship. Perhaps you are in over your head, without enough saved for retirement, a zero balance in your emergency fund, and the nagging feeling that things will only get worse from here.

There's only one way out of a financial mess. Your situation probably didn't form overnight, and it may take time for you to resolve your financial problems. Some of your money problems may even be someone else's fault. It's good to acknowledge that reality, as well.

Regardless of who caused the problems or why they exist, it's your responsibility to take ownership of the situation and move through the process of building a healthy financial life for yourself. Understanding and building credit is part of the kind of solid financial situation that will see you through the normal ups and downs of everyday life.

No matter where you are, it's possible to improve. The first step is understanding the landscape of credit in today's world. Knowing the rules of the game is a crucial part of winning in every area of life. You can start right now by looking at your credit situation, your lack of knowledge, and your past decisions as an opportunity for change.

WHY WOMEN SHOULD HAVE THEIR OWN CREDIT

Many women just haven't taken their credit situation seriously. They meld and mix their finances with their spouse or partner, letting the other person make major financial decisions and handle the day-to-day money management issues.

Others are so focused on paying the bills so they can keep the lights on and the collectors at bay that they've put off caring for their credit or trying to build good credit. Whether you are well-off or not, it's essential to create a credit identity that is only yours.

CONSIDER ALICE'S SITUATION

Alice is thirty-nine and newly divorced. She and her ex-husband didn't have large amounts of money, and he handled all of their investments, debts, and the regular bill-paying duties. The couple married the summer after graduating college, and Alice turned over the finances immediately.

She never believed she had a head for numbers, and much preferred that her husband handle everything that had to do with money. Over the years, when she would ask questions or try to learn about their joint financial life, he would get annoyed, and they'd end up arguing. This cycle confirmed Alice's belief that money was not her forte.

When they decided to separate, Alice searched for an apartment near her place of employment. She didn't want to stay in their small rental home, located forty-five minutes from her job and far away from the heart of the city. Her list of criteria for the new apartment was short. She wanted a secured-entrance, second-floor, two-bedroom apartment that would let her keep her small dog, Ellis. If the place offered access to free Wi-Fi, and there was a decent coffee shop within walking distance, those would be nice bonuses.

After finding her ideal apartment home, Alice put in an application. The property manager called a few days later to say that her application was denied because she had no credit history. Alice then realized that since her husband handled all their finances, he hadn't put her name on any of their accounts. She couldn't even furnish a history of on-time utility payments in her name. She had opened her first solo bank account just weeks earlier.

Her only options were to get a cosigner, or pay a much larger security deposit that would deplete her small personal savings account.

Establishing and maintaining credit separate from their spouse or partner is imperative for women. Without your own credit identity, life changes and relationship status changes could be financially devastating.

Alice had the choice to establish credit in her name earlier in life. It was more comfortable to avoid the topic altogether. Now, she'll have to pay a high deposit to get an apartment and spend extra time and effort trying to build up her emergency fund.

Alice made the same choices as many women who let their partner handle the finances. Over time, it becomes easier to ignore the reality of credit. Women need and deserve a solid credit history of their own.

WHAT MAKES UP GOOD CREDIT

When Americans talk about having "good credit," they are probably referring to their FICO score. The Fair Isaac Corporation (FICO) creates these scores. Lenders use them to determine how much of a risk they'd take by extending credit to you, or offering you a secured loan, like auto financing or a mortgage.

This number ranges from 300 to 850. Based on the information in your credit reports generated by TransUnion, Equifax, and Experian credit reporting agencies, the numbers offer a representation of your history of how often you've borrowed money, how you've handled repayments, and how much you've borrowed.

Here's an approximate breakdown of the FICO score tiers:

300-579: Very Poor
580-669: Fair
670-739: Good
740-799: Very Good
800-850: Exceptional

While you may think that bad credit is reserved for the younger generations, the average age of a person with excellent credit is forty-one. The average age for a person with bad credit is fifty-two. The average overall credit score in America is between 669 and 699. Those scores are the highest since the Great Recession in 2008, showing that Americans are slowly getting back on their feet financially.

The Fair Isaac Corporation doesn't just generate scores for the lending industry. Certain types of FICO scores may also be used by insurance companies to help determine your rates.

People with good credit have some financial habits in common. They pay their bills on time, every time. They don't max out their credit cards, and they tend to not carry much of a balance from month to month, either.

While no one understands the details of the credit scoring model, we do have enough information to make a rough estimate of what makes up a good credit score.

The two most important factors are your payment history and the amounts owed on your accounts. Whether you pay your bills on time accounts for about 35 percent of your total FICO score.

Late payments and bankruptcy are two things that can drop your credit score by hundreds of points in a short amount of time. Making payments on time also helps boost your score.

The amount of money you owe on accounts makes up about 30 percent of the FICO score criteria. A big part of this portion of the credit score is your total credit utilization. So, if you have four credit cards with credit limits of $3,000, $3,500, $5,000, and $2,500, you have $14,000 of available credit. Personal finance experts say that charging more than 30 percent of your total available credit hurts your FICO score. So, in this case, it's crucial to keep balances under $4,200 total.

The length of your credit history also has an impact on your credit score. It makes up 15 percent of the FICO score criteria. This part of the score is determined by the average age of all accounts, in addition to how long you've had your oldest account. If you open a few new accounts, this portion of your score may drop as they lower the average age of your accounts.

Ten percent of your credit score is determined by the "mix" of types of credit you use. Showing that you can responsibly use different kinds of credit helps boost your score. Lenders want to see history with auto loans, bank credit cards, installment loans, and mortgages.

The other 10 percent of your FICO credit score is determined by how many new credit inquiries you authorize. FICO keeps track of the number of times you apply for a credit card or loan. Their research shows that applying for many new accounts within a short period means you may be more likely to make late payments or even default on a loan or credit card agreement. The scoring model only counts credit inquiries for the past twelve months.

While your credit score provides a quick summary of how you've handled credit in the past, your credit file offers a great amount of detail about your current and past accounts. Your credit file contains the details used by the FICO scoring model to come up with your three-digit credit score.

So, if your credit score drops, the reason for that change is in your credit file. There, you may find a number of hard inquiries, missed payments, or charge-off accounts. All of these things contribute to a falling FICO credit score.

Having a good credit score (generally classified as a score above 700) doesn't necessarily mean you've made all the right decisions with your money. Also, having a low credit score doesn't mean that you've made completely terrible decisions.

For example, someone who is deep in debt could have a great credit score because they make every payment on time each month. They may only be making minimum payments and racking up a ton of interest, but the fact that they make every payment on time has a huge positive effect on their credit score.

Having a low credit utilization rate could mean that you keep your balances low, or it could mean that you have high balances, but a lot of access to credit across many cards. So, someone who owes $50,000 in credit card debt can have a great credit utilization ratio if their credit limits add up to $200,000.

You may make all of your mortgage payments on time, but if they take up a large percentage of your take-home pay, you won't be able to save for emergencies or retirement. This is how borrowing too much money can do long-term damage to your overall financial health.

HOW TO COPE WITH YOUR SPOUSE'S BAD CREDIT

If your spouse or significant other has bad credit, you may have many questions about how their financial history could impact your future together. Technically, marriage does not merge your credit histories.

When you apply for a loan together, the lender considers both of your FICO scores, income, and financial histories separately. While one person's excellent credit may carry the other person's average credit through the approval process, black marks like missed payments, defaults, judgments, or bankruptcies could mean denial for you as a couple.

Even if you and your spouse keep your finances completely separate, you'll eventually understand how important it is for you both to take good care of your credit. This basic maintenance limits the negative effect on the other person's financial life. If your spouse's credit score is lower than yours, or if they have bad credit, you don't have to worry that it will directly affect *your* credit.

There are some negative aspects to having a spouse with bad credit, however. If you want to buy a home together, the other person's credit score will help determine the interest rate you pay on a mortgage. If you decide to use *only* your credit to apply for the mortgage, the lender will consider *only* your income when they decide how much money you can spend on your new house.

You could choose to apply for loans on your own, but in most cases, you will be the one liable for the debt. Depending on the laws in your state, your spouse may be off the hook, legally; even if they live in the home you own, drive the car you own, and use the credit cards that are in your name only.

It's also important for the health of your relationship for you to approach maintaining good credit as a joint effort. Set a goal together and work toward it as a couple. For example, you could make it a goal to get both of your credit scores above 750. At this level, you could maximize your financial opportunities and make the most of your future income by minimizing the interest you pay on the debt.

You *both* need good credit to move forward with your financial life together. If you have a spouse with bad credit, consider working together to boost their score.

HOW TO HELP YOUR SPOUSE RAISE CREDIT SCORES

The first step is to get a full credit report for each of the three credit reporting agencies: Experian, Equifax, and TransUnion. Accessing these documents is free once every twelve months if you visit www.annualcreditreport.com. Plan to dedicate time toward looking closely at each credit report for you and your spouse.

Do this together and try to suspend judgment. *Your* credit score may be great for a variety of reasons, but that doesn't automatically grant you the right to judge your spouse's financial past. In fact, if they agree to sit down and look at all three complete credit reports with you, it probably means they trust you to keep your personal opinion of them separate from your opinions about the information contained in their credit reports.

Remember: Bad credit isn't permanent, if you are willing to put a bit of time and effort into correcting the situation.

HERE'S ONE METHOD FOR QUICKLY EVALUATING THE INFORMATION IN YOUR SPOUSE'S CREDIT REPORT:

1. Print each of the three credit reports.
2. Sit down with one report, a red pen, a green highlighter, a yellow highlighter, and an orange highlighter.
3. Underline, in red, any information in the credit report that you believe is incorrect, or that appears more than once on the report.
4. Look up the statute of limitations on debt in your state, and with a yellow highlighter, mark any entries that are no longer legally valid.
5. Mark accounts in good standing with a green highlighter.
6. Mark accounts that you know to be correct that are past-due or in collections with an orange highlighter.
7. Repeat the process with each credit report.

Items underlined with red require your immediate attention. Go to the website of the credit reporting agency and start the process to report the incorrect information. The credit reporting agency will contact the company and notify them of their legal obligation to prove that the information is correct. If they fail to provide that proof, the credit reporting agency must remove the information from the report.

Items marked with yellow can also be immediately reported to the appropriate agency. If the last payment made on the account is outside the time limit imposed by your state's statute of limitations on that type of debt, the credit reporting agency must immediately remove the entry.

Contact accounts marked in orange one by one to ask them to provide proof that the debt is reported to the credit reporting agencies correctly. If you and your spouse can do so, make payment arrangements. Start by offering to settle the debt for a small percentage of the amount the collection agency claims is owed.

Keep in mind that over 40 percent of credit reports in America include at least one piece of incorrect FICO-score-lowering information. It is your legal right to see, understand, and request validation for each and every piece of negative information reported to credit reporting agencies.

When you pay a charged-off account that's in collections, get your agreement in writing before making the payment. Here's the information that should be included in the agreement:

- The original account holder and account number
- The total amount of debt
- The amount of debt that the collection agency will accept as "payment in full"

Pay the collection agency with a cashier's check sent by certified mail. That way, they can't take more money out of your account than indicated in the original agreement. When dealing with a collection agency, it's important to be cautious. If they are a reputable firm, they won't mind abiding by the law, nor will they be offended when you take steps to protect your bank accounts by paying with a cashier's check.

Keep your records of all communication—the letter about your payment agreement, certified mail receipts, and your cashier's check receipt—with your financial records. This debt may pop up again with a different collection agency, and you'll need to be able to prove that you've already settled it.

Once you and your spouse have started the process of cleaning up the three credit reports, you should start to see improvement in their FICO credit score within a few weeks.

ADD YOUR SPOUSE AS AN AUTHORIZED USER ON YOUR OLDEST CREDIT CARD ACCOUNT

Two important aspects of the FICO credit scoring model are payment history, and length of credit history. To help your spouse with both of those things, add them as an authorized user on the credit card you've had longest.

You'll simply have to call the credit card issuer or log into your account online and have your spouse's birth date and Social Security number on hand. Credit card companies don't conduct credit checks, so your spouse's current credit situation isn't a factor in this process.

For the best results, the credit card needs to have a long history of perfect on-time payments. If more than 30 percent of the card's total available credit remains outstanding from month-to-month, or if there are any late payments, adding the card to your spouse's credit file could hurt their FICO scores.

Also, be sure to verify with the credit card issuer that they regularly report on-time payments to the credit bureaus. Some credit card companies only report how long the account has been open, the amount of available credit, and any associated derogatory payment information.

The next time the credit card company reports financial activity on your account to each of the credit bureaus, they'll enter the same information into your spouse's credit reports. They'll also add the credit card's entire payment history into your spouse's reports. This should help immediately boost their FICO credit score.

REDUCE YOUR CREDIT UTILIZATION RATIO

Contact the credit card companies that you and your spouse have accounts with to ask for an increase in credit limits. If they grant any credit limit increases, this will immediately help your credit utilization ratio and give both of your FICO scores a boost.

You can also open a new credit card account with this goal in mind. Don't carry a balance on the new credit card, or you'll defeat the purpose. For example, if you have a total available credit of $15,000 across all of your credit cards, and you carry a balance of $10,000, adding a card with a $5,000 credit limit would help lower your total credit utilization from 75 to 50 percent. Ideally, you would never charge more than 30 percent of your total available credit. If you opened a second new credit card adding another $5,000 to your available credit, you'd have a new credit utilization ratio of 20 percent.

Also, it's important to seek out a credit card with a $0 annual fee. Be smart about raising your credit utilization number. Your goal isn't to go on a shopping spree or increase the buying power in your wallet. It's to raise the available credit on your credit report and boost the FICO score.

Another way to accomplish this goal is to pay down outstanding balances on your and your spouse's credit cards that are in good standing. Start with the cards that have the highest interest rates.

If you are on a strict budget, employ the traditional "snowball" method of decreasing your total credit utilization. Pay the minimum due on each card before the deadline each month. Dedicate the rest of your debt payoff budget to the card with the lowest balance. When that card is paid off, move on to the next. It's critical to pay the minimum amount due on each account on or before the deadline each month. Not only does this prevent you and your spouse from getting charged hefty late payment fees, but it also prevents further damage to the FICO credit score.

Moving forward, make sure that every bill gets paid on time. How you pay your bills makes up 35 percent of your FICO credit score. New information matters more than old information, so now is a great time to put your credit cards on autopay. You can set it up so that the minimum payment is paid a few days before the due date through an automatic withdrawal from your checking account. When you want to make an additional payment, you can do so manually by logging into the credit card portal.

Even if you and your spouse decide to keep part—or all—of your finances separate, it's important for you to take care of the health of your FICO scores by making on-time payments, cleaning up credit reports, and maintaining a healthy credit utilization ratio.

CREDIT "DOS AND DON'TS"

Women face unique challenges when it comes to credit, even with laws in place to level the playing field. The agreeableness and nurturing nature of many women allows them to put off taking care of their financial health. It's possible to take care of family members and meet the needs of others without sacrificing your personal wellbeing. Doing so requires proper boundaries, and that's difficult when juggling a lot of high-priority tasks. While it's terrific to put family first to create a stable household, it's also necessary to prioritize your personal wellbeing. This includes taking care of your credit.

Part of empowering yourself to take control of your credit is understanding which steps to take, or not to take, to lay a foundation for healthy credit. Here are some things to keep in mind as you move forward with the process of establishing and maintaining healthy credit:

Do: If you can't get approved for a traditional credit card, get a secured credit card with no annual fee that transitions to an unsecured card. This will help boost your score by building a good payment history with the credit bureaus.

Do: Put your credit card minimum payments on autopay to help you make every payment on time.

Do: Take twenty-four hours to think about major purchases, especially if you need to use credit to make it happen.

Do: Avoid store-branded cards. They have high interest rates, and many don't have a grace period for new purchases.

Do: Call the credit card company if you accidentally miss a payment. Chances are, they'll refund the late charge if you ask nicely.

Do: Read the entire contract before making a significant purchase with credit.

Do: Consider your income when adding a new loan or credit line payments to your budget. If your total monthly debt payments go over 10 percent of your income, adding to that number could push you into a downward spiral of debt.

Do: Take full advantage of free credit tracking services from the credit card company. Some companies even offer monthly newsletters, tailored to your financial situation with suggestions about how to raise your score.

Don't: Max out your credit card. Your credit score will take a dive within a couple of months if your credit utilization ratio goes too far over the 30 percent mark.

Don't: Wait for your credit card bill each month to pay the bill. You can check your account activity online once a week to keep track of your spending and make sure all account activity was authorized by you. Pay down your balance more than once every month on an account that you use often to keep your credit utilization ratio in a safe zone.

Don't: Put off looking at your credit card statement. Even if you choose paperless billing and autopay, look closely at the transaction history for every account. If you find unauthorized purchases, you have a limited window of time to alert the fraud department.

Don't: Pay interest on your credit card charges. Learn about the grace period on the account and pay off your balance before you get hit with interest.

Don't: Open a credit card just so you can get the sign-up bonus. Unless the ongoing benefits offer advantages, skip it in favor of a card that will serve you better in the long run.

Don't: Open a credit card account with an annual fee while you are trying to build credit. It's much better to find a secured credit card without an annual fee. At some point, you'll have to choose between paying the fee and canceling the card, which could hurt your credit score.

Don't: Fill out a credit card application before you know if you are pre-approved. The pre-approval process won't hurt your score, but applying for more than one or two credit cards will bring it down.

Don't: Cancel your credit card accounts. Even if you worked hard to pay them off, leave the accounts open. Closing accounts could shorten the average length of time you've had credit, which will hurt your FICO score. It could also damage your credit utilization ratio.

Don't: Avoid using credit out of fear. Not having a credit score means you'll pay more for utility deposits, and you may not even be able to rent an apartment. It's much smarter to learn about how to use credit responsibly.

Don't: Use credit cards to cover everyday expenses like gasoline and groceries. If you are using credit as a replacement for income, you are setting yourself up for financial distress.

Don't: Carry a balance on rewards credit cards. Cash-back credit cards are a great addition to your wallet if you pay the balance in full each month. Otherwise, interest charges eat up your rewards, and you end up paying for the privilege of swiping that card.

WHY CREDIT MATTERS, AND WHAT TO DO IF YOU DON'T HAVE ANY

Your credit score lets lenders, insurance companies, potential landlords, and employers know how you've handled money in the past. This information gives them clues as to how much of a risk they may take on if they enter into a business relationship with you.

CONSIDER LINDA'S PREDICAMENT

Linda lives in a two-story home in a nice neighborhood with her three teenage daughters. She decided to stay in the family home after her husband died suddenly five years ago. At age fifty-one, she considers herself fairly financially stable. She doesn't use credit cards, she makes her utility payments on time, and she owns her ten-year-old SUV.

She plans to let her oldest daughter drive the SUV to school next year, so she'll need to purchase a new vehicle for herself. Linda wants a maintenance-free car with advanced safety features, so she's been shopping the latest models at the local Toyota dealership.

Since she doesn't drive more than 10,000 miles per year, and she'd like to have a new car every three to four years, she's considering a lease. The payments would fit nicely into her budget, and her good driving record and long history with her insurance company mean she gets a great deal on full-coverage premiums.

When Linda visits the dealership to work out the details of her lease, she learns that with her current FICO credit score of 610, she doesn't qualify for the best lease terms. This doesn't make sense to her; she doesn't even use credit, so how could she have a "low" credit score?

The salesperson tells her that the best lease terms go to people with credit scores above 700. He offers her a "subprime lease" that requires a much higher amount of cash upfront, as well as a higher monthly payment.

LINDA'S OPTIONS FOR BUILDING HER CREDIT SCORE

Linda has a few months to raise her score, so she has some options. She should take a close look at her credit reports with TransUnion, Equifax, and Experian by accessing them at no charge through www.annualcreditreport.com. It's important to make sure there aren't any mistakes or old information that could be hurting her score. If she finds errors in her credit report, disputing the information with the appropriate credit bureau through their online portals could be enough to raise her score within one to two months. Chances are, opening a new credit card would boost her score, and even with a credit score in the low 600s, there are a lot of options. Here are some important criteria to consider when choosing a new credit card:

No annual fee

When building credit, prioritize cards without an annual fee. As a FICO score rises, it becomes easier to get approved for credit cards with better terms. Canceling a card with an annual fee may make sense after working to build good credit, but closing accounts can hurt scores. It's a better idea to choose a card with a higher interest rate and no annual fee, so it doesn't cost anything to leave the account open, even if it's unused.

Secured credit cards

This type of card can be a great help to people who want to build good credit. Look for a card that transitions to an unsecured card within a predetermined amount of time when the issuer sees that a certain number of monthly payments have been made on time. If possible, avoid secured cards with high annual fees, as well.

Department store credit cards

While they are easy to get, store cards typically charge the highest amount of interest allowable by law. Read the fine print before pursuing this type of credit. Many store cards, managed by a single credit card issuing company, do not have a grace period for purchases.

While the welcome offers sound enticing in the store, it's possible that even the retail associate offering you 20 percent off your entire purchase today if you apply for their store-branded credit card doesn't realize that the 29.99 percent interest rate begins accruing the same day you use the card. This means that by the time you receive a monthly bill, the credit card company has already added a hefty amount of interest to your purchase.

Credit-builder loans

This forced-savings program doesn't involve charging purchases to a credit card or using possessions as collateral. A credit-builder loan servicer, usually a credit union or community bank, deposits a predetermined amount of money into an account. This money is "lent" to the account holder, but isn't accessible until the payment plan is complete.

For example, if you borrow $1,000 for twelve months through a credit-builder loan, you'll make twelve monthly payments of $85. At the *end* of twelve months, the credit union or bank will send you a check for $1,000 and keep $20 as a finance charge for servicing the loan. Every month that you make a payment on time, the credit union or bank reports that activity to each of the credit reporting bureaus, which helps build a credit history and boosts your FICO score.

Any of these quick and easy credit-building options will help someone without a credit history establish a documented pattern of financial responsibility.

Without a history of past credit mistakes or financial hardship, Linda has a lot going for her. She should talk to her local credit union or bank about a credit-builder loan. With this type of loan, you don't make a security deposit, but you also don't get the money right away. The credit union or bank holds your payments in an account until you fulfill the terms of the contract. Each month, when you make a payment on time, they report that activity to the three credit bureaus. When you've made your contractual payments, and the loan term is up, the credit union or bank returns your money minus fees in a lump sum.

She should also ask them if she qualifies for a credit card with no annual fee. Having those two things reporting to the three credit bureaus in her name each month will help her score start to rise in just a few months.

Also, she should ask a trusted friend or family member with excellent credit if they would be willing to add her as an authorized user to their oldest credit card account.

If Linda does these three things, and is committed to making every payment on time, she should be able to qualify for better lease terms in just a few months.

Keep in mind that building credit doesn't have to cost money. Choosing the right credit cards and paying off the balance each month should make using credit with the goal of raising your FICO score a cheap—or even free—process.

Linda has a low credit score not because she was financially irresponsible, but because she didn't understand how or why to make her FICO score a priority. While paying utility accounts on time and managing bank accounts are crucial components of financial responsibility, they don't help raise credit scores. At this point, it's important for Linda to learn as much as she can about how credit works. While there's a great deal of information online about credit, she may benefit from taking a class or participating in a workshop about how to build credit, as well.

HOW TO REPAIR CREDIT

Wouldn't it be nice if you could just hand your credit files and your financial information over to a group of experts and let them work their magic to boost your FICO scores up past the 750 mark? It would be ideal if they could accomplish this in just a few months, of course.

What if you didn't have to pay your old debts at all? Maybe you could pay just a fraction of those bills to make them go away.

These are the promises that credit repair companies make. People who don't understand credit, or who carry the false belief that credit is too complicated to ever really understand, fall for these expensive, time-consuming, and disappointing schemes.

CONSIDER KAMALA'S PROBLEM

After spending nine years pursuing her education, Kamala has landed her dream job, is happily single, and is ready to buy her first home. She works in a medical complex near several recently-renovated historic buildings, and would like to purchase a loft about two blocks from her job. There's a small grocery store nearby, several good restaurants, and plenty of entertainment within walking distance of her new potential home.

Her mortgage broker says she'd qualify for a much better interest rate if she could clear up a few black marks on her credit report. She has an old medical bill from her freshman year in college that went to collections, a recent missed payment on her credit card, several duplicate entries for debt that she paid off last year, and she is still listed as an authorized user on her sister's Mastercard, which is maxed out.

Kamala's broker insists that clearing up her credit report problems is a simple matter of hiring the credit repair agency that works with many of his clients. There's a one-time setup fee of $250, and a monthly fee of $150. The service includes credit-monitoring and security alerts. After the mortgage is complete, the firm will even put a credit freeze in place to protect Kamala from fraud.

Kamala writes her mortgage broker a $500 check and fills out the forms to authorize the credit repair company to access her credit files and communicate with creditors on her behalf. Afterward, Kamala wonders if she made the right choice.

Removing old accounts, making a phone call to a credit card company to remove herself as an authorized user, alerting credit bureaus to duplicate entries, and placing a free credit freeze after getting a mortgage are all things Kamala could have easily accomplished on her own in just a few hours with online resources. She paid a very high price, and will continue to pay a monthly premium for services that she has a legal right to obtain at no charge.

Credit repair agencies do things that individuals could accomplish if they wanted to take a hands-on approach. Kamala would have been much better off—and saved $500—if she had told her mortgage broker that she'd like to think about the possibility of hiring a professional to fix her credit.

After spending about ten minutes online, she would have learned that she could do everything that the credit repair agency offered. She also would have gained a great deal of knowledge about her own financial situation by taking the do-it-herself route.

If you are a woman with very little knowledge of how credit works, you are at risk of falling victim to a credit repair company. There's only one way to move from fear into certainty, and that's by learning. You must learn about your personal financial situation, your credit history, your FICO score, how credit works, and how to improve your situation. No one has as much at stake in this situation as you.

Credit repair isn't complicated. It's also not quick. There are a few things you can do right away to start the process, but real and lasting change takes months, and in some cases, it takes years.

Here are five free things you can do today to jump-start the process:

1. **Ask TransUnion, Experian, and Equifax for the free copies of your credit reports that the law promises.** You can do this at www.annualfreecreditreport.com. Many online services offer you a copy of your free credit report, but they may require you to enter payment information and join their credit alert subscription program. This is unnecessary. Federal law guarantees everyone

with a Social Security number a free copy of each of their credit reports once every twelve months.

2. **Look closely at each of your credit reports.** Do you see accounts you don't recognize? Is there inaccurate information on the report? If you find one or more mistakes, dispute them through the appropriate agency's online portal.
3. **Research the statute of limitations for your state on debt.** You can accomplish this with a quick Google search (*ex: What is the statute of limitations on debt in Washington?*). Now, look through each of your accounts. If a debt collector is reporting an old account to your credit reports and it's past the statute of limitations, ask the credit reporting agency to remove it. They must do this at your request, by law.
4. **Add up your debt payments.** Look at your budget. Can you allocate more money toward paying down your revolving charge accounts—like credit cards—each month? If so, you'll improve your credit utilization ratio for a nice boost to your score. If not, you'll at least understand how much money you'll need to spend each month to cover those bills and keep your FICO score from dropping.
5. **Identify accounts that are delinquent within the past twenty-four months.** These unfavorable items do a great deal of harm to your FICO score. If you can afford to pay any of these accounts to bring them current, do so. If you are only a month or two behind, call the creditor and ask them if they would be willing to remove the late payment from your credit report and refund any late fees. If you can't afford to make payments to fix those

accounts, you'll at least be aware of exactly who you owe and how much you owe.

Recent entries on your credit report make more of an impact on your FICO credit score than older information. Keep this in mind if you feel discouraged when you think about repairing your credit. *Decisive action will yield results.*

Proceed with caution when you want to pay off accounts that were sent to collections more than twenty-four months ago. By law, the collection agency must keep detailed records of how much you owe and how those charges accrued over time. They must prove that you authorized the charges. If they can't produce proof of these things, they have no legal ability to force you to pay the debt, and they must remove it from your credit report.

Also, be on the lookout for duplicate entries. Before paying a debt held by a collection agency, make sure you get the total amount of the debt, the name of the creditor, and the account number attached to the original debt in writing. It's common for one debt collector to sell the debt to another while continuing to report to credit reporting agencies. You'll no doubt want to pay money that you owe, but paying attention to duplicate entries will prevent you from paying the same debt more than once.

If you feel unsure about any debt that appears on your credit report, you can dispute it, and the creditor that owns the debt will provide the proof you need to move forward with making payment arrangements to clear the debt, or they'll remove it from your credit reports.

After you've confirmed that you owe the debt, you can proceed by making arrangements to pay the collection agency so you can get the amount owed cleared from your credit report. It's possible in some cases to settle the debt by paying only a portion of the total amount due. Contact the collection agency directly with your offer. *If they accept, get the agreement in writing before you make the payment.*

After the transaction is complete, you'll need a receipt or letter showing that the debt is paid in full. If the account reappears on your credit report, you can send a copy of proof that you paid the debt to the credit reporting bureau and ask them to remove the derogatory information immediately.

Accounts without new activity typically "fall off" your credit report in seven years to ten years.

- **Foreclosures** are incredibly damaging to a credit report. As time goes on, this type of derogatory report has less effect on your credit. It helps to add new, positive information by making on-time payments. A foreclosure will remain on your credit report for seven years past the final discharge of the debt.
- **Bankruptcies** (Chapter 7, 11, and 12) remain on your credit history for ten years following the day you file. In most cases, Chapter 13 bankruptcies stick around for seven years.
- **Judgments** appear on your credit report for seven years from the filing date. When you pay the debt in full, the company that sued you will update the entry.
- **Collections accounts** will be on your report for seven to ten years from the date it was sold by the original creditor to the collection agency. When you make any payment, the clock resets. When you pay the debt in full, it should appear in your credit file as "Paid Collection," and it will probably show up on your report for seven years from the day you pay the debt.

- **Tax liens**, enforced by federal, state, or local government when you fail to pay your taxes, stay on your credit report for a minimum of ten years from the date they were filed with the court. Paid tax liens stick around for seven years from the time you cleared the debt.
- **Credit inquiries**, although necessary to get a new credit card or most types of loans, may knock your FICO score down a few points. They stay on your report for two years from the date of the original inquiry.
- **Late payments** on revolving debt—like a personal line of credit or a credit card—show up on credit reports for seven years from the date the creditor reported the information.
- **Late payments** on installment debt—like car loans, mortgage loans, or student loans—stay on a credit report for ten years from the date the creditor reported the information.
- **Lines of credit**, like a credit card or student loan that you pay according to the terms of the original agreement, stay on your credit report for ten years from the last time the creditor sent a report to the credit reporting agency. If you close a credit card account, your payment history will still show on your credit report for ten years past the date you closed the account.

HOW TO HANDLE CALLS FROM COLLECTION AGENCIES

If you know you'll need to communicate with a collection agency to clean up your credit report, it's wise to learn a bit about the Fair Debt Collection Practices Act, enacted in 1978. This set of laws lays out specifics about how collection agencies and other debt collectors must conduct themselves when communicating with consumers.

A debt collector is a third party that contacts you or makes an entry about a debt you owe. They purchase the debt for pennies on the dollar, and they retain the legal right to attempt to collect the money. Because the debt collection industry has a long history of taking advantage of consumers, you are protected by the FDCPA.

This is an area of credit repair and credit maintenance where you may have to stand up for your rights. It's crucial to understand the laws about what collection agencies can do, and what they can't do.

If a debt collector calls you, ask for the following in writing:

- The amount of money they say you owe
- The name of the original creditor
- Instructions about what you should do if you don't believe you owe the money

They have five days to comply. *Never pay a debt over the phone, on the spot, or under duress. Never give your personal financial information to someone over the phone, no matter how "official" they sound.*

When you get the document, review it to make sure it's correct. If you aren't sure, you have thirty days to send the debt collector a letter by certified mail saying you don't believe you owe the debt. Keep a copy of the letter for your records. If you send the letter by regular mail, you have no way of knowing if they received it.

If they can prove you owe the money by sending you a copy of the bill from the original creditor, they can start collection activities and continue to report to the credit bureaus.

Keep a file on any collection agency that contacts you about a debt. Make notes about when they called, who you spoke with, and what was said. If the collection agency breaks the law, you'll need those records.

Here's a list of things that a representative from a collection agency cannot do according to law:

- Call you before 8 AM or after 9 PM without your permission
- Contact you at work after you tell them you can't receive that typc of call at your place of employment
- Talk to your friends, relatives, neighbors, or coworkers about your debt
- Make false claims about their status as a credit bureau representative, law enforcement official, or attorney
- Lie about how much money you owe
- Harass you with obscene language, abusive language, or repeated calls
- Threaten to take your property, unless it's named explicitly as collateral in the original loan document
- Threaten to send you to jail
- Threaten to sue you, unless they actually plan to do so
- Threaten to contact your employer

If debt collectors are bothering you, it may be helpful to form a script to help you communicate. These professionals know how to be intimidating and are experts at manipulating you into offering information.

Remain calm and polite, but remember that you don't have to answer their questions. Ask for everything in writing. It bears repeating: *Never give a debt collector a payment over the phone. Do not, under any circumstances, provide a collection agency access to your bank account, debit card, or credit card.*

If you believe you are the victim of unfair debt collection tactics, you have several options. First, contact your state's attorney general's office. They will collect your information and tell you how to proceed. You can also contact the Consumer Financial Protection Bureau and the Federal Trade Commission to report the collection agency's misconduct.

HOW TO BUILD CREDIT

Once you've worked to remove negative information from your credit report and correct any mistakes, you can move on to building new credit. If you have a personal loan, car loan, lease, mortgage, or credit card, and you pay the bill on time each month, you are already laying the groundwork for a healthy credit score.

New information reported to each of the credit bureaus weighs more heavily in your credit score than old information. So, the best thing you can do to build credit is to make every payment on or before the due date.

If you accidentally make a late payment, don't panic. Send the payment immediately. Call the creditor and explain the mistake. Tell them you are working hard to build your credit and ask them to remove any negative report from your credit file.

By the time you get to this stage, you should be familiar with the information in your credit file. If you don't already have a credit card in good standing, now may be a good time to add one to your credit mix.

This benefits you in several ways. Since 10 percent of your FICO credit score is a reflection of the different types of credit on your reports, adding one credit card and making each payment on time will help you build credit over time.

Remember, it's vital to never charge more than 30 percent of your total available credit. Pay the entire balance each month to avoid interest charges, as well. Since it's so important to establish a solid payment history, at least set your minimum payments to autopay so there's no chance you'll forget. If you know you'll be able to pay off the total balance due each month, go ahead and set that up in the credit card payment portal.

THE *FASTEST* WAY TO BUILD CREDIT

Building credit takes time. In some cases, you just don't have the luxury of waiting months—or even years—for your FICO score to reflect your hard work. When you need to raise your credit score in a hurry, there's one tactic that many people use with great success.

You'll need a close friend or trusted relative with a credit card that has a low balance and a perfect payment history. If they add you as an authorized user on that account, you'll inherit their entire payment history. Their available credit on that account will show up on your credit report as an addition to your available credit.

If you need to establish a history of responsible credit card use, but you can't qualify for a traditional credit card, and you aren't able to become an authorized user on someone else's spotless account—consider a secured credit card.

While you'll start from scratch with a brand new account, you also won't take on some of the risks of opening an account with a cosigner or becoming an authorized user. When shopping for a secured card, choose a credit card that automatically transitions to an unsecured account after a certain number of on-time payments. Some secured cards never transition and carry hefty annual fees. For someone building credit, this type of card could cause problems later on. Canceling a credit card could shorten the average length of the credit history.

With a secured card, your spending limit will be the same as the amount of cash you send the credit card company as a deposit. You won't be able to charge more than you provided as security on the account. Secured credit cards function like unsecured credit cards in every other way, though. If you carry a balance from month-to-month, you will be charged interest on that debt. Late payments incur fees ranging from $25 to $40. If you charge more than 30 percent of the card's total available credit, you'll end up hurting your credit score.

Credit-builder loans, mentioned earlier, are usually available at credit unions or local community banks. They offer another way to show that you are capable of making payments on a financial account as promised.

WHAT ABOUT REWARDS CREDIT CARDS?

With sign-up bonuses, travel perks, and even cash back on your purchases, rewards cards are a tempting option when you are shopping for a new credit card. Making a smart choice involves knowing your spending habits and understanding how you've handled credit in the past. If you are confident that you can pay off the balance each month, a rewards card may offer advantages that outweigh any potential negatives.

There are several main types of rewards cards. People who love to travel may find that a great match in a card with a miles or points system they can use for free airline tickets, free hotel stays, various upgrades, and discounts on tickets to events. Shop for a card with a great welcome bonus, but make sure you can fulfill the criteria within the required timeframe.

Cash-back cards often have rotating spending categories that allow you to earn bonuses. Make sure that the rewards rate on everyday purchases is good, so you can get the most benefit out of the card without having to meet any spending requirements. Pay attention to limits, too. Most cash-back rewards credit cards offer a certain percentage of each purchase in the form of a cash reward up to a predetermined spending limit.

No matter what type of card you choose, take time to read through the details before applying. You can find reliable information online at credit card review websites about minimum requirements for getting approved for a certain type of card. Research the card before you apply. This may save you from losing a few points from your FICO score with a hard credit inquiry.

Do the math and figure out whether the potential rewards with normal spending cover the annual fee. Some rewards cards with the most lucrative programs also have steep annual fees. Also, be aware that if you plan to carry a balance on the card, you'll pay interest on your purchases. These costs can quickly outweigh the advantage of any rewards.

LOANS TO AVOID WHILE BUILDING CREDIT

There are a few types of loans that aren't good for people trying to build credit. Subprime auto loans are notoriously difficult to navigate. This type of financial product isn't designed with the consumer's wellbeing in mind.

CONSIDER SAM'S SITUATION

After cleaning up her credit report and paying off some lingering bad debt, Sam feels shaky about her credit score. After her divorce, she couldn't get approved for even a small credit card because her FICO score was 480. It's been a year since she got denied for a car loan, and her vehicle needs new tires as well as brakes and rotors. The car is only worth about $2,000, and with over 300,000 miles on the engine, Sam doesn't believe that putting another $1,000 into the car is the best choice.

There's a small dealership in town with decent used cars and a "no credit check" weekly payment plan. Sam's afraid that her credit isn't quite good enough to get a traditional car loan, so she stops by one Saturday to investigate.

She learns that while payments for a newer car with low miles fit into her budget, the interest rate on the loan is 29 percent. The salesperson explains that people with credit problems have a terrible time getting loans, and he's seen so many people get denied that he tells most folks to skip the headache and just buy a car the easy way.

Terrified of getting denied credit yet again, Sam buys the car and commits to several years of weekly payments.

Living in fear of your credit score isn't productive for women. Sam's emotions led her to accept less-than-favorable terms on a car loan that she'll be tied to for the next few years.

What could she have done instead? A quick application through her credit union's online auto loan site would have given her instant information about whether she was preapproved for a car loan. This type of credit inquiry wouldn't count against Sam's credit score, either. Armed with the facts about her credit situation, Sam would have been able to make the best decision about her money and her future. She also would have saved thousands of dollars over three years while driving a much nicer car.

Women who go through a divorce often find financial matters especially tricky. It isn't easy to explain your money situation, and it's not pleasant to talk to strangers in banks and credit unions about the fact that you are recently divorced. It's understandable that many women avoid the situation entirely.

Divorce can be one of the most devastating things a woman goes through in her lifetime. Facing credit problems or learning about how to manage credit can be incredibly empowering. If you've been through a divorce, be especially cautious about making quick decisions about money. It's alright to take your time and think about your next move. How money and credit fit into your personal vision for your future is entirely up to you.

CREDIT OR CASH? HOW TO CHOOSE

There are some definite advantages to using credit cards instead of cash. Credit card companies must provide fraud protection for unauthorized purchases exceeding $50 if your credit card or credit card numbers are stolen. If a thief takes your cash, it's gone for good.

When you pay with cash, your spending is limited by how much money you have available at the moment. With credit, it's easy to overspend. For many women, using *cash only* is an important aspect of their success with a budget.

The Envelope Method of budgeting has been around for hundreds of years, and there's a reason it works so well for some people. When the money that you planned to spend in a certain category is gone until your next payday, the spending must stop. When you spend cash, you are never over budget.

If you are deep in debt and need to find your way out, budgeting your money each pay period and spending only cash is a foolproof way to get your spending under control. Using a credit card makes thinking through your choices with money optional. With cash, you have to prioritize your purchases.

If you have a track record of sticking to a well-thought-out budget and are ready to start building credit, swiping a card instead of handing over cash for purchases is probably okay. Make sure you can pay off the balance each month, though. High interest rates can undermine your financial goals, and credit card debt may hurt your credit score if your credit utilization ratio goes over 30 percent.

HOW TO MAINTAIN CREDIT

There are two aspects to maintaining good credit: spending within your means, and making your payments on time, every time.

The only way you can spend within your means is to understand your real income and your actual spending entirely. Budgets are a great tool for calibrating income and spending, but it can be challenging to be honest about where your money really goes.

If you need to set up a budget, don't estimate how much money you've spent in various categories in the past. Don't make a forward-looking budget with your spending goals in mind. Instead, go through your accounts to get an accurate picture of your real spending over the past few months.

Using this information to make a budget, you'll be ready to face the reality of the amount of money you spend in each area of life. Living within your means prevents your spending from getting out of control. If you can spend less than you earn, you'll have money to pay down debt, save for emergencies, and meet your day-to-day living expenses. You'll also avoid the debt trap that many women fall into when they overextend themselves financially.

If you find that your budget is just stretched too thin to live within your means, it's time to take a different approach. You have two options: reduce expenses, or increase income.

Try to leave your preconceived notions about both options behind as you explore the possibilities within your life. So many women live in a mental and emotional place of scarcity. When you think about making more money, let your mind wander a bit. Is there a side gig that could add income to your budget? Are you underpaid and overdue for a raise?

Consider your expenses, as well. Is your expensive habit stealing power from your income? Are you tied to high-priced real estate, or living with a lot of debt?

If you want to change your financial circumstances, you must honestly consider the possibilities. Fixing, building, and maintaining good credit requires a healthy attitude toward money and debt. Cultivating that attitude requires you to take action on your own behalf.

For many women, that kind of self-care just doesn't come naturally. If you have long-term goals, it's not just *permissible* to cut your spending and pursue a more substantial income—it's necessary.

It doesn't matter how old you are, or what kind of financial past you have. You have the right to move forward with confidence as you seek to improve your current financial situation. Ask for help or clarification when you need it and expect to be treated with dignity and respect by financial advisors. If you come across an individual that isn't helpful, simply move on until you find someone who is willing to help you succeed.

Remember, no one is born knowing how to handle their

finances. Your journey belongs to you, and you have the right to build the financial future that you want.

CHAPTER FOUR

REAL ESTATE: THE BEST WEALTH-BUILDER

Sandra Luna
Real estate agent

Whether we know it or not, the messages we receive as children directly impact our financial decisions as adults. My story is a perfect example. My mother grew up during the Great Depression. This had an enormous influence on her sense of risk and her work ethic. She strived hard to get all A's in school, and to be the first in her family to graduate college; and she always found ways to support not only herself, but her parents as well, as they got older. My mom believed education, hard work, and perseverance would take you places.

My grandparents had owned a store and cafe in their prime years. Before that, they picked cotton. Picking cotton was grueling, hard work. Their hands bled from hours of backbreaking effort in the fields to feed themselves and make a life for their three daughters. They worked long, hot hours under the glaring sun with no health benefits and no safety net, relying upon their will and their body to sustain them. Witnessing this firsthand, my mother grew up aiming for a job that would have her working in a climate-controlled office. My mother's goals did not include owning her own business or earning money without trading time.

To make ends meet, she often had a "side gig" that earned her a solid second stream of income. She held part-time jobs as an office administrator or bookkeeper, and she was always someone's employee. My mom found rewarding employment working for the city where we lived. This employment gave her a healthy paycheck, a pension, paid time off, and lifelong health insurance. The price she paid was years of her life. She was smart and hardworking, but she always traded time for money. Somehow, she even sent me to private school.

As an adult, I sought a better way for myself. Unlike my mom, I wanted an independent means of earning an income. I rented an apartment for fifteen years and had rewarding, fun jobs that paid the bills, but never moved me forward. I worked full-time and went to school at night, and in six years, I earned a bachelor's degree with no student loan debt.

I came to realize that I needed to own real estate to build a stable financial future. I was thirty-six years old when I started to think about retirement. I believed that if I applied my organizational and administrative skills to a job in real estate, I'd learn everything about investing from the inside out—and that's exactly what happened.

Though my mother had been successful, her repeated advice to me was to get a good job; sacrifice and work for years; and collect a paycheck and pension. I wanted fun and interesting work. I viewed any repetitive job as mental death. As a young adult, I saw frequent corporate layoffs in the news. That showed me that I couldn't rely on a company for a solid financial future, even after years of dedicated employment. What I learned through people I met was that I needed to leverage my efforts and investments so that I did not have to continue to work so hard. I decided to get into real estate. Years later, after buying and selling properties and homes for many clients, I sold my mother's mobile home. Though it was located in the expensive San Francisco Bay area, where median home prices at the time (in 2011) were $500,000, I could only net $45,000 for the mobile home. Unlike other properties, the mobile home had barely appreciated. Although it provided shelter to our family, it was not a great equity investment.

CHOOSE FRIENDS WISELY

When I was sixteen, I had a sign in my bedroom that read, "Choose your friends wisely, for they are who you will become."

At sixteen, I understood this to mean, "Hang out with cool people." As an adult, I reflected on the idea and refined it to mean, "It's who you know." *You only know what you know because of who you are and your environment.*

It is rare that we get an Oprah Winfrey out of an impoverished community. For someone to expand beyond their environment—to have the capacity to consider new ideas outside of their conditioning—they often need a helping hand, or a mentor. Education was that opportunity in Oprah's case: hours of reading, research, and self-determination lead to landing a great first job, which led to another, and so on.

In 2004, I met two accomplished women. One of these women had used a credit card for a down payment on a home in the 1980s, and now owned several properties. The other woman also owned many properties. I also met a couple who owned eighteen units and collected $40,000 a month in rents. Wow! Why was I working forty hours or more every single week, and never getting ahead? I wondered why I didn't think of buying a property sooner.

This was the turning point for me. Since meeting these phenomenal people many years ago, I purchased my first place; rented it; sold it; and bought another. I also co-own a third home: a rental. My primary home is a duplex, and I rent out the other half, nearly allowing me to live mortgage-free. I received help to purchase my first place, and I was creative in how I did it.

As a professional real estate agent, I help couples, single people, divorcing people, family members or friends who choose to co-own, and developers to buy and sell condos, single-family homes, units, and apartment buildings—to live in, or as investments. Nothing makes me happier than finding a great investment for someone, or selling their investment as they cash out or trade up. My aim with this chapter is to meet you where you are right now and gently nudge you to the next step in wealth. You may rent now; own now; or have owned for many years. You may have one investment, or several. Wherever you are right now, there is room for improvement. Take ninety days to figure this out for yourself and make a plan.

GETTING STARTED

For 90 percent of the population, real estate is their greatest asset.[1]

To get started in real estate, you need to assess your assets, income, time frame, and desired outcome. What do you hope to accomplish by owning property?

Nothing can take the place of one-on-one professional advice, so

Assets by wealth percentile group in 2023: Q4

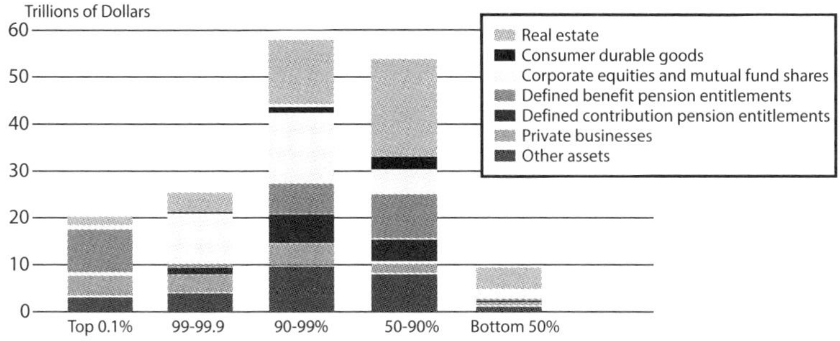

Wealth component	Top 0.1% (US$ trillions)	99-99.9 (US$ trillions)	90-99% (US$ trillions)	50-90% (US$ trillions)	Bottom 50% (US$ trillions)
Wealth component	1.81	4.15	13.67	20.40	4.81
Consumer durable goods	0.61	0.38	1.70	3.34	1.85
Corporate equities and mutual fund shares	9.34	10.39	14.97	4.83	0.41
Defined benefit pension entitlements	0.31	0.99	6.62	9.26	0.47
Defined contribution pension entitlements	0.19	1.41	6.04	5.07	0.60
Private businesses	4.49	3.88	4.97	2.26	0.16
Other assets	3.43	4.19	9.64	8.35	1.31

Note: Distributions by generation are defined by birth year as follows: Silent and Earlier=born before 1946, Baby Boomer=born 1946-1964, Gen X=born 1965-1980, and Millennial=born 1981 or later.

make sure you elicit help from a financial advisor or a successful person you know and trust. Who do you know who leads a good lifestyle? Ask them how they did it. If you choose to work with a professional financial advisor, choose someone who is putting *you* first—not only their financial gain. The wealthiest people always own real estate, and it should be an important part of your overall financial plan.

Real estate is a big part of most successful portfolios. This is because for most people, living expenses—mortgages or rent—are the largest expense we have every month. Why not leverage the biggest cost you spend each month, instead of trying to squirrel away some "extra" money and save?

Having a great real estate agent is vital. I emphasize *great* real estate agent—not just good. Does your agent own their home? Do they have investments? How long have they been in real estate?

Take note that simply because someone is fifty or sixty years old, does not mean they have been in real estate for twenty years. How many transactions have they negotiated, written contracts for, and successfully closed? Ask these questions of your real estate agent in a respectful manner. Nine times out of ten, the broker is closely monitoring a new agent; but since this is most likely your biggest investment, go with a real estate agent who has both experience and the time to work with you.

If you are a seller, ask who will host your open houses and handle calls or emails from online marketing. Get your agent's direct cell phone number. Inquire about who is on their team and what role each person plays. Ask these questions up front to avoid surprises.

Now that you have decided to buy, you need to get to know your market, at least superficially. Do the property values go up? How quickly do they rise, and at what approximate percentage? What were the values in the last recession? How quickly did the local market recover? How solid is your income or nest egg if you have to cover the mortgage for a few months (if it is an investment)? Is an out-of-area investment wise for you? Do you live in a second home market, or do your neighbors mostly live locally? Answering these questions will help guide you to your next decisions.

Most professionals are happy to give you a free consultation. Ask questions; take notes. If you choose to go out of the area because of prices, make sure you have the time and money to handle an out-of-area purchase, and specifically, the management of the property, including repairs and tenant issues.

HONESTY & TRUST

Your efforts to grow wealth through real estate will yield dividends when rooted in honesty and trust with a professional real estate agent centered on your needs. It is a relationship built on candor and confidence. Pick someone you like, and in whom you can trust. Be upfront, open, and honest with them. The agent will not have access to your Social Security number, bank account numbers, or direct credit report; but you need to tell your agent if you have a bankruptcy, a low credit score, a pending divorce, or an issue that may affect your buying power. Your agent will be in contact with your lender and many times refers you to a lender they know from prior transactions. For many reasons, it is helpful to have a local real estate agent, local lender, and local escrow company. You may be surprised at the personal experiences you will share with your real estate agent as you move through the process of sharing financial hopes and dreams, and overcoming real-life obstacles that arise during the process of your real estate journey. That is why it is so important to pick someone you trust and like.

INCOME, DEBT, AND TAXES

When mortgage brokers assess your creditworthiness, they are going to review all of your debt and all of your income streams. Lenders generally want to see two or more years of solid employment, often in the same job or same industry.

You may spend days or even weeks completing the loan application and gathering the list of requested documents. It can be overwhelming, but take heart—these are important steps to changing your future. Once you gather these documents, it is wise to save them in a cloud-based computer folder or hard drive of your preference so that you do not have to go looking for them again. You will need bank statements, credit card statements, tax returns, pay stubs, copies of your ID, and more. You might even consider naming the PDFs of these documents on your computer in a clear and organized manner so it's easy to understand what the file is just by looking at the file name.

Get organized before you complete the application so you do not forget about any credit accounts, liabilities, or debt. The lender, or lender's assistant, will collect the information you provide, and will, in a timely manner, provide you with a loan amount and terms that they can offer you. Ask questions, *always*.

Remember, only declared earnings to the IRS are viable for loan consideration. This means that if you made any income that you did not claim on your tax return, that income will not help you qualify for a loan. For example, you may have made money with a tip-based business, or you may have a self-employed small business—but if you did not claim this income on your tax return, you cannot use those funds to qualify for a loan.

However, all of your debt can easily follow you! Do you own your car, or make payments? Do you have credit card debt? School loans, child support payments, alimony, and other loans or liens will all be considered by the lender—and the deal killer: back taxes owed, or unfiled tax years. Make the effort to file all tax years before you apply for a loan; this will save time and headache later.

Next, the lender will consider cash balances. If you save money in an account, the lender will also want to see that cash "season," or remain on deposit, for at least two or three months. Part of the documentation a lender will request includes all bank statements for the last sixty days—or for one year, if you are using income and not taxes to qualify.

Consult your mortgage broker about any cash gifts, cash savings, or other "undocumented" funds that you'd like to use toward your down payment. If parents or grandparents are helping you out, let the mortgage broker know as soon as possible. If you recently came into a large financial sum, you simply need to document how you came into this money for the lender. Again, a good mortgage broker will be able to walk you through the best timing and approach to best handle any situation.

Keep in mind that interest rates on loan options change often, as do lending parameters. The reserves and credit scores lenders require will also change, depending on the market. This all will impact which loans may be offered to you. Therefore, there are easy times to buy, and more difficult times to be qualified. If it's a difficult time in the lending environment, the lender may require more of a down payment—thereby potentially limiting your buying power—or require more cash reserves than originally anticipated.

Lenders also prefer to see your income at a thirty-seventy up to fifty-fifty ratio compared to your home payment, depending on the loan amount. They will want to consider the loan's entire PITI (principal, interest, property taxes, and insurance) payment. The PITI is your whole amount due every month for the term of the loan. Your loan rate may be fixed (unchanged) for three years, five years, seven years, fifteen years, or thirty years. For this period of time you can count on the principle and interest remaining the same. Once that time frame is up, your payment may go up, so be prepared. Property taxes can also fluctuate slightly. Homeowners often pay if your county or city votes to fix the roads, schools, hospitals, or police and fire services.

My first home purchase had a five-year fixed-rate loan. That means after five years, my payment went from $1,350 to about $1,900. I maintained the higher amount for quite some time, but it wasn't easy or fun, and I eventually found a renter. Talk to your real estate agent and your loan broker about how stable you need your payments to be. If you plan on selling and trading up, you may only need a three-, five-, or seven-year fixed loan. If it is your dream home and you'll never want to sell it, the payment may be higher initially, but perhaps a thirty-year fixed interest rate is the way to go. Talk to your loan agent about their opinion; and talk to your accountant about your new tax write-offs, as a homeowner. It is so important to have a good accountant. There are many tax deductions related to real estate.

If you are self-employed and have a legitimate reason for a home office, this can be a positive deduction for you as well, including possible home additions and improvements. When you sell your primary residence, improvements and remodels may offset your taxes on the profit, as the improvements will increase your tax basis on the home. For example, if you paid $500,000 for your home and you spend $75,000 on improvements, your tax basis is $575,000. When you sell, and it sells for $875,000, you are taxed on the $300,000 difference, not the $375,000 difference from your original purchase price. This would have your profit at $300,000.

In California, at the time of this writing, current tax codes permit single people to shelter $250,000 of profit, tax-free, from the sale of their primary residence. A married couple can shelter $500,000. Therefore, if a single person owned this home, she or he would only be taxed, at their tax rate, on $50,000. A couple wouldn't be taxed at all. California law SB520 allows couples to maintain this $500,000 tax free amount, even if one spouse has been relocated due to disability (such as assisted living) or work.

Talk to your tax advisor about depreciation and recaptured depreciation for properties used as a rental. *This book is meant to guide you, not give tax advice, so always seek out a local professional to discuss your personal tax implications.*

Taxes work differently if you own a rental property. You cannot shelter any amount when you sell; however, you may be able to do a "1031 exchange," which allows you to roll over the profit to purchase another property and not pay taxes on that gain. Should you choose to cash out some, you will be taxed on that amount, for both federal and state taxes. California can be very tricky with their 1031 exchanges, if you plan to take the money and 1031 exchange out of state. California requires a form be filed with your taxes each year, and requires notification upon sale, even if the sale is outside of the state of California! Please consult a 1031 specialist for the implications, including future possible requirements for reporting and responsibilities for a sale.

1031 exchanges are a fantastic way to increase your real estate portfolio. Just imagine: You can buy a property and own it for several years while you collect rent. Then, that property increases in value and you sell, keeping all that value, and you then roll it into a larger investment, potentially doubling or even quadrupling your rental income. There are fees and strict timelines that apply, but this can be a very profitable option, and this practice is quite common among investors. Your experienced real estate agent should be able to refer you to a 1031 specialist and a good tax advisor. Read more about 1031 Exchanges on Page 132.

1031 EXCHANGE

Section 1031 of the Internal Revenue Federal Tax Code, the ability to exchange "like-kind" property and defer paying taxes on the gain accrued. For example, if an investment property is purchased for $100,000 and then sold for $500,000, there is a gain of $400,000 on which income taxes must be paid. Alternatively, if property is exchanged for "like-kind property," then the gain exists but is not recognized and no tax is due at that time. The idea is to delay the income until your tax basis is lower, perhaps in your retirement. The sold property is called the "relinquished property," and the new purchased property is called the "replacement property." There is currently no limit on the number of exchanges one can do in a lifetime and properties must be kept for two calendar years, or twenty-four months. Consult your real estate agent to see if a 1031 exchange is a good option for you. A good 1031 exchange specialist can be a key component on your real estate investment team.

GETTING YOUR DOWN PAYMENT TOGETHER

As I mentioned earlier, I had help with my first purchase. I co-owned with a friend, and she had provided the down payment. I paid the taxes and mortgage and I occupied the property. I lived there for a few years, and then we both rented it out to a tenant.

When we eventually sold the property, we split the profit fifty-fifty after she recouped her initial down payment. Because it was my primary residence, I did not pay taxes on the gain, since it was less than $250,000. She did an IRS form 1031 exchange with her funds into a new investment.

With my second purchase, a friend lent me funds for the purchase. We agreed that I would pay her back within three years when I sold or refinanced the property. Fortunately, I was able to pay her back with my work earnings, but the value of the home had gone up after three or four years, and I could have refinanced if that had been necessary.

Get creative when you need a down payment. I stated earlier that I knew someone who got a cash advance on a credit card. This is unlikely to be sufficient in today's environment—in the Bay Area, or in most parts of the United States.

Several of my clients have obtained loans, or an early "inheritance," from their parents. I've had clients who co-own with their parents, similar to my first purchase. Arranging financing with a friend for the down payment can be a profitable investment for both, and you may negotiate paying them an interest rate for the opportunity. Your friend may even be okay with an interest-only payment, allowing you to have lower payments.

Always have an official promissory note created by an attorney or your escrow officer, and have all parties sign the written agreement with a notary. This note can be a lien against the property.

Don't think you have any wiggle-room for a down payment? Consider the opportunities from a little creative thinking. Can you sell that extra car? Can you sell a piece of jewelry or art which does not have sentimental value? Can you pick up an extra job and save all of that money for a down payment? How about doing your own nails or hair, or limiting meals out at a restaurant to once a month? Where there is a will, there is a way to find the extra cash. Individuals are generally able to take some money out of their retirement plans for a home purchase—within limits—without tax implications. Consult your tax advisor. Be creative, and don't give up.

Remember, you are not spending this money; you are moving the funds into another investment. Your investment is now in a different form, but it is still your asset. If retirement is years away, it might better serve you in real estate. If you do this right, the asset will grow—whether it is your primary residence, or in a rental earning you income. By leveraging your housing costs, you can create a much greater return. Will your stock options or bonds increase in value as fast as the home prices in your area? Highly unlikely. Consider that this property will either house you, or provide wealth opportunities in the form of rental income and tax deductions through depreciation over time. If you buy and your mortgage is low or high; if you own long enough and time it right—you will sell and get all of that money back, plus a healthy profit. Do some calculations and see where you stand.

CO-OWNERSHIP

Many people don't know this, but the idea for co-ownership began in Europe centuries ago. Today, in Europe, it is called "joint tenancy." Joint tenancy has several parameters around which people can own property together, whether they are related or not.

In the United States, "tenancy in common" (TICs) gained legitimacy in the Law Property Act of 1925. In New York, "cooperatives" (co-ops) are very common in buildings as a way for people to own together. Co-ops, TICs, and condominiums are the most affordable way for many people to begin ownership in high-value real estate markets.

Co-ownership can be the answer for many people, and it has unique qualities to consider when deciding whether it's right for you. If someone has a little capital and would like to invest in real estate, but comes up a bit short of overall funds, interested parties can choose to co-own together. You can co-own by buying one house, one unit, or a multi-unit property. Each buyer could have rights over one unit, a specified number of units, or a percentage of the whole, to be determined by the buyers. To own a percentage of the property is called a "tenancy in common." You can be a party in a TIC with friends, family, or business partners. A couple can also hold a title as TIC partners.

Tenancy in common is merely a way to hold a title. In practice, its form is similar to owning a condominium. When a single person owns a property, it is often held as fee simple, or perhaps in trust. When a married couple owns a property, often they hold title as joint tenants, so that if one of them dies, the other still owns the property. A TIC allows any number of people to own a percentage of a property, and the deed will indicate exactly who has how much of the total ownership. The occupancy rights to each part of the property, and what percentage each person owns, will also be listed in the TIC agreement. Always meet with a TIC attorney and create a TIC agreement if you choose this method of ownership.

The TIC agreement will spell out the arrangement, including rules, a map of the property's common and "exclusive use" areas, and even what to do in the event of foreclosure. This is the opportunity to document all agreements as well as shared costs and acceptable property uses. The TIC agreement may have as few as five pages, or as many as a hundred, depending on the owners, property, and arrangements.

This document is not recorded with the deed, but it should be notarized. All parties can choose to ignore the document—until there is a disagreement, and then the document can be enforced. For example, the Agreement may say that the patio

is the only place residents may grill; but if there is a deck, too, and everyone wants to have a party there, then the grilling can happen on the deck, if all parties agree. The agreement can be updated by amendment at any time with attorney involvement, or by all parties initialing the change.

TICs can be wonderful—or they can lead to huge problems, if people are not respectful and agreeable. Knowing your TIC partners, and meeting and discussing issues prior to owning together, is an important part of co-ownership.

If you are entering into a shared ownership of an existing TIC building, most existing TIC agreements describe all areas of potential disagreement and remedies for resolution. Read the HOA meeting minutes, if provided. Basic safety, common respect, and applicable laws steer any agreement toward rules that protect the safety, sanity and right to peaceful habitation for any future resident. If you are creating a new TIC with a partner, I cannot stress enough the value in a TIC agreement. Your real estate agent should be able to refer you to an attorney who is experienced in TIC formation.

As mentioned earlier, TICs are similar to condominiums. The most significant difference is the deed. Both TICs and condos have common areas, shared expenses, and homeowner association fees (HOA fees), as well as potential assessments for common maintenance, improvements, or repairs. Generally, HOA fees are expenses any homeowner will have to pay; however, in certain developments, HOA fees may pay for amenities you don't really need, so decisions to get involved with an HOA should be thoughtfully considered. Expenses every homeowner will need to pay include building insurance, water, garbage, sewer service, and common electricity. At times, an HOA fee may include TV or cable service, telephone service, heat, gas, and exterior maintenance; as well as items you may or may not want to pay for, such as a pool, doorman, security system, or extensive landscaping. A good real estate agent will help you assess a property and, together with a home inspector, help you decide if a property is in a condition suitable for your situation. Prior to making an offer, you should be able to read the HOA documents, which will include the bylaws, budget, meeting minutes, and other governing documents. Read them! A buyer's due diligence when buying property is the responsibility of the buyer to research, understand and ask questions. Do not rely on others to do proper investigations.

In a TIC, you own a percentage of the property with an exclusive right to occupy a particular portion; whereas with condominiums, you own the condo yourself with other common spaces on the land. In either, you will have HOA fees, shared expenses, and rules in place for everyone's protection. Also, you usually are able to do any decorating or remodeling inside your unit (with architectural plans and a structural engineer, if you plan on any structural changes). There are often similar rules in both, such as the need to match the type of existing window frame material and exterior paint colors; and rules and restrictions about storage areas, where you can grill outdoors, hours of quiet time, guest parking, and more.

A condo or a TIC may not be your "dream home," but it can be a great first step to get ahead. Remember your first purchase is just that: Your first purchase. Keep your first purchase for five years or so, then trade up. Talk to your real estate agent about the timing of your local market and which other properties you could next trade up to. They keep their eye on the market constantly and can even provide you with an estimated closing statement from an escrow company so that you will know your taxes, fees, and profit before you sell. Knowing this will help you make a decision about what level of purchase you might next consider.

GET YOUR FOOT IN THE DOOR

According to a report by the National Association of Realtors (NAR) in 2023, 19 percent of first time buyers were single women and 20 percent of repeat home buyers were single women. This represents the second-largest home-buying group after married couples, who make up 52 percent of homebuyers.[2]

Consulting with your real estate agent is important before you make any big decisions. Often there is so much information available to us online that we think we have done our research on a number of topics like investing, real estate, the local market, or even financing. Ask the experts. A second opinion never hurts, but you could have some major blind spots and not realize it. Sometimes reading national news and national real estate updates can give you ideas that simply do not exist in your local real estate market. Find that real estate agent you trust and ask them what they think. If they are a good real estate agent, they know the market and its intricacies.

Markets can also change on a dime. Something you learned about the market three weeks ago could completely turn around; and only someone who has access to other agents and company-wide sales trends, and who is out in the field working in real estate full-time, can possibly know the up-to-the-minute news.

The most important thing is action. I knew a couple who waited eight years to buy. Eight years! They were convinced the market was just about to go down . . . just about to go down, for eight years. Finally, I decided to show them how much equity they had lost. A flat they liked, but decided to wait and not buy, was selling again—and after those long eight years of waiting, they essentially had a $700,000 loss in equity. They ended up paying $800,000 *more* for a property than when we were originally looking. Don't be too cautious! Take a chance and get your foot in the door.

"No, it's not your dream house. It's your wake-up-and-smell-the-coffee house."

CartoonStock.com

GIVE UP THE FIREPLACE!

If money is no object, by all means, be picky. If you have a budget, please be realistic and see the bigger picture and your long-term goal.

Two significant things you cannot change are location and, often, square footage. There are instances where you may add square footage to a property, but can you afford to build? The current building price is $900 to $2,400 or more per square foot of new construction in the San Francisco Bay Area. Any number of things can create a delay or increased repairs, including waiting for permits. If you find a home or investment in a good location, consider if you can work with it. If you know it is too much work, back off.

For your own home, you want it all. You probably have fond memories of a fireplace, and now you think you've got to have a fireplace to be happy. And if it's your second purchase, you can be more choosy, because chances are, you have a bigger down payment from the sale of your first place.

Touring many properties is a great way to compare and to spot a good deal. Seeing the properties in person is important, too, because photos only tell half the story.* If your time is limited because of your work schedule, or your family is a concern on weekends, tell your real estate agent exactly what you want, and they can scope things out for you.

Also, do everyone a favor—*please* do not base everything on price per square foot. Price per square foot tells us nothing about the finish of a property. This metric says nothing about the type of flooring, kitchen counters, paint on the wall, appliances, views, outside space condition, lot size, neighbors, or parking. So, it is one part of a whole that you'll consider when defining value.

You may not find the perfect place. Let me restate that: you *will* not find the perfect place—at least, you won't think it is perfect. But it will be, because you can afford it, and it checks several boxes. It fits your overall vision. You may just have to give up something, but strive to see the bigger picture and the equity you'll be earning. Your first place will not be your last place—at least, not usually—so it is worth it to give up the fireplace, if you have to.

Don't ever feel it is too late! Unless you're five years from death, purchasing real estate can still pay off. I know a woman who was a sixty-five-year-old first-time buyer. It has been three years, and her property is already worth about 10 to 15 percent more. Would she have saved as much in her savings accounts during the last three years? Doubtful.

COVID SHOWINGS

During the COVID-19 outbreak beginning in 2020, the real estate industry had to maneuver and adapt to safe practices. In 2024, showings are in person, and you can tour again with your real estate agent; but during the height of COVID, most "showings" were done virtually and by appointment. It's a good idea to drive by the house and check out the neighborhood if you do not know the exact location. Most listing agents now provide virtual tours or 3-D tours so that people are able to virtually "walk through" the home online. Disclosures and reports are often read before seeing the home in person. I use online map programs to "walk" down the street and see if there are businesses in the area, or busy streets. Your real estate agent will guide you through this process to ensure that you are informed and knowledgeable about the home before exposing yourself to an in-person showing, if this is a concern.

THE DANGEROUS GAME OF USING EQUITY

Equity, like credit, can be a sound asset—or a part of your downfall. Your home is not a bank account. Yes, you can use a home equity line of credit (HELOC) to do repairs or upgrades; but make sure you are able to afford to make the payments later. If you have a good interest rate, using your equity can be an inexpensive source of funds. I've seen property owners with waning income refinance and refinance, until finally, they can't make the larger payment; and now they do not have sufficient equity, either. Even if they sell to downsize, owners still may not come out ahead.

Use equity only if your income is solid and you want to borrow money. If you *need* to borrow money, beware. The subtle difference between the "want" and the "need" to borrow should be clearly weighed against your income stability before deciding to leverage your home equity for funds. Sometimes selling a large home is better than refinancing, because you will be able to put more cash down for a smaller, more affordable home and still have money in the bank.

Every situation is different, and market timing is important. Often the best timing is your own personal timing. Making a move is best when you need to make it, rather than waiting for a market shift that may or may not come. As always, seek a professional opinion.

TYPES OF INVESTMENTS IN THE RIGHT LOCATION

It is hard to make blanket statements about your home search, and even harder with potential property investments! Every investment has to be looked at individually. There are many things to consider, such as GRM (gross rent multiplier) and CAP rates (capitalization rate), but investigating current tenants is important, too.

In California, there are strict tenant laws, rent control, and in certain places, even eviction moratoriums. Understand your rights as a landlord before buying any property that is already tenant-occupied. Further, you always need to investigate the condition of property, because repairs will be your cost, too.

There are several locations where rentals perform well—and you cannot beat a good location: anywhere near colleges, public transportation, shopping and business districts, or tourist areas. Renters are often young; often, they have no car, and therefore prefer to walk or bike to places. Choose responsible people who will care for your property and not consider it a party place. If you can find a building in decent shape, in a good location, you may have struck gold. Be aware that tenant profiles can make or break an otherwise good scenario.

As with any investment decision, you should crunch the numbers. Ultimately, you need to go with your instinct. Know the rent control laws and eviction procedures in your area. Be aware that these laws may change at any time.

It is important for you to talk to your real estate agent and get data on different types of properties. For example, I discussed earlier that I had to sell my mother's mobile home for $45,000, when the average price for a single-family homc in the area was about $500,000 at the time. This is because mobile homes do not appreciate as quickly as single-family homes or condos.

Technically, mobile homes are personal property. You used to register them with the Department of Motor Vehicles because they are considered a type of vehicle. This is changing in some areas and the need for annual registration for mobile homes may change to paying actual property tax instead.

Many times, mobile homes, tiny homes, or modular homes reside in an RV park or mobile home park and you pay rent on the space, which includes a private yard, parking, and a designated address and mailbox. There could be an HOA fee. Less common are mobile homes where the owner also owns the land. If you have a limited income and need a safe, clean place to live, a mobile home may be a good option for you; but it won't necessarily grow wealth like a condo or single-family home. However, sometimes that is not the only important thing to consider, so mobile homes have an important place in our housing market. Real estate agents can help you navigate these decisions, so ask yours which option is the best for you in your area, and ask how mobile homes have performed, comparatively. Since COVID, the mobile homes in my area have greatly increased in price and in retail prices. Mobile homes will be your property and may protect you from eviction in your old age. They may also provide a supportive community as well. These purchases should not be dismissed if you are on a strict budget.

CHOOSING A REAL ESTATE AGENT

I was recently discussing with a colleague what an intimate and unusual job we have as real estate agents. Our clients invite us into their home. They give us a key and let us invite strangers inside to show the property. We learn about their finances, dreams, debt, and family dynamics, and we see how they deal with the stress that inevitably comes with making large financial decisions and transitions in life.

Be aware of how you best handle stress, and check yourself throughout the process. Selling and buying real property may take one month, three months, or a year. An accommodating real estate agent will go as fast or as slow as you want to go.

As I said earlier, choose a real estate agent who is experienced and in whom you trust. They do not have to be the person you would want to go to dinner with, but they have to be the person you would trust with your checkbook. If you do not trust their advice, you will be fighting them every step of the way. Trust them to make good decisions and to be up-front and honest with you. They may tell you things you do not want to hear. If you are a couple, let them in on your decision and thought process.

If you question their judgment, ask them why they believe as they do. Most real estate agents can tell you about a past experience which is guiding their cautious (or risk-taking) behavior today.

BUYER BROKER AGREEMENTS

Beginning in August 2024, there is a nationwide practice for every buyer's agent to sign a Buyer Broker Agreement with every buyer. This means if you want an agent to engage with you and show you homes, you need to make a commitment and so do they. These are not new agreements. For decades the way we have initiated transactions is by placing properties (listings) in the Multiple Listing Service (MLS). As a member of three of my local Realtor Associations, I belong to three MLSs. In the MLS, a listing indicates very specific details of a property (square footage, lot size, APN number), as well as artsy linguistics "advertising" the property. It also includes any photos the listing agent wants to showcase and the legal identification of the listing broker and brokerage. For the past several decades, the MLS has included the CSO (commission for the selling office). Up until now, the buyer has been mostly unconcerned about the commission process. In other words, for decades buyers have searched for a home, analyzed comparable sales, and then offered a price they agree to pay. The seller's broker then, at close of escrow, has shared the commission via escrow with the buyer's broker as advertised in MLS listing. This fee historically has been 2.5 to 3 percent, depending on various factors, including effort and negotiation. The buyer has paid the price of the house and their closing costs such as appraisal, escrow fees, notaries, recording fees, the lender fee, and perhaps prepaid insurance.

What has changed? Beginning August 2024 and forward, the seller's agent is not able to offer compensation to the buyer's broker in the MLS but is still able to offer it via email, fliers, websites, verbally, etc. It is negotiable. It now must be written on a new form that you will submit before or with your offer of purchase. To summarize, a buyer's agent will need to investigate if sellers are willing to pay the buyer's agent's commission and even if they do not say they are willing or offering, buyers can always request a credit in escrow within the contract for this or other NRCCs (non-recurring closing costs). This is one more reason why you need an experienced agent who is good at negotiation and deal making. Let your agent advise you on the best way to proceed with the right property.

Signing an agreement with an agent you want to work with should be a no-brainer. First: If they are licensed, they have a fiduciary duty to you, so put it in writing. Second: If you were to buy an off-market property, the agent would have to ask for the commission from the seller's agent, too. (This is another item to discuss, but it's not that far from how we do business now.)

I am an agent in the Bay Area. Our housing is expensive, and our markets are competitive. In California, commissions have always been negotiable, and for the last fifteen-plus years there have been services who will list your house for a flat fee or small percentage. The consumer has even had the option of listing their own property. Given that selling and buying property are such important, high-risk and high-reward transactions, make sure you have solid professionals behind you to support and advise you.

WHAT IS ESCROW?

In Southern California, "title" and "escrow" are often two separate entities. "Title" refers to the deed of a property. "Escrow" is a period of time that the property is transferring ownership once it is in contract, but it can also be referring to the company handling. When you are "in escrow," you are either buying or selling. In Northern California, where I live, escrow and title are usually handled by one company, and there are several good firms handling this sort of work. Your real estate agent will have a handful of favorite escrow officers and companies and will open a pre-escrow if you are selling. If you are the buyer, you choose the escrow company; but often if the sale involves a trust or foreclosure, the existing escrow company has perhaps done a lot of work already and your real estate agent may be satisfied using the company where the pre-escrow was opened. The escrow officer is another spoke in the wheel of your successful real estate portfolio! They are often very experienced professionals who know almost everything, it seems. They will accept all monies from the buy side, pull a Preliminary Title Report, handle all signings related to the transfer of the deed, and so much more. A Preliminary Title Report is a document showing all ownerships and liens on a property as well as egresses and other information including the tax assessor's map. This report is gathered for every sale. Your escrow officer will most likely have a team behind them, and their office typically operates under regular business hours. Ask questions! Make sure you understand the next steps. Always ask your real estate agent to answer some baseline questions.

PAYING YOUR PROPERTY TAXES

During my first purchase of real estate, no one explained to me how much property taxes would be, and how often the bills would be due. Twice a year sure comes up often! It left me scrambling every six months to come up with thousands of dollars to pay them.

I tell every client I have to save for property taxes all year long by opening a new bank account just for the property. Before you close escrow, your loan agent should be able to tell you what your "PITI" is: principle, interest, taxes, and insurance. Open the account by saving one to two months of these payments.

Each month, on the first, put in your PITI payment. Have your mortgage auto-deduct on the fifth of each month. When your taxes become due, the amount will be in the account; you can write a check and send it in.

Nothing is worse than stressing over how to come up with thousands of dollars to pay your taxes. You can check your city and county tax rate online. In California, property taxes are based on your purchase price, so before you purchase, you can know this approximate amount. If you have questions, your loan agent, real estate agent, or the escrow officer should be able to help.

CALIFORNIA PROPOSITION 19

In California, the passing of Proposition 19 in 2020 created an invaluable opportunity for many homeowners. You may recall that since the passing of Proposition 13 in 1978, property taxes are stable for any homeowner, save local initiatives. Proposition 13 prohibits reassessment (tax assessing, thereby setting property taxes), except upon change of ownership or for new construction. That means that when you buy your house, the assessed value of your home becomes the sales price (plus any permitted work you do), and your property tax is based on that value and will not change until there is a change of ownership. For homeowners on a fixed income, this was a meaningful ruling.

This stable property tax cost makes homeownership affordable for many; but it also can create "golden handcuffs." That low cost locks you in, so homeowners are paying a low cost compared to sales prices years later.

For several years there have been five counties within California that will allow the transfer of the property tax rate if you move within or to a county. Meaning, if I own my home and have since

1980 and I pay a low property tax rate, I can sell my home and buy a new home, but still pay my property tax rate from my 1980 house. For seniors, this is a game changer, but with only five counties participating, it limited where one could move.

Proposition 19 allows any homeowner age fifty-five or older, and anyone with a disability or who has been a victim of a natural disaster, to buy a new home and transfer their original tax basis. Again, game changer. Now you can move anywhere in California, downsize, and still pay the property taxes that you've been paying. There are certain conditions one must meet, and the caveat is that you apply for the tax rate after you buy the new property. Meet with your tax advisor and see if this law is an option for you. People are just starting to take advantage of this opportunity.

As an agent, it pains me to see elderly or disabled people "trapped" in their homes because of stairs or unsafe accessibility issues. If you live up stairs, on a hill, or in a multi-level home, perhaps you should see the negative impact that could have if you injure yourself or have any mobility issues now or in the future. Falling greatly impacts older folks and if you can address this before it becomes a problem, you may save yourself harm and inconvenience.

I cannot stress enough that you must think ahead and plan accordingly. A single-level home, a condominium building with an elevator, or a flat lot can help prevent accidents and falls. By being proactive and downsizing yourself to a safer environment, you will be helping your heirs not have to deal with a large property full of things that will need to be sold or given away.

FACING YOUR FEARS

Nothing is more sad to me than people who get paralyzed with fear and do nothing—change nothing; accomplish nothing. You can analyze, and "what if," and think of the worst case scenario until you are blue. It does no one any good—especially you.

If you want to grow a chunk of money and you do it thoughtfully, there is no better way than through real estate. Some people love the stock market and are good at it, or just lucky. Real estate is a tangible, endlessly useful, and necessary possession that we all need: a place to live. You can bet people will eventually need their cash that is in the stock market, and you can also bet that people are not going to start living in caves again.

Yes, there will be a percentage of people who go into tiny-home-living or RV-living; but most people want a home to call "home"—a place to return to after a busy day, and a place they'd love to "staycation" in. Every market is different. Understanding trends in industry and commercial business—i.e., jobs—in your market is important. If your area is reliant on one industry or one company, understand the long-term ramifications if that company moves or shuts down.

"Nothing ventured, nothing gained" are the wise words of Benjamin Franklin. There has never been a more accurate statement. You have to take risks in life. I am not saying that if you came into $300,000 from an inheritance, you should invest it all; but $100,000 is 20 percent of $500,000, and in most markets, $500,000 can get your foot in the door. So research, evaluate, decide, and go for it. No one will make it happen except for you.

MAKING AN OFFER

Making an offer is an important step, and can be exciting, exhilarating—and stressful.

As I mentioned before, you should see as many properties as possible. Take into account the location, the size of the home (both square footage and number of rooms), position to sunlight, yard, lot size, existing condition, phone signal strength, possible updates you could do, the market, and the level of competition.

How long has it been on the market? If a property is on the market for more than about three to four weeks, chances are you may get some money off the price. If it's new on the market, or less than two to three weeks, you may need to offer full price—or even more. Check with your real estate agent and they will be able to provide you with comparable properties and direct advice about your local market. Your real estate agent will check with the listing agent for the property you like and find out what the interest level has been.

When you find a property you like, review the disclosures. Disclosures are facts about the property that the seller needs to provide regarding the condition, history, and any upcoming issues about the property that may affect your decision whether or not to buy the property. There are several state, county, and city disclosures that are mandatory. There are other disclosures that you will only receive if the seller has lived in the property, or did not inherit the property. People who inherit property may be exempt from having to answer certain questions that they most likely do not know the answer to. Find out which category your property falls under.

After you read the disclosures, you can decide whether or not you want to perform inspections of your own. Having inspections on the property, particularly if you are a first-time buyer, is important. The inspection will teach you things about the property that every homeowner should know, such as how to turn off the water, where the gas shut-off valve is, or where the sewer line or septic system is placed. A good inspector will point out things about the home that are good in nature, and things that need immediate attention or future repair.

Buying a house is like having a baby, and it may give you

psychological "stretch marks." You'll need to take care of the property, and knowing the state, workmanship, and condition is imperative. Your real estate agent is not a contractor, most likely; but they can suggest which inspections you need, and when.

As you write your offer, you will decide on a price to offer and the terms of the contract. Within the contract, you will write stated and default contingencies. A "contingency" is an event or condition that the contract is based upon, or *contingent* upon. For example, your contingencies may include loan, appraisal, inspections, and other certain reports or events such as selling the property you own now. A loan contingency will mean that if you get approved for your loan, you will buy the property. If the home appraises for the right value, you will buy the property. If you can sell the home you own now, you will buy this new property. It will include purchase price, number of days to close of escrow, and timelines for all contingencies. It will include a title officer and company, and you will sign a form stating you agree to work with your agent's broker and your agent.

If your inspection or any due diligence during your inspection contingency period uncovers new information about the condition, or a significant defect about the property, you can cancel your contract and not be obligated to buy it. Always talk to your agent if you're getting cold feet. Although terms and price are agreed upon at ratification, everything is negotiable, and the seller may help cover the cost of an issue—like the roof you now realize you need to replace. Every transaction is different, and this is why you need a good agent with experience, negotiation techniques, and a diligent work ethic.

With the help of your real estate agent, you will determine the market, competition, and contingencies you want to have within your offer. You need to be comfortable with your risk; and unfortunately, in hot markets, contingencies may lose you the deal. No house comes without some issues, generally, so weigh your risk versus your desire to be in the house, and then go for it.

After submitting an offer, the seller will respond with either a counter, a signed contract, no response at all, or a "thank you, but we accepted another offer." A counter-offer can change any terms of your original offer, so read it carefully. It may request to change the price, the time of your inspection contingency, or the down payment; or it may add in other terms, such as a seller conducting a 1031 exchange, which will require you to sign related documents (at no cost to you).

Your real estate agent may advise you on how to respond to any counter or addendum to the contract, but the ultimate choice is yours. Many times, a counter period can last up to a week or two, or in rare cases, even longer. Other times, with several offers in play, the counter-offer may have a fast-approaching deadline to respond—sometimes even a few hours!

Don't be discouraged by counter-offers, and don't take them personally. Some people let their ego take over in this process and refuse to communicate. Be an adult and respond, unless the price they want is so far-reaching that you can no longer see the value. This process is business. Some people love to negotiate, and they assume you'll counter back and forth a few times; others hate it, and refuse to play ball. My point is: Don't lose out on a good opportunity simply because the seller wants to make things a little difficult for you. If the home is right for you, it is worthwhile to engage.

Once all terms are decided and agreed upon in writing by all parties, the contract is ratified. The following day is Day One, and all contingency periods begin simultaneously. Your real estate agent will send the ratified contract to your lender. If you have inspections to do, they will set about scheduling them. Your lender may immediately ask you for more documentation on income or reserves. It can feel like a part-time job, but try to get to your lender anything the company asks for without delay. Lost time waiting for your documents can slow down the process, so try to get things done day-of, and not at the end of the day, which effectively means losing that day.

Read and reread the disclosures. Ask questions. You will most likely be speaking to your real estate agent on a daily basis or every other day. Stay positive and let them know your concerns so they can address them. You will be asked to sign everything; and truthfully, you really cannot possibly read all the fine print, but ask your real estate agent which documents are property-specific and which documents are state disclosures or mandated disclosures. Pay particular attention to the property-specific ones. Always ask questions.

Within a couple of days of your offer being accepted, you will be asked to fund escrow. This amount is often 3 percent of the purchase price, but it can be more or less depending on what your real estate agent wrote on the contract. Discuss this amount with them *as you write the offer*, not after.

Wire fraud is a real thing, and you will most likely sign a disclosure about it. Never transfer funds without first initiating a call to your escrow officer and confirming wire instructions. Confirm with them the best and most secure methods to get them the large amount of money. Dropping off a personal check may be the easiest way.

This initial deposit is also known as "earnest money" or "good faith money." Escrow, who is technically a third person, acts as a neutral party to hold the funds in an escrow account. This means that your agent will not hold the funds; their agent will not hold the funds; and the seller does not yet receive the funds. Rather, the funds will be held in a separate escrow account until the transaction is closed or canceled.

Should you cancel your contract within the contract parameters, you will receive one hundred percent of your funds back after all parties sign and agree to release the funds. Should you not follow the contract as written, and you cancel the contract after contingencies are removed, your deposit may be in jeopardy. Discuss with your agent what your time frame is and when and how this money of yours becomes nonrefundable.

During the escrow process, your escrow agent is available to talk to you if you have any questions. The company should provide you and your agent with an estimated closing statement, showing all your fees, closing costs, and the final amount you'll need to fund escrow. Sellers and buyers have different fees at close of escrow, and these fees are negotiable at the time you write up your offer contract. Normally, sellers must pay for mandatory reports—such as a natural hazard report, and often a permit history report from the building department—but not always. Every locale is different, and local ordinances will specify what needs to occur and who is ultimately responsible.

Once you remove your contingencies, your deal is pending and you are about to close escrow. While you are in escrow, it is important that you maintain good credit. Do not buy a new car or make any large purchases, such as financing furniture. Don't open any new credit accounts, as it can show up on your credit report. Your lender will most likely pull your credit again, just before close of escrow, so keep that credit score high.

Talk to your real estate agent about when or if to give notice to your current landlord if you are a renter. Is there any reason why your transaction may not close? Maybe there is a disgruntled heir that will refuse to sign? A transaction is not closed until it is *closed*, so be cautious about buying new furniture or appliances until your home is closed and you get the keys and possession.

Your agent and the agent on the other side will give escrow instructions to escrow. These will include purchase price, who pays for which fees, your name, and any tenant information, if applicable. Your lender will also be in touch with escrow, and they will send the loan documents directly to the escrow company. The escrow or title company will record the new deed in the buyer's name at the county recorder's office, and immediately release funds to the seller. Once this happens, keys can be given to the buyer, and the buyer can now occupy, make any updates, paint, or move in.

BEFORE MOVING IN

Before you move in, you may want to make some changes that you don't necessarily want to be present for, if the work is extensive. These changes may include floor updates, re-sanding wood flooring, painting, or any loud indoor work. If you can live in your original home as this work is being performed, it may save you some noise, dust, and annoyance.

Ask your real estate agent for a good moving company. Ask your real estate agent for referrals of *any* kind, including gardeners, haulers, electricians, painters, plumbers, or a window covering company. Your agent will have experience with hundreds of moves, and should have a network of reputable and reliable tradesmen for everything from major construction to window replacement, roof replacement, gutters, and pest control. You are not in this alone, and your agent wants to help, so just ask.

The time after you close escrow is exciting! You're moving in, setting up, and making it home. After talking to your agent every day, you may lose contact; but be assured they would probably love to hear from you, see pictures of your new house, or even get an invite to come see it (and you!) in person. I love when I get an invitation to see a home I sold, and I feel so honored and appreciated when I hear from a happy client.

FUTURE USE

Many people today are realizing how rewarding it feels to have the financial security that comes with a second stream of income. If you cannot purchase another property, perhaps you are able to add a unit to your current property? Use caution, and understand that zoning laws are subject to change; you may need to make a trip down to the building department in your county to confirm any information you find or go online. It is your responsibility as the buyer to do some investigative work, but your real estate agent is able to point you in the right direction.

There are property lots and zones where you may be able to add on an entire new building structure, or you may be able to turn a basement into a second or third unit. Helping you imagine a possible configuration with an entry location from the street, parking, possible separate outdoor space, and the like is something your real estate agent should be able to help imagine. An architect or designer can help accomplish this, too, and will work to fully unveil a property's true potential. Local architects should know local zoning codes, and they will have worked with the planning department in your community. Accessory dwelling units, or "ADUs," are popular and trendy now, with housing being at an all-time high and people seeking extra income. ADUs work well for college students, aging parents, or tenants.

"Worst-case scenario? The renovation goes three years and two million dollars over budget, one of you bludgeons me to death with my own hammer, and you both get the electric chair."

WHERE ARE YOU ON "THE SPECTRUM"?

To come up with the ninety-day plan that is right for you, consider whether you want to buy, or sell, or both! Take these ninety days to plan. Your rolling goals should include milestones for property appreciation, tax savings, and potential income. You may even create a business plan for rental property acquisitions and management.

For those of you who are ready to buy an investment or a second home, or maybe help a friend to buy, congratulations! You have won the small battles and are on the other side.

I check in every so often with my mentor to get tips on how she thinks, how she plans, and what she looks for in a new property. For example, one of the things she taught me was not to rush to pay off my mortgage. *What*?! Don't we all want to pay off our mortgage? Depending on your age, yes or no. If you have more working years ahead of you, owing money on your home may not be a bad idea. First of all, you can write off the interest on your loan. Secondly, you can use your money to buy another property—aiming, of course, for positive cashflow. It is the old lesson of "other people's money." Using money from other people—in this situation, the bank—is helpful. In other words, some debt is good. If you are nearing retirement, perhaps you'll be living on a fixed income; and then, yes, you may want to pay it off. Always consult with a professional.

WHEN YOU'RE THE SELLER

Selling your house can be just as much a patience-exercise as buying. Hopefully you are the kind of person that makes a decision and sticks with it but knows when to pivot. Listen to your real estate agent regarding fixes and updates you may want to make before going on the market. If money is an issue, let them know and maybe consider a personal loan to make these updates. There are loan programs created just for sellers to prep a property. You will more than likely recoup any money you put into the home when you sell, but market conditions matter. There are other factors, such as location, so you don't want to make any unnecessary updates, either. Again, ask questions and trust your real estate agent. You may read articles or listen to the news about the market but if you have an experienced and active agent, they deal with the real estate market on a daily basis. They hear market updates from lenders, watch rates, and hear about off-market sales that you cannot possibly know about. They also speak to other agents and hear what open house traffic was like over the weekend, and learn about new strategies people are pulling out of their hats. A lot goes into knowing the market, and the market changes from week to week, so get an expert opinion and listen to it.

HOME PREP

The biggest thing about selling is getting your property ready to see. Do whatever you can to increase your curb appeal and show the buyer it is "move-in ready." Your real estate agent will take photos or videos and do all the marketing such as advertising copy, floor plans, and so on, so it's important that you like their marketing skills. Before you sign anything, make sure you like their branding and the marketing of their past listings, and that you trust their negotiation skills. Do they know other agents? Are they actively helping sellers and buyers right now? Consider the timing of the market and ask them when you should prep to go on the multiple listing service (MLS).

Prep your house. Consider, at minimum, painting. Fresh paint removes most existing odors and creates a fresh, clean look and blank slate for the new buyer. Stage, too, if you are able—it will do wonders for your home's impression on the public. The photography will look better if you stage, and in-person buyers won't need to guess if a queen or king bed will fit in your bedrooms. Staging is about emotion and you will want to engage all five senses when a person walks into your beautiful home.

DISCLOSURES

California puts the impetus on the seller; any and all facts the seller or agent knows about a property, they must disclose.

For example, if your neighbor's teen is in a band and they practice every afternoon for an hour—that's a disclosure. If there are racoons that knock over garbage cans—that's a disclosure. If you can hear the freeway or a busy intersection from your home or yard—that's a disclosure. If anyone passed away in the home, or you had a pet, or you had a past fire or mold issue—those are all disclosures! Anything that may sway the buyer's decision whether or not to purchase is a disclosure.

Your agent will explain items as you answer numerous questions about the home on disclosure forms. Ask them for help and advice on how to word things properly. For example, I never say "fixed"; rather, "repaired." If you had a leaky roof, you may want to say it's "fixed" . . . but what if it again leaks next winter?

ON THE MARKET

Once the home is on the market, leave your agent alone and expect updates. You want your agent speaking to other agents and buyers about your home, not just you! Trust the process, your agent, and the universe to bring you a buyer. It will happen! Ask your agent if they'd like help watering plants, sweeping, and cleaning. If you want frequent updates, ask your agent for frequent updates; if you're busy too, let them know you're okay to hear from them when there is actual news or an offer to review. The less time your agent spends taking care of your feelings and helping you process the time it may be taking, the more they can market, talk to other agents about your listing, and share the listing with potential buyers. Yes, your agent is your agent and is there for you, one hundred percent, but they've got a job to do and it includes marketing and getting the word out. Be aware and check your expectations. Be positive and patient and see the big picture. Don't get caught up in the staging you may not like, for example; the art is supposed to be neutral and boring. Don't worry, you don't want a buyer to see the art—you want them to see the house, and to get a feeling that they could see themself there.

If you are selling an investment, you may stage one unit—but let's just be real: it mostly comes down to numbers in this case.

Have your mortgage broker run some numbers to see what the mortgage will be at different list prices with the 25 to 35 percent you expect an investor to put down as a down payment. Are the potential or current rents going to cover that possible PITI for the next buyer? Ask the lender if they want to provide an estimate sheet, so they get a marketing opportunity for helping you. There are many agents that only do investment-type properties, and if your agent is experienced, they will know how to market them.

PRICING

Your real estate agent will help you decide pricing. You'll review several comparable properties; but ultimately it's up to you how you price your property. Consider the market climate for homes or investments, other sold properties in the area, and other listed properties that are your competition.

"Obviously the price of this property is a reflection of it's very desirable location."

ACCEPT THE OFFER

If you are lucky, you'll get five to ten offers and wish you could accept more than one. If you get more than ten offers, it's either a super-hot market or the list price is low. If you have one offer, work with it! Your agent will be able to guide you if a possible counter is wise, but don't immediately discount the offer if it seems low to you. In my area, if a property has been on the market for two to three weeks or more, it may be priced too high. I'm not at all saying to accept any offer because you have to. In the San Francisco Bay Area, low-ball investors are plentiful and they routinely want to pay 45 to 65 percent of market value. That doesn't work for most sellers who are alive. Unless your property has issues such as habitability that would make it difficult to finance, or the property is just not moving, these types of buyers are irrelevant. Every situation is different. Listen to your agent.

In a few situations, buyers expect a counter, so they may come in low. Your agent's job is to communicate with the other agent and see if there's a possible meeting place. Don't lose a legitimate buyer over a seemingly low offer. See the big picture. You may ask your agent for an Estimated Closing Statement (ECS) to see what your proceeds from the sale will be. Think about it, but remember that a buyer's interest may diminish as time goes on, so be respectful and reply to the offer within a reasonable amount of time.

It's impossible for me to lay out every strategy or tactic you can use in dealmaking, and there are other books on the topic, but if you trust your agent, consider the comparables, and market the property well; and if many viewers have seen it, consider taking the offer rather than countering. Trust your agent and your gut. The longer a property stays on the market, the less likely it is you'll get a high offer. Forget your pride and make a good business decision.

LET'S RETURN TO INVESTING

Let's remember that taxes work differently if you own a rental property. You cannot shelter any amount when you sell; however, you may be able to do a "1031 exchange," which allows you to roll over the profit to purchase another property and not pay taxes on that gain. Section 1031 of the Internal Revenue Federal Tax Code grants the ability to exchange "like-kind property" and defer paying taxes on the gain accrued. In our former example, if an investment property is purchased for $100,000 and then sold for $500,000, there is a gain of $400,000 on which income taxes must be paid. Alternatively, if property is exchanged for "like-kind property," then the gain exists, but it is not recognized and no tax is due at that time. Consult your real estate agent to see if a 1031 exchange is a good option for you. A good 1031 exchange specialist can be a key component of your real estate investment team.

WHAT IS A 1031 SPECIALIST?

The objective of a 1031 exchange is to roll your profit from one investment into another investment without paying capital gains. Capital gains are taxes you pay from selling an asset such as a stock, mutual fund, or real estate. It can also be from selling an exchange traded fund, or EFT, such as gold bars, treasuries, and now even cryptocurrency. The tax rate is determined by your income level and how long you have held the investment. Optimally, you will "cash out" and pay these taxes after retirement age, when you are (presumably) in a lower tax bracket. In 1991, the code was amended to allow the investor to have up to 180 days to complete a real estate transaction of "like kind" and greater value. In 1989, Certified Exchange Specialists (what we commonly refer to as "1031 specialists") became the overseers and the certified experts in tax and exchange laws. This specialty takes away a lot of the guesswork for us common folk. In other words, you or I don't have to know every detail of the code, nor do we file the paperwork. A 1031 specialist will work for a brokerage handling 1031 exchanges, educate the client, and provide most necessary paperwork. The 1031 specialist will work in concert with the title company and cooperate with the exchanger (investor) to manage deadlines and hold funds. Funds from the first sale will go directly to the 1031 specialist's brokcrage account until the purchase for the exchange property is needed to be funded, both for the initial deposit and for the final funds. Any unused funds may be taxed. Forms must be completed to identify the potential exchange properties; the investor has forty-five days from the first close of escrow to identify a potential replacement property, and up to 180 days (from the first close of escrow) to close the second escrow. Your experienced real estate agent should have a handful of qualified and competent 1031 specialists that they can refer you to. These timelines may cause you some panic, but rest assured your real estate agent is used to the pressure and will make your exchange their top priority. Ask questions! Your 1031 specialist is another valuable spoke in the wheel of your successful real estate portfolio team!

ANALYZING INVESTMENTS: GRM / CAP RATES

Many factors go into analyzing whether an investment is a good opportunity. Location is key. Existing tenants can have a lasting impact, and the grounds themselves will either be a draw to future tenants, or not. Remember, price per square foot tells us nothing about the neighborhood, the outdoor space, views, walkability, aesthetics, or the overall feeling you get on the property. Once you've chosen the area and set some parameters for what you're looking for, the "numbers game" starts. That said, some property investors only care about numbers. "What else is there?" is what some investors are thinking right now. True, it's the bottom line, but some investors consider buying a place to move into in the future, or to make available for an aging relative. In this case, you'd want to consider more items than existing rents—am I right? If you have deep enough pockets to handle whatever repairs come up, perhaps you are less concerned with the condition and more with immediate incoming rents.

GRM Gross Rent Multipliers (GRMs) are a simple review metric to calculate and compare value ratios of properties. The GRM is the value of the property divided by the annual rents. The lower the GRM, the better the income. You often round up or down to create a whole number value, rather than using a decimal point.

AT PURCHASE:

$$\text{GRM} = \frac{\text{PURCHASE PRICE}}{\text{YEARLY GROSS RENT}}$$

SUBSEQUENT YEARS:

$$\text{GRM} = \frac{\text{MARKET VALUE}}{\text{YEARLY GROSS RENT}}$$

For this example: Let's imagine two different four-unit buildings, each valued at $2,000,000.

BUILDING A: In this building, two units have long-term tenants and two units have newly signed leases. Rents are $960, $1,020, $3,460, and $4,250. This is a total monthly income of

$9,690, which is $116,280 annually (monthly rent multiplied by twelve).

If the property is valued at $2,000,000 (list price or potential purchase price), the GRM for this is 17.20.

Value, divided by annual rents = GRM. i.e. $2,000,000 divided by $116,280 = 17.19986, or simply 17.

BUILDING B: If rents were higher, though—let's say $3,460, $3,850, $4,250, and $4,500—then that is $16,060 monthly, or $192,720 annually. The GRM here is 2,000,000 (value of property), dividcd by 192,720 (annual rcnt) = 10.3777, so thc GRM is 10.38, or 10.

The lower the GRM, the better the income and profit. Practice these calculations and it becomes easier. I consider any GRM between 4 and 9 to be very good. If you are looking at a GRM of 10 or above, factor in other things such as potential for the price to go up in value over time (equity gain) and the potential to raise rents soon (fixing it up, upcoming vacancies, overdue rent raises, etc.) before making any decisions. Also, understand where property values in the area went last time we had a recession. Ask yourself: Did the area hold its value, or did prices plummet? Are the employment opportunities in the area a steady gain, or does one need to travel for shopping and industry? Walkability is a big factor for most tenants, too. Think about all of these things. Your real estate agent can lead you in the right direction, but ultimately, it's your decision.

CAP RATES Capitalization rates are another metric to quantify value. The goal is to quantify the *yield* of a property for a period of one year. To get a more accurate assessment as to whether the investment is profitable, cap rates calculate operating costs: electricity, water, trash, sewer, insurance, yard maintenance, and so on. The cap rate is equal to the net operating income divided by the value of the property (the list or purchase price). This metric is similar to GRM, but we are taking into consideration the costs to operate.

$$\text{CAP RATE (\%)} = \frac{\text{NET OPERATING INCOME (NOI)}}{\text{PROPERTY VALUE}}$$

First, find your net operating income (NOI) by subtracting your expenses (utilities, maintenance, etc.) from your income (annual rents). Then divide your NOI by the purchase price. This is your cap rate.

EXAMPLE:

Building A: Cost is $2,000,000. Income is $116,280. Expenses are $19,800. NOI is 96,480.

96,480 divided by 2,000,000 is .04824 x 100 = cap rate 4.824, or 5 (round up).

Building B: Cost is $2,000,000. Income is $192,720. Expenses are $19,800. NOI is $172,920.

172,920 divided by 2,000,000 is .08646 x 100 = cap rate 8.646, or 9 (round up).

In this case 9 represents a higher yield than 5, so unlike GRMs, a higher number is better.

MORE ON PROP 19

Not only does Prop 19 let you downsize and pay the same tax rate, but it also allows heirs to afford the tax bill. If you inherit a property and choose to live in it for two years, you may be able to pay the existing tax rate. Consult a tax specialist as to what your options are and if it's worthwhile for you to move back into your parents' house.

IN CONCLUSION

There is no right or wrong way to do real estate. I know extremely successful property owners who only buy and never sell. I know successful owners who sell one property every two years and do a 1031 exchanges. I know eighty-year-olds who refuse to pay taxes and won't sell. I know owners who finally cash out and don't want to deal with ownership any longer.

It's a personal choice and a preference. For some, it is a hobby; for others, it is the best, easiest, most pleasurable and profitable way to make money that they can possibly imagine. Take advice, listen to the advice, and ask questions. Listen to your gut, not your fear; and most importantly, try to know the difference.

SUMMARY/LESSONS

For a quick personal assessment on where you are, answer these questions and reflect.

- What did you learn from your parents about money?
- Which parent handled the money and bill-paying, and why?
- Was there stress or abundance around money in your household?
- Are you a saver or a spender?
- What was your method of handling money once you became an adult?
- Where is your money going today?
- Where is your income coming from today?
- Do you keep a written record of your expenses and debt?
- Do you have unreasonable or unnecessary debt?

- If you have debt, do you have a plan in place to pay it all off?
- Can you visually see the list of where your debt is to manage it better?
- Do you know the difference between good debt and bad debt?
- Where is your good debt? Where is your bad debt?
- How should you best leverage your income?
- When is it time for you to buy, as opposed to renting?
- Is there anyone you know who would be a good financial mentor?
- Is there anyone you know whose financial state can teach what *not* to do?
- What are your fears around money?
- Are you taking any risks with your money to get ahead?
- When is it time for you to invest in an income property?
- When is it time for you to invest in a second or third income property?
- Is pride getting in your way of downsizing to a more affordable place to live?

CHAPTER FIVE

FINANCE THAT PROPERTY!

A Mortgage Broker's Pro Tips

Ashley Card Dimas

Buying a home is exciting, but financing can be anything but a thrill. Securing the perfect mortgage and the best mortgage broker for you and your family requires patience, attention to detail, and character judgment. Because things move quickly when a seller accepts your offer, getting the loan may feel like a full-time job, between gathering financial documents and endless forms to complete.

Eliminate some of this stress by being prepared. It is important to build a relationship with your mortgage advisor, as they can help guide you as you build your real estate portfolio and consolidate debt. You will most likely purchase several properties, and refinance more than once, in your lifetime; it is important to work with an advisor you trust, and who has your best interests in mind.

In this chapter, I will give you an overview of the loan process, types of loans, loan products, mortgage qualifications, and what details make up a mortgage.

YOUR NINETY-DAY MORTGAGE CHECK-UP

In the ninety-day, goal-oriented approach that this book proposes to wealth-building, you will assess whether you are ready to obtain your starter home, or a forever home; whether it is time to purchase an investment property; or whether you should consider refinancing. The steps I will outline largely describe the process associated with purchasing a single-family home, condominium, or two- to four-unit residential property.

In identifying your current financial situation and your future goals, you will need to determine the following:

- How is your credit score?
- How significant are your cash reserves and other collateral?
- What is your current income and debt?
- If you have an existing mortgage, how much interest are you currently paying compared to today's interest rates?

These are all questions a mortgage advisor will walk you through so you have a solid understanding of how you can achieve your goals.

KEY TO BEING FINANCIALLY PREPARED

Add up your monthly expenses
Calculate your housing expenses
Add in the extras
Know your max spending comfort level

If you decide to get a mortgage loan for the purchase of a property, or to refinance your current property, the first step is choosing a mortgage advisor. When choosing a mortgage advisor, you should consider the following:

- It is wise to choose a local lender—one who is known to the real estate agents in your community. Using a local lender with a good reputation could benefit you in a competitive offer situation. Local lenders are also familiar with the lending guidelines in your area.
- Choose someone that is responsive and available.
- Choose someone who takes the time to answer all of your questions, so you can completely understand the process and your options. You are partnering with a lender who is making an investment in you as well as the property. In this transaction, you will initiate a relationship to build wealth over time.

Of course, every borrower wants to get the lowest interest rate possible. However, it is most important to choose a lender who can deliver what they promise; perform in the required timeframe; and, ultimately, close the loan. So, when you are shopping for a mortgage, make sure you look at the lender as a whole and do not just consider the lowest interest rate. Speak with your real estate agent and ask for lender recommendations. Agents work closely with specific lenders who they have confidence in.

There are three main types of lending establishments from which you can choose.

- **Traditional retail banks** (Bank of America, Wells Fargo, Chase, etc.) underwrite and fund loans with their own capital. However, the borrower is limited to that bank's loan programs and rates. If, for any reason, the borrower has to switch to another lender during the process, it is costly and time-consuming.
- **A mortgage broker** acts as an agent for the borrower to arrange the transaction with traditional banks and niche lenders. This offers the borrower multiple choices of possible lenders, programs, and rates. However, the broker has little control over the loan process when working with a third-party service provider.
- **A direct lender** offers a combination of what a traditional retail bank and mortgage broker have to offer. A direct lender offers an extensive range of both banked and brokered products resulting from established relationships with major banks, niche lenders, and private investors. This gives the direct lender a wider range of loan programs and competitive rates. On the banked products, a direct lender originates, underwrites, and funds the loans in-house, maintaining control of the entire loan process.

DETERMINING HOW MUCH YOU SHOULD PUT TOWARDS THE DOWN PAYMENT

When determining how much to put down, it is important to evaluate how much you have in the bank, how much you want to keep in the bank after you purchase the property, and what is a comfortable monthly payment. Some clients prefer to keep more money in their bank and put less towards the purchase. The monthly payment will be higher, but when interest rates are low, it may make more sense to keep your money in investment accounts if you have a better return on your investments.

Traditionally, 20 percent of the purchase price was the required down payment. However, today there are programs available which allow for as little as zero to 3.5 percent down. For most programs, when you put less than 20 percent down, the lender will require private mortgage insurance, also called "PMI." PMI protects the lender, reducing the risk of default by the borrower. PMI is arranged by the lender and provided by private insurance companies.

DETERMINING WHEN YOU SHOULD REFINANCE

What you should consider:

1. How much lower is the interest rate?
2. How much would it lower the monthly payment?
3. How much are the closing costs?
4. Do you have enough equity?
5. Do you want to switch from an adjustable rate mortgage to a fixed product, or vice versa?
6. How long do you plan on staying in the property?
7. Do you want to take extra cash out?

WHAT ARE THE DIFFERENT TYPES OF LOANS?

1. **Conforming loans** (loan amounts vary by county) are loans that are equal to or less than the dollar amount established by the limit set by the Federal Housing Finance Agency under the guidelines of the government-sponsored enterprises (GSEs) Fannie Mae and Freddie Mac.
    - Loan limits effective 2024: $1,149,825 = 1 unit, $1,472,250 = 2 units, $1,779,525 = 3 units, and $2,211,600 = 4 units. (The loan limits are adjusted yearly.)
    - Key takeaways: Conforming loans require lower reserves, lower credit score, less preexisting credit (as measured by open credit accounts), and higher debt-to-income ratios.

2. **Jumbo loans** are loans that exceed the maximum conforming loan amounts (as stated above), which vary per county. Jumbo loans typically have higher qualification standards than conforming loans, since lenders take on additional risks. Because of this, lenders are looking at several key factors to determine your risk level.
    - Key takeaways: Jumbo loans require higher reserved amounts, higher credit scores, minimum credit tradeline requirements, and lower debt-to-income ratios.

3. **FHA loans** are federally-backed mortgages designed for low- to moderate-income borrowers who may have lower-than-average credit scores. FHA loans have two types of mortgage insurance: an upfront MI (which is rolled into the loan amount), and a monthly MI.

    - Key takeaways: FHA loans require lower minimum down payments, and permit lower credit scores. These loans require as little as 3.5 percent down, and debt-to-income ratios of no more than 50 to 55 percent. No reserves required.

4. **VA loans** are mortgage loans that are guaranteed by the United States Department of Veterans Affairs (VA). There is no mortgage insurance, but they do charge a funding fee that serves a similar purpose.
    - Key takeaways: VA loans require zero percent down, and debt-to-income ratios of no more than 50 to 55 percent. No reserves required.

LOANS THAT FIT YOUR LIFE

FIXED-RATE MORTGAGES

- Fixed rates available for terms of fifteen to thirty years
- Same payment every month
- Sound long-term investment
- Impervious to market volatility

ADJUSTABLE-RATE MORTGAGES (ARMS)

- Three-, five-, seven-, or ten-year fixed terms offer a custom timeframe
- Traditionally lower initial rates than comparable thirty-year fixed products
- Lower monthly payments during fixed period
- Annual lifetime rate adjustment caps of 2 to 5 percent

SECOND-TIER MORTGAGES

There are two types of second-tier mortgages. They can be acquired in conjunction with the first mortgage, or as a standalone mortgage.

Fixed-Rate Second Mortgage

- Fixed rates available for terms of ten to thirty years
- Same payment every month
- Usually need to draw the entire amount at funding

Home Equity Line of Credit (HELOC)

- Adjustable rate, which is tied to the federal prime rate (plus a margin)
- The draw period is usually ten years
- Payments comprise of interest only for the first ten years and principal and interest for the remaining twenty years
- There are no initial or periodic caps and the lifetime cap is usually 18 percent annual interest

WHAT IS "AMORTIZATION"?

The term "amortization" refers to the process of paying down debt with regular principal and interest payments over time. An amortization schedule is used to reduce the current principal balance on a loan through installment payments, allowing the borrower to build equity in the property over time. Using a tool called an amortization schedule calculator, you can estimate the amount of your payments, as well how much of your repayments will go towards the principal and how much will go to pay interest.

Amortization Calculator

Loan Amount	$500000
Loan Term	30 years
Interest Rate (APR)	3.25 %

Calculate

Monthly Pay: $2,176.03

Total of 360 Loan Payments	$783,371.37
Total Interest	$283,371.37

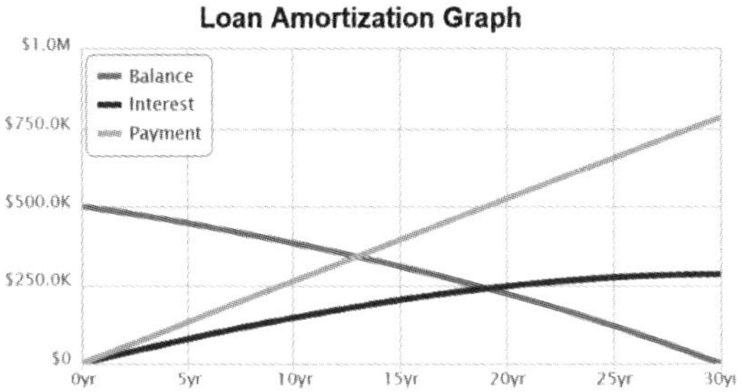

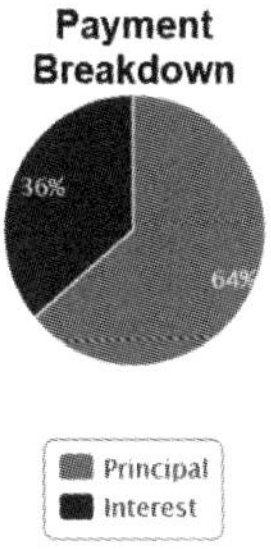

Annual Amortization Schedule

Annual Schedule | Monthly Schedule

	Beginning Balance	Interest	Principal	Ending Balance
1	$500,000.00	$16,101.77	$10,010.59	$489,989.38
2	$489,989.38	$15,771.53	$10,340.83	$479,648.52
3	$479,648.52	$15,430.39	$10,681.97	$468,966.53
4	$468,966.53	$15,078.00	$11,034.36	$457,932.16
5	$457,932.16	$14,713.99	$11,398.37	$446,533.79
6	$446,533.79	$14,337.99	$11,774.37	$434,759.39
7	$434,759.39	$13,949.58	$12,162.78	$422,596.58
8	$422,596.58	$13,548.34	$12,564.02	$410,032.54
9	$410,032.54	$13,133.86	$12,978.50	$397,054.02
10	$397,054.02	$12,705.72	$13,406.64	$383,647.37
11	$383,647.37	$12,263.45	$13,848.91	$369,798.44
12	$369,798.44	$11,806.62	$14,305.74	$355,492.67
13	$355,492.67	$11,334.67	$14,777.69	$340,714.96
14	$340,714.96	$10,847.20	$15,265.16	$325,449.76
15	$325,449.76	$10,343.60	$15,768.76	$309,680.99
16	$309,680.99	$9,823.42	$16,288.94	$293,392.03
17	$293,392.03	$9,286.06	$16,826.30	$276,565.72
18	$276,565.72	$8,731.00	$17,381.36	$259,184.33
19	$259,184.33	$8,157.60	$17,954.76	$241,229.56
20	$241,229.56	$7,565.31	$18,547.05	$222,682.48
21	$222,682.48	$6,953.46	$19,158.90	$203,523.57
22	$203,523.57	$6,321.44	$19,790.92	$183,732.63
23	$183,732.63	$5,668.57	$20,443.79	$163,288.82
24	$163,288.82	$4,994.15	$21,118.21	$142,170.60
25	$142,170.60	$4,297.47	$21,814.89	$120,355.71
26	$120,355.71	$3,577.85	$22,534.51	$97,821.19
27	$97,821.19	$2,834.48	$23,277.88	$74,543.29
28	$74,543.29	$2,066.57	$24,045.79	$50,497.48
29	$50,497.48	$1,273.33	$24,839.03	$25,658.44
30	$25,658.44	$453.94	$25,658.42	$0.00

HOW DO YOU QUALIFY FOR A MORTGAGE?

HOW WE DECIDE

Credit Score

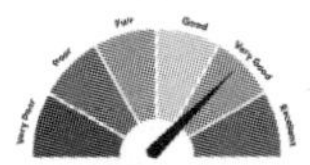

Credit score
While there is no specific credit score minimum for first-time homebuyers, you'll have a much better chance of securing a mortgage on the terms you want if your score falls into the following ranges: Good 670 -739 Very Good 740-799 Excellent 800-850

Monthly income
If credit scores reveal the likelihood of making future payments on time, then income (and savings) are the engines that enable you to make those payments. It's very important that you can show lenders that your income is stable.

Debt-to-income ratio
You can't mention income in the context of mortgages without quickly pivoting to debt-to-income ratio (DTI), a measurement of monthly income vs. recurring monthly expenses (including the proposed mortgage premium) expressed as a ratio or a percent.

Savings and assets
Savings are the backbone of any large purchase, and lenders will need to know how much money you have in reserve. Having enough savings to show your mortgage provider that you're prepared to make monthly payments even if an emergency arises.

CREDIT

Much of the time spent qualifying a borrower for a loan is spent on judging creditworthiness. Credit reports provide a lot of valuable information. The lenders pull a tri-merge credit report from all three of the credit bureaus (Experian, TransUnion, and Equifax). The credit score factors in the borrower's monthly liabilities and ability to repay debt. Underwriters will pay close attention to your score, but they will also examine your credit history in the form of a detailed credit report to determine if there are any red flags such as late payments, bankruptcies, foreclosures, or overuse of credit.

TIP: Do No Harm—Always talk with your lender first before closing existing accounts, opening new accounts, or paying off debt.

INCOME

The lenders look at all types of income when qualifying a borrower. Below is a non-inclusive list of the different types considered.

- Salary: hourly, weekly, or monthly
- Passive income, which consists of:
    - Rental income from investment properties
    - Disability insurance payments from private or government sources
    - Retirement income from Social Security, pensions, or investments
    - Child support/alimony (must continue for at least three years from application date)
- Averaged income: Income averages for last twenty-four months
    - Bonuses
    - Commissions
    - Overtime
    - Dividends/Interest
    - RSUs (restricted stock units)
    - Stock options exercises

Self-Employment Income: Standard loan programs typically require income to be calculated based on a twenty-four-month average of the borrower's reported income on the most recent tax returns. The lenders look at the "net" income, not the "gross" income. The lenders also require the current year profit-and-loss statement to document that the income is stable. However, more lenders are creating new programs designed to help self-employed borrowers qualify for a mortgage. Some of these programs use twelve or twenty-four months of bank statements to document the business owner's deposits and expenses, rather than a more conservative approach using tax returns.

DEBT-TO-INCOME RATIO

When judging whether a borrower can repay the loan, lenders will consider the borrower's debt-to-income ratio.

The ratio considers the borrower's total monthly mortgage payment (PITI) and other monthly debt (identified on the credit report), divided by gross monthly income.

A borrower's total PITI, plus other debt
"PITI" stands for "principal, interest, (property) taxes, and insurance." The debt-to-income ratio is one of the metrics that lenders use to measure an individual's ability to manage monthly payments and repay debts.
$6,670(PITI) + $310(Debt) = $6,990 = 41.94%
$16,666 (income)

Allowable debt-to-income ratios (DTI) for the different loan programs

- **Conforming loans:** DTI up to 45 percent, can go as high as 50 percent on an exception basis
- **Jumbo loans:** DTI typically up to 43 percent, however more lenders are expanding to 45 percent and some to 50 percent
- **FHA/VA loans:** DTI up to 50 percent, can go as high as 55 percent on an exception basis

SAVINGS AND ASSETS

The lender will then qualify the borrower's household financial assets. This review considers funds available for the down payment, closing costs, and cash reserves. Lenders will need to verify the source of the funds by reviewing the most recent two months of bank statements. Borrowers will need to explain the source of any recent large deposits into their bank accounts.

The Down Payment: These funds can come from a variety of sources.

- Savings/checking
- Mutual funds—brokerage accounts
- Sale of property
- Secured loan proceeds (HELOC, 401(k))
- Retirement plans
- Gifts from a family member
- Liquidations of employer compensation in the form of restricted stock units or vested stock options

The Reserves: The reserve funds can come from any of the above-mentioned sources except from gifts. The borrower must maintain his or her own cash reserves.

BENEFITS OF PREAPPROVALS

Borrowers like preapprovals because they provide validation of their financial power and perceived creditworthiness by the lender. Sellers like them because they provide the necessary proof that the borrower has the financial might to make the purchase, allowing them to compete with cash buyers. Without a preapproval, many borrowers experience unforeseen last-minute obstacles when trying to get approved for their mortgage.

Lenders like preapprovals for the same reasons, as well as the added bonus of having an opportunity to establish a methodical, step-by-step process for reviewing and verifying the many files that accompany the underwriting process without the last-minute crunch. Ultimately, this makes it easier to spot issues and submit conditions ahead of time—issues that could otherwise cause delays during the final phase of underwriting.

Given the inherent complexity of the homebuying process, prospective homeowners and those looking to refinance need to do all they can to avoid unexpected issues that may contribute to potential delays. Delays are almost never advantageous to the borrower; they invite seller anxieties, and may put your loan approval at risk. This is precisely why you always want to do everything you can in advance to ensure a smooth process.

STOP! CHECK WITH YOUR LENDER FIRST!

When you are applying for a loan, be very careful not to do anything that might impact your loan. Making big purchases or changing your income could affect your ability to qualify for a loan.

So, once you have applied for a loan but before the deal has closed, DO NOT do the following without checking with your lender first.

WHAT NOT TO DO!

- Buy a car
- Take on more student loans
- Open a new credit card or close a credit card
- Co-sign on a loan for someone else
- Max out your credit cards
- Forget to make your payments on time
- Quit your job without a written offer in hand [3]

PROPERTY (COLLATERAL)

Appraisal: The lender will order an independent appraisal to confirm the property value, the property type (single-family, condo, two- to four-units). They will determine whether all construction has been done with permits and conforms to building codes. The appraiser will also judge whether the property poses any health and safety issues and verify that the property meets specific standards as collateral.

Preliminary title report: The real estate agent will open escrow and order the preliminary title report from the title company. This report shows if there are any liens on title arising from unpaid balances for property taxes, utilities, completed construction work, or child support. The title report will also show any deed restrictions (live/work) and abatements (unwarranted units or other construction done without permits).

HOA documentation: If the property is a condominium, the lender will review all of the condo documents, which consist of the deed "Covenant, Conditions, and Restrictions" (CCRs), homeowners association budget, bylaws, articles of incorporation, and certification letter. The lender needs to make sure there are no problematical restrictions in the CCRs, and that the association maintains enough reserves. Finally, the lender will verify there is no pending litigation against the homeowner's association.

Insurance: The lender will confirm what type of insurance is required and the amount of coverage needed. Here are some types that might be required:

- Fire/hazard
- Master HOA (property, fidelity bond, liability)
- Walls-in or HO-6 for condos (which covers the property from the studs inward and the owner's contents)
- Flood

Closing Costs

Buyer is responsible for:

- Escrow fees
- Title Insurance
  (owner and lender policies)
- Lender Fees
- Appraisal Report
- Pre-paid Interest
- Points, if applicable
- Homeowner's Insurance

Seller is responsible for:

- 100% County Transfer Tax
- Both Buyer and Seller Realtor Commissions

City Transfer Tax differs per area, check with your realtor on who is responsible for paying.

As an estimate, closing costs are approximately 1-2% of the purchase price.

WHAT YOU NEED TO DO

For most lenders you can start either with an online application or speak to a loan officer. An official mortgage application will supply your lender with the necessary documentation to perform a comprehensive review of your financial situation.

PRE-APPROVAL CHECKLIST

These are the primary documents you'll need for a pre-approval:

- Paycheck Stubs
- Copies of W2's
- Tax Returns
- Bank Statements
- Loan obligations (student loans or mortgages etc.)

TIMELINE OF THE LOAN PROCESS

PRE-QUALIFICATION

- Meet or talk about finances
- Discuss possible loan programs

PRE-APPROVAL

- Complete loan application
- Run credit
- Provide financial documents
- Receive an automated underwriting approval

CREDIT APPROVAL

- The loan will be submitted to the underwriter for credit, income, and asset approval

OFFER ACCEPTANCE

- The lender can lock in your interest rate and order the loan disclosures itemizing the fees associated with the loan
- Appraisal will be ordered
- File is updated with any missing documents
- Loan will be submitted for final loan approval
- The lender issues the closing disclosure (CD) with final fees
- Loan documents ordered
- Signing the loan documents
- Funding and recording of your loan
- Congratulations! The keys are yours!

WHAT CAUSES INTEREST RATES TO MOVE?

ECONOMIC DATA

BAD ECONOMIC NEWS = LOWER INTEREST RATES

GOOD ECONOMIC NEWS = HIGHER INTEREST RATES

Below are the key data points the markets watch that impact the mortgage rates:

- Employment (non-farm payroll (NFP) number)
- Inflation (CPI and PPI)
- Gross domestic product (GDP)
- Housing starts and new home sales
- Existing home sales
- Manufacturing and services growth
- Retail sales

BOND MARKET TECHNICALS

- Federal Reserve monetary policies and guidance
- Foreign central bank monetary policies and guidance
- US Treasury Bill and Bond auctions
- Corporate bond issues
- Contract timing—end of the week/month/quarter/year
- Stock market lever: risk-on vs. risk-off—"flight to safety"
- Fiscal policies (proposed or current)
- Over-sold/over-bought stock market

30-YEAR FIXED RATE MORTGAGE AVERAGE IN THE US FROM 4/2/1971-12/01/2022

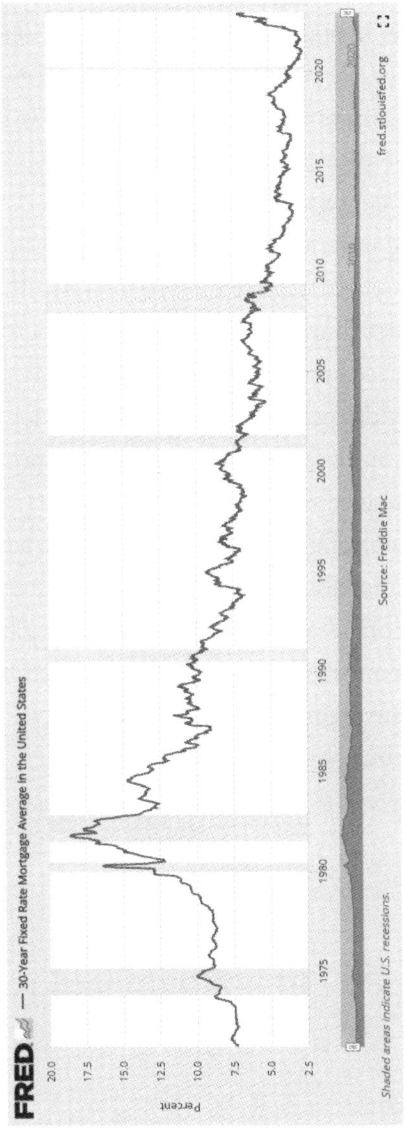

WHAT'S YOUR FINANCING PLAN?

After reading this chapter, you may feel more prepared to ask a lender for advice on a loan. Consider using your lender as your strategic partner in building wealth over time. Solicit insights not just about the specific transaction for which you are preparing, but for the relationship you will build for each successive transaction. Seek to improve your credit scores and lower your interest rates with each financing decision you make.

Once you are pre-approved, your mortgage advisor will help you determine where you are in your plan to either acquire real estate for the first time, purchase another property, or refinance. Establish goals; accomplish them; then roll to the next set of goals for a new ninety-day period. Working with your lender is a lifelong process of building relationships with trusted professionals who can help you achieve your goals.

The most important job I have as a mortgage advisor is to help my clients successfully navigate the lending process and set them up for success on all real estate transactions. The relationship you build with me can endure many years and for many more transactions. Buying real estate is a sound investment, so let's start building your wealth together.

CHAPTER SIX

TAXES

Tamara Hull
CPA

TAMARA'S TOP 10 TAX CHECKLIST

1. Have you filed all of your tax returns—for federal (with the IRS), and your state of residence? Call the IRS and the state tax agency to find out. You may also be able to look up your account online.
2. Have you paid all of your taxes for past years? Call the IRS and the state tax agency to find out. You may be able to check online.
3. Do you owe money to the IRS or your state tax agency, but can't pay? Set up a payment plan. You may be able to set it up online.
4. Have you heard about ways to reduce what you owe, but want to learn more? Keep in mind that the IRS has programs, but many states do not. Most of the IRS programs require you to provide financial information—and supporting documents like bank statements, credit card

statements, and more. The IRS will usually "settle" for what your net worth is (assets less liabilities). So if your net worth is more than what you owe, you are probably not a good candidate for reducing your taxes owed.

5. Have you paid enough taxes for the current year? Use an online tax calculator to double-check, or consult with a tax professional to do a tax projection or tax plan.
6. Do you have enough withheld from your paychecks so that you don't owe when you file? If you have recently filed your tax returns and you had a balance due, you may need to adjust your withholding.
7. If you do not have taxes withheld from your paychecks, or if you are an independent contractor, then you may need to make estimated tax payments throughout the year. You can usually make these payments online or by mailing checks.
8. Do you e-file your tax returns? E-filing is the best way to thwart identity theft, as well as avoiding data input errors by the IRS or the state tax agency. If you mail a paper tax return, the IRS or state tax agency will take much longer to process your tax return, and take longer to issue your refund. And tax returns that are mailed in are either scanned by the tax agency, which often results in misread amounts; or they are hand-entered by an employee, which also often results in mistakes.
9. If you get a letter from the IRS or your state tax agency, open it immediately! Your first line of defense is to call them and ask them to explain what was sent, or ask for extra time to respond. If you don't contact them, they will ramp up their efforts to get your attention.

10. If the IRS or your state tax agency has levied your bank account, the bank can't help you. You need to contact the IRS or the state tax agency and make other arrangements to pay (like a payment plan) and find out what they need from you to release the levy and send the release to your bank. The bank is supposed to hold the levied funds for twenty-one days—not twenty-one business days, but twenty-one days, *including* weekends and holidays. So the clock is ticking to get the release.

MY NINETY-DAY PLAN FOR YOUR TAXES

WEEK ONE

Assess your situation by reviewing items 1, 2, and 3 of my "Top 10 Checklist." Do you have any of these issues that need to be addressed? If not, then you are already doing great with your taxes!

If you do have any of these issues that need to be addressed, and you don't have a tax advisor, or you can't afford a tax advisor, contact the IRS and your state tax agency to find out the status of your tax returns that need to be filed and any taxes that need to be paid. If you do have a tax advisor, ask them to help you address these issues.

When you call the IRS or your state tax agency, tell them the truth—whatever that truth is. Ask them for assistance. Ask them to put a hold on your account if they are threatening to do any type of levy or lien so that you can figure out what you need to do to get your account up-to-date.

WEEK TWO

Review your taxes for this year as mentioned in item 5 of my "Top 10 Checklist." Has your income increased or decreased compared to last year? Your taxes withheld from your paycheck, or your estimated tax payments, should increase or decrease, too.

Look at the last tax returns you have filed and compare them to what you expect your income to be for this year. Will they be similar? If so, are you on track this year to pay the amount of tax you owed for the last year?

If your marital status has changed—from single to married, or married to single—you should review your payroll tax withholdings. It does not matter how long you were married or single during the year; all that matters is what your marital status was on December 31. If you were married all year, and then you got divorced in December, then your marital status is "single" on your tax return for that year.

Note: If you were married at the beginning of the year, but became single by the end of the year, and you have been having payroll taxes withheld as "married" for your allowances, then you are probably going to owe when you file your tax returns.

If you were single most of the year, and then got married late in the year, then your marital status is "married" on your tax returns. If you have been having payroll taxes withheld as "single" for your allowances, you should see a decrease in your total tax for the year, and possibly a refund—if you file jointly with your spouse.

WEEK THREE

Optimize ways to reduce your taxes.

HSA/FSA

Does your employer offer a Health Savings Account (HSA) or a Flexible Spending Account (FSA)? Do you expect to have medical expenses or other expenses that are covered by the HSA or the FSA plans? If you do, then you should seriously consider contributing to the HSA or FSA plan. The reason is that the contributions reduce your taxable wages, similar to contributing to your company's 401(k) plan.

Withdrawals from the HSA or FSA plan are not taxable if they are used for medical expenses or other expenses (i.e., dependent care) allowed by the plan.

There can be pitfalls to contributing to a HSA or FSA plan, so definitely review the rules and see if contributing to either makes sense for you.

401(k)/ Profit-Sharing/Pension Plans

Does your employer offer some type of profit-sharing or pension or 401(k) plan? If you contribute to the plan, those contributions reduce your taxable wages.

If your employer offers a matching contribution, don't leave that money on the table! The employer's matching contribution is not taxable to you, unless you withdraw it from the plan.

Withdrawals from 401(k), profit-sharing, and pension plans are usually taxable. But also be careful about withdrawing before you are the correct age, or you can be stuck paying "early withdrawal" penalties, which are assessed by the IRS and most state tax agencies.

WEEKS FOUR THROUGH SIX

Learn more about what is taxable income, and what is not.

Investment sales

If your investments are publicly traded, then the sale is probably being reported to the IRS. You will need to report your investment sales. You need to report how much you paid for the investments and how much you received for selling them, net of selling costs. If you made money on the sale, you may have to pay capital gains taxes on the money you made.

If you lost money on the sale, you will only be able to deduct $3,000 of the loss, after offsetting your loss against any gains. You don't "lose" your loss—you carry it forward to future tax years and tax returns, until it is all deducted or offset against other gains.

Dividends

Dividend income is taxable income, and you need to report it on your tax returns. The payer of the dividends will usually have reported the dividend income to the IRS.

Interest income

Interest income is taxable income, and you need to report it on your tax return. The payer of the interest will usually have reported the interest income to the IRS. However, if the amount of interest you earned that year is under ten dollars, then the payer does not have to report it to the IRS. Technically, you should still report it as taxable income even if the payer did not have to report it.

Child support

Child support is not taxable income—as long as it is called "child support" in your divorce agreement. See "Family support" below.

Alimony

Alimony may be taxable income. If your divorce was final in 2019 or later, then your alimony is probably not taxable income. If your divorce was final before 2019, then your alimony is taxable income.

Note: If you and your spouse are dividing your assets, that distribution, allocation, whatever you call it, is usually not taxable when you take your share of the marriage's assets, and your spouse takes theirs. However, if you sell any of the assets you receive in the divorce, you may have to pay tax on the gain. For example, if you had a joint investment account and you split up the investments when you divorced, and now you have your own investment account, you don't owe tax on the splitting of the investments; but you could owe tax if you sell any of the investments.

Read your divorce paperwork before you sign it! Make sure it says what you think you agreed to.

Family support

If your child support and alimony are combined and called "family support," and your divorce was final before 2019, then all of it is taxable income. I have had several clients go back to court to get it separated into child support and alimony so they wouldn't have to pay taxes on the child support when they normally would not. Some divorce attorneys have gotten creative, and the spouse who receives the money is surprised to learn it's all taxable—and their former spouse gets to deduct it all on their taxes.

Social Security payments

Social Security payments might be taxable income. If you are also receiving pension payments or withdrawing money from 401(k) plans or IRAs, then your Social Security payments are probably taxable income. If you are still working, then your Social Security payments are probably taxable income.

Note: You will often hear people talking about waiting to take their Social Security payments when they reach full retirement age. Your "full retirement age," in the eyes of Social Security, depends on when you were born. There is a misconception that if you wait to take your Social Security payments when you reach Social Security's full retirement age, then your Social Security payments won't be taxable. This is not true. No matter what age you are when you receive Social Security payments, they may be taxable depending on the other income (taxable and non-taxable) you receive.

One of the benefits of waiting until you reach Social Security's full retirement age to start taking your Social Security payments is that if you are still working, your earnings won't reduce your Social Security payments and benefits.

Social Security disability payments

Social Security disability payments might be taxable income. If you receive a Form SSA-1099 that reports the amount of disability payments you received, you need to report those payments on your tax returns.

Private insurance disability payments

If you receive disability payments from an insurance company, your payments may be taxable income. The determining factors are (1) how the insurance premiums were paid; (2) who deducted the premium payments; and (3) if the premiums were "after tax" payments.

For example, if your employer paid the disability insurance premiums, then you need to find out if they added the premiums as a taxable item to your paychecks. If they did not, then the disability payments are probably taxable income to you.

And if you paid the premiums, but it was through your paycheck; and the premiums were deducted before determining your taxable wages, or they were paid through a cafeteria plan—then the disability payments are probably taxable income to you.

If you paid the premiums through your paycheck, but they were *not* deducted before determining your taxable wages, and were not paid through a cafeteria plan, then they may not be taxable income to you.

Unemployment

If you receive unemployment payments, those payments are taxable income—at least for the IRS. Some states do not tax unemployment payments.

Stock options

Stock options can be very tricky. You really need to talk to a tax advisor who understands stock options *before* accepting them or signing any documents. The company who issues the stock options—usually, your employer—often has multiple ways they can issue the stock options to you. Some of the ways benefit them, some benefit you, and some benefit both of you. The most common types of stock options are incentive stock options and non-qualified stock options.

With stock options, you need to understand how and when your company will grant them to you; how the options vest; and what happens when you exercise the options to buy the company's stock. Exercising the options to buy the company's stock is where mistakes are often made, especially if you hold onto the stock instead of selling it.

Restricted stock units (RSUs) and restricted stock awards (RSAs)

Same advice as for stock options—restricted stock units and restricted stock awards can be tricky, and you really need to talk to a tax advisor who understands them *before* accepting them or signing any documents.

Life insurance proceeds

In general, life insurance proceeds are not taxable income to the beneficiary. However, if the life insurance proceeds include any interest income, that is probably taxable. (See "Interest income.")

Inheritances, in general

Except for inherited IRAs and pensions, most inheritances are not taxable to you as the recipient. You may inherit assets that *create* taxable income—like inheriting a business, partnership, or LLC. But inheriting the business, partnership, or LLC does not usually create taxable income to you by itself.

Inherited investments, such as publicly traded stocks and bonds, are not taxable when you inherit them, but you may have taxable capital gains when you sell them.

Inherited real estate is not taxable when you inherit the property, but you may have taxable gains when you sell the property. Inherited rental real estate will probably generate taxable income as you take over as the landlord.

At the time that I write this, your "cost basis" for inherited stocks and bonds, businesses, partnerships, LLCs, real estate, and other assets is usually the fair market value (the value they were trading at) on the date of death for the person from whom you inherited them. This is often referred to as the "step up in basis." This tax provision can be repealed, so double-check with a tax advisor before selling any inherited assets.

Inherited non-Roth IRAs and pensions

Inherited non-Roth IRAs and pensions are taxable income to the beneficiary. If you have inherited the non-Roth IRA from your spouse, then you have the option of taking over the IRA account and treating the IRA as though it was yours all along—which means that the required minimum distribution rules will follow your age, not your spouse's age, and you don't have to withdraw the IRA within five or ten years.

For non-spouse inherited non-Roth IRAs, you may be eligible for the "five-year rule" or the "ten-year rule." The five- and ten-year rules for inherited non-Roth IRAs allow the beneficiary to withdraw all of the IRA over five or ten years—depending on the age of the original owner of the IRA (i.e., who you inherited it from), if they started taking required minimum distributions before they died, and what year they died. Consult with a tax advisor to see what options are available to you.

Inherited Roth IRAs

If you inherited the Roth IRA from your spouse, and are the sole beneficiary of the Roth IRA, then you can treat the Roth IRA as your own and follow the rules as if it was your own Roth IRA. If you are not a spouse, then the distribution rules will depend on the age of the deceased when they died, the year they died, how long they held the Roth IRA, and if they had started taking required minimum distributions.

Selling your house

You need to report the sale of all real estate, even if it is your personal and primary residence. The escrow or title company will be issuing a Form 1099-S to you and the IRS that reports the sales price of the property.

With the sale of any property, it is very important to add up all of your costs for purchasing and improving the property in determining your cost basis.

If the property was a rental property that you reported on Schedule E, then you should already have the purchase price and improvements reported on a depreciation schedule. Note that your cost basis is reduced by the depreciation expense, but the depreciation expense may be "recaptured" when you sell the property. Consult your tax advisor before selling any rental real estate to estimate the tax consequences of the sale.

If you are selling the house that is currently your personal and primary residence, you should calculate your cost basis by adding your purchase price and any improvements you have made over the years. If you've lived in the house for a long time, I recommend physically walking through each room to help jog your memory of the improvements you have made over time. Don't forget carpets, floors, bathroom remodels, kitchen remodels, new appliances, new roofs, fence replacements, landscaping, walkways, patios, windows, window coverings (if you are including them in the sale), doors, light fixtures, upgraded electrical outlets, added insulation, HVAC upgrades or replacements, water heater upgrades or replacements, driveways, trees, etc. All of your improvements, upgrades, and replacements helped increase the value of the house, and should be included in your cost basis.

Once you have determined your cost basis, then you can start estimating your gain or profit on the sale. Another factor in determining the gain or profit on the sale of your home are the selling costs. Most sellers have to pay real estate commission, and various and sundry city and county fees, to sell their home; all of these are deductible in determining the gain or profit.

If you are single and are the sole owner of the house, and you have lived in the house for at least twenty-four of the sixty months before the date of the sale, then you should be able to claim a $250,000 capital gain exemption on the gain on the sale of your house.

If you are married, and *both* of you have lived in the house for at least twenty-four of the sixty months before the date of the sale, then you should be able to claim a $500,000 capital gain exemption on the gain on the sale of your house.

If you are recently widowed, then you may be eligible for the $500,000 capital gain exemption if you sell the home within two years of the date of your spouse's death, provided you and your spouse both lived in the home for twenty-four months before your spouse died. If you are widowed and sell the home more than two years after your spouse dies, then you should be eligible for the $250,000 capital gain exemption under the same rules as single owners.

Selling your car

In general, the sale of your car is not taxable income. However, if you sell your car for more than you paid for it (including the money spent improving and upgrading it), then you may have to pay capital gain on the profit. And if you sell your car through an auction house (i.e., RM Sotheby's, etc.), then you need to report the sale on your tax returns because the auction house is probably reporting the sale's proceeds to the IRS.

Selling items on eBay, Pinterest, Etsy, et al.

If you sell items on eBay, Pinterest, Etsy, et al., you probably need to report the sales on your tax return. If you purchased the items and sold them for a profit, you probably can report them as capital gains. If you created the items and sold them, then you need to report them on Schedule C—but don't forget to deduct all of the costs of creating the items you sold.

Airbnb, Vrbo, HomeAway, and other income from rental of your home

Any rental of your home that creates income is taxable as rental income and should be reported on Schedule E. Some people mistakenly report Airbnb, Vrbo, and HomeAway income on Schedule C and needlessly pay self-employment taxes on the net income. But some people report the income on Schedule C because they *want* to pay self employment taxes (for Social Security benefits later).

Roommates

If your roommates are paying money to you, then you might be their landlord. If you are their landlord, then you need to report their payments as rental income on Schedule E. However, if you have roommates that are only sharing household expenses (cable, housecleaning, gardening, food, internet, etc.)—not paying you rent—then that money is not taxable income to you, and does not have to be reported. If you choose to report the shared household expenses reimbursements, be sure to include the household expenses for which they were reimbursing you (which should result in a net of $0).

Renting your car to others

If you rent your car to others (i.e., Turo), then that income is taxable income to you. However, you can deduct direct expenses related to the car rental plus a portion of the costs of owning and operating your car. Don't forget to consider gas, electricity (if it's a non-gas car), insurance, tires, repairs, maintenance, registration fees, etc.

Lyft, Uber, delivery services

Any income from delivering people, food, or things is taxable income to you. If you are using your own car, then you can deduct a portion of the costs of owning and operating your car. If you are renting a car, then the rental costs of the car are deductible. Don't forget to consider gas, electricity (if it's a non-gas car), insurance, tires, repairs, maintenance, registration fees, etc.

Donating your car

This is not an income item, but something to be carefully considered. If you do not itemize your deductions (i.e., you claim the standard deduction), *do not* donate your car, because you will not get to deduct the donation. Also please note that if you do donate your car, the donation you are allowed to deduct is limited to how much the nonprofit received from the sale of your car—not the Blue Book value. You can claim the Blue Book value only if the nonprofit keeps the vehicle and uses it.

Your final tax return

Not to be morbid, but . . .

The year you die is the last year that someone can file a tax return for you. If your beneficiaries decide to sell all of your assets after you die, those sales do not get reported on your final tax return. The sale of your assets, post-death, are reported on a fiduciary tax return (IRS Form 1041) or on the beneficiaries' personal tax returns. Your beneficiaries cannot file a tax return in your name and Social Security number in the years after your death.

The things you learn the hard way. This is the story of how I screwed up my own taxes.

When I was in my early twenties, I was working full-time and starting to take some night classes at the local community college. I wasn't making a lot of money, so my budget was pretty tight. I hadn't been taught much about personal finance except that you should only buy what you can afford, and you shouldn't go into debt. I had no credit cards and no credit history.

When I learned that I was eligible for a student loan if I carried a certain number of units, I decided to obtain one; the terms were good, and I could use the extra funds as a nice cushion. I dutifully signed up for the extra classes and then applied for the student loan.

I was denied.

At first, I was sad that I was denied; but then I was shocked when I found out the reason for the denial—I had a bunch of delinquent store charge accounts and credit card accounts on my credit report. But I had never applied for any of them!

It was the beginning of a nightmare.

I soon learned that there were default judgments against me, and that late fees and interest had been accumulating for years, in addition to the debts. I tried to prove that I had not applied for the credit cards or made any of the charges, but my mother's forgery was just too good. She still lived at an address that was part of my credit history; and she refused to confess to her crimes.

The total debt was about $40,000 when I found out about it.

I worked with the various stores and credit card companies to try to reduce the debts, and I got it reduced to a little over $30,000. But my annual salary was just $26,000.

I was devastated.

My paychecks were already barely covering my expenses *before* I had to pay the credit cards, so I started cutting my costs as much as I could. I moved in with a friend to reduce my living costs; I cut back on my splurges and trips. But the biggest change I made was to reduce the amount of federal and state income taxes being withheld from my paychecks to $0.

That was a *big* mistake!

I loved having the extra money every paycheck, and there weren't any problems for a while. Then I filed my tax returns, and I owed both the IRS and the state.

But instead of having federal and state income taxes withheld from my paychecks again, I kept the withholding at $0. After all, I now had tax debts to pay along with the credit card debts, and I could use that extra cash.

What I didn't know at the time is that the IRS and the state were filing tax liens against me. I didn't know; my credit was horrible anyway, so I wasn't applying for anything. I moved a couple of times during this period, and I didn't always get the letters that the IRS and the state were sending me. I didn't always open the ones I did get. I also changed jobs a little too frequently, and the wage garnishments didn't catch up to me.

Until one day, when it all imploded.

An IRS revenue collection officer was waiting at my apartment one night when I returned home from class. He walked through my apartment looking for things I could sell. Sadly, I had nothing of value. My roommate had to prove that some things were hers, not mine. He made me show him all of my jewelry to prove that it was all cheap costume jewelry with no value.

I learned that he had been to my bank, and had learned that I had less than one hundred dollars in my bank account, so he decided not to seize it.

He took photos of my car—its odometer, the tires, the interior and the exterior—to document its condition so he could determine what it was worth. He let me keep the few dollars and coins I had in my wallet.

He tried to make me sign a bunch of documents, but I refused to do so and promised to read them and return them to him later.

Fortunately, I had recently started working for a CPA as a part-time bookkeeper. He helped me set up a plan to pay my back taxes. It took a while, and in the meantime, the IRS started levying my bank account. I had to quit using my bank account and pay for everything in cash, or buy money orders and cashiers checks.

Eventually, my CPA boss was also able to get the IRS to reduce a lot of the penalties and interest they had added to my tax bills. He also made me file for federal and state income tax withholding from my paychecks.

Back then, the IRS rarely allowed you more than one year for any payment plans. The IRS also would not let you have a payment plan if you owed taxes for another year. The IRS rarely approved an Offer in Compromise back then.

In hindsight, I should have filed for bankruptcy to wipe out the credit card debts. My credit was already awful, so a bankruptcy wasn't going to make it worse; and it took me much longer than seven years to pay off the credit card debts and the tax debts. At least a bankruptcy would have been off of my credit report after seven years.

LESSONS TO LEARN FROM MY MISTAKES

I don't recommend bankruptcy if you owe back taxes. One reason is that the taxes have to be old—at least three years past due—but in those intervening three years, the IRS will file tax liens, seize your bank accounts, and garnish your wages.

Instead, set up a payment plan. The IRS now lets you pay your past-due taxes in a payment plan of up to seventy-two months (six years) if you owe $50,000 or less. And, the IRS will let you add additional taxes from subsequent tax years to an existing payment plan if your total debt will still be $50,000 or less.

As for your state taxes, check to see if your state offers a payment plan. California currently offers one if you owe $25,000 total for all unpaid years, for up to sixty months (five years).

Better yet, don't get behind on your taxes!

MY ADVICE

- File your tax returns every year, even if you owe money and can't pay any of it. You will avoid penalties for filing late (as opposed to additional penalties for paying late).
- File your tax returns on time. Do not request an extension if your only issue is that you don't have the money to pay your balance due. The extension is for filing, not paying.
- If you have a balance due, set up a payment plan. The IRS lets you set up a payment plan online; or, you can mail in a form 9465.
- If you set up a payment plan, go with the option to let the IRS make an automatic withdrawal from your bank account every month. The setup fees are lower, and you are less likely to screw up the plan by missing a payment and having to start over.

- If you set up a payment plan, first do the math on the minimum amount you *have* to pay every month—the amount you owe, divided by seventy-two. Then, figure out a higher but reasonable amount you can *afford* to pay every month, and choose this amount as your payment amount.
- You can always pay off the balance due sooner, even if you have a payment plan, with no penalties. The IRS likes to get their money as soon as they can.
- Remember that if you have a refund for any tax year after you set up the payment plan, if there is still a balance due on the payment plan, the IRS will keep your refund and apply it to the balance due.
- If you receive a paycheck, then adjust your withholdings so that you have more income taxes withheld to hopefully reduce or even avoid having a balance due in the next year.
- If you are self-employed, be sure to pay all of your quarterly estimated tax payments; and be sure that your quarterly estimated tax payments are enough to cover what you owe.
- If you prepare your own tax returns, print out a copy and keep it in your files. I have had way too many people become my clients and not be able to provide me with a copy of a tax return because it was in that computer that crashed, or the software had expired. If the IRS audits you, they will want you to be able to provide a copy of the tax return you filed.
- Contribute the maximum you are allowed to your company's 401(k) plan, your IRA, and your Roth IRA. There are limits to how much you can contribute to

> an IRA or a Roth IRA based on your age, your income, and a few other things; so check with a tax advisor to help you figure out the maximum you can contribute.

What I learned in the process of cleaning up my tax mess was that I wanted to help other people and share what I had learned, so I became a CPA and have been helping people with their taxes—and their tax problems—ever since.

CHAPTER SEVEN

WHY DO YOU NEED AN ESTATE PLAN?

Jennifer Cowan

People tend to procrastinate around estate planning. Studies by the American Bar Association have shown that only 30 percent of us die with a will or trust in place. As an estate planning attorney, I have seen and heard countless examples of why it's critical to write an estate plan long before you approach the end of your life. Here is just one example:

Kate, a woman in her mid-sixties, is going in for an operation for cancer. She lives in California, is divorced with three daughters, and is financially secure. Her house is paid for, and she has a stock portfolio. However, she has not spoken to two of her daughters in years. And she has no estate plan.

Dying without a will or trust (otherwise known as "intestate") can result in your assets going to whomever the state considers your "heirs at law"—family members recognized under state law ("intestate heirs"). In the state of California, the probate code spells out what happens to someone's property if they die without a will. The statutory scheme makes sense, but of necessity, it is very general and depends upon who survives you: your spouse and children will be first in line to inherit, but if they have predeceased you (or you never married/had children), then more distant relatives will inherit.

This means that if something were to happen to Kate during her surgery, under the California Probate code intestacy provisions, her three daughters would split her assets equally three ways. This is not her desire. She wants all of her property to go to the only daughter that she is still in contact with. In order for her wishes to be given full effect, she needs to set up a will or trust to change the default estate plan in the Probate code.

Having all the necessary documents in place before you encounter times of loss or uncertainty means you will feel more relaxed, with the knowledge that your wishes will be met.

WHAT IS ESTATE PLANNING?

While most people associate "estate planning" with leaving assets to chosen beneficiaries, it also means naming people to make decisions for us (either medical or financial) if we are incapacitated. If you become incapacitated, even temporarily, and you don't have an estate plan, there may not be any single individual legally authorized to make decisions for you.

A cohesive estate plan should allow for the care and management of you and your assets in the event of your incapacity, as well as the management and distribution of your property after your death.

Since the majority of people in the US apparently do not have a will or trust in place, what is the "tipping point" that causes people to finally act? In my experience, it is usually because they've seen a problem in administering the estate of a family member or friend. When people see firsthand how things can go wrong, they don't want to cause similar problems for their loved ones.

The goal of this chapter is to set a course for you to create a cohesive estate plan now, so you are ready in case of an emergency. We will be covering the three key components of estate planning:

- Advance Healthcare Directive: Designating someone to manage your healthcare and end-of-life decisions if you are unable to do so.
- Durable Power of Attorney: Designating someone to manage your financial affairs should you become incapacitated.
- Will or trust: Leaving your assets to chosen beneficiaries.

If you take one thing from this chapter, I want you to know that estate planning is for everyone. Whether we are rich or poor, we all need to name someone to act for us if we become incapacitated, even temporarily.

ADVANCE HEALTHCARE DIRECTIVES

Our goal for the first month involves the most basic estate planning—preparing what in California is called an Advance Healthcare Directive (AHCD) or a Durable Power of Attorney for healthcare. This document authorizes someone to act on your behalf if you are legally incapacitated, such as in a coma, or when you are unable to make medical decisions for any reason.

We are all familiar with the unfortunate examples that make the news when a person on life support has no named agent for healthcare, or when there is no document specifying whether the patient would want to be on life support. Under some state laws, two or more people (such as the spouse and the parents) have an equal right to make medical decisions, and sometimes they disagree about whether or not to terminate life support. No one wants to go through the difficulties and disputes that can arise from such a situation.

Of course, these are sad—and fairly rare—examples; but less dramatic examples can still be painful. One person I know watched her relationships with her siblings end over the decision about what sort of memorial to have for their mother. At the time of their mother's death, each sibling followed a different religion. Since their mother had not specified what sort of memorial she wanted, the siblings each argued for their own chosen faith. If their mother had a legal document specifying what sort of memorial was important to her, her children would have had to follow her wishes. There might still have been hard feelings, but it would have been out of their control and so (hopefully) easier to move on from.

In California, the AHCD allows you to legally specify either, or both, of two important decisions:

- First, you may name a person who will have legal authority to make medical decisions on your behalf if you are unable to make them yourself. This person is known as your "agent." Unless you explicitly limit your agent's authority, it is quite broad.
- Next, you may specify your wishes with regard to what type of medical treatment you wish to receive and end-of-life decisions. Your wishes may be expressed in as much detail as you desire. Your doctor and agent must follow your instructions.

The AHCD has other optional sections concerning organ and tissue donation, designation of a primary care physician, and consent to disclose medical information. It may be effective immediately; for a specified period of time (i.e. during a hospital stay); or upon your incapacity. Incapacity is defined by your primary physician when they state that you are unable to make your own healthcare decisions. The AHCD may be revoked or replaced at any time.

The California Medical Association recommends that you discuss your end-of-life choices with your agent (and any named successors), physicians, and family. Give a copy of the document to your agent, your primary care physician, and your local hospital. Ideally, your family would also be told who you have chosen to speak for you, and where a copy of your AHCD can be found.

MAKING END-OF-LIFE AND HEALTHCARE DECISIONS

It is important to have a discussion with your agent about your end-of-life decisions and what is important to you regarding your care. Neither you, nor your AHCD, can possibly anticipate all medical decisions that may need to be made, or the options that will be available. This is why it is important to have a discussion with your agents about your values and wishes.

A tool many clients have found helpful as they discuss their wishes for end of life care is the "Go-Wish" deck of cards available through the Coda Alliance. These cards have simple value statements, such as "to have close friends near" and "to be treated the way I want." You sort the various cards into piles depending on how important they are to you.

There was an opinion piece in *The New York Times* by Jessica Nutik Zitter, M.D., suggesting that death education be offered in schools to teach young teenagers about the realities of the ICU—as compared to a medical TV show "save," which is often thrilling, romantic, and idealized, and *not* realistic.[1] In Dr. Zitter's view, we are not able to plan for the death of our choice, or at least a death consistent with our values, because we often do not know how close we are to dying. Many patients end their lives in the ICU, burdened by costly medical procedures that are not likely to prolong life. In contrast, studies indicate the majority of Americans say that they would prefer to die at home.

I believe that doctors also need death education, but the focus for doctors would be on communicating with patients how close they are to the end of their lives. Many doctors are calling for a new approach already, pointing out how medical school necessarily focuses on saving lives and preserving health, leaving little time for training on end-of-life issues and palliative care. These discussions would likely be difficult—which is all the more reason to include training on this topic.

When I prepare clients' Advance Healthcare Directives, we typically talk about how they can best ensure that their healthcare wishes are followed. I recommend honest, soul-searching conversations with their named agents regarding end-of-life wishes. Whoever you have named as your agent must be ready to stand up for your choices and values with medical personnel. If your agent does not feel that they could do so, that person may not be the best choice for your agent.

For example, would a close friend or family member be able to argue for the removal of life support (if that is your wish)? Or, alternatively, are you concerned that your agent would be someone who would be too fast to "pull the plug?" Do you want pain relief, or do you want your mind to be as clear as possible? These are all topics that need to be discussed with your agent.

Regardless of whether doctors and medical personnel are able to discuss end-of-life issues, it is important for us to think about what we would want; take responsibility for our own wishes; and take the steps needed to make sure that our wishes are followed.

FIRST-MONTH GOALS

PREPARE AN ADVANCE HEALTHCARE DIRECTIVE IN FOUR STEPS

1. Think about who you would like to make medical decisions for you. This could be a spouse or partner, a close friend, or a family member. Ask that person if they would be willing to act on your behalf.
2. Discuss possible scenarios with your proposed agent. Make sure he or she can honor your wishes. Try the "Go-Wish" game online.
3. Contact your primary care physician or healthcare provider for a form to nominate a healthcare agent, or contact an estate planning attorney to draft one for you.
4. Once you have completed the form (appropriately witnessed or notarized, whatever is required in your state), give a copy to your doctor, your local hospital, and your agent. If you are comfortable, let your family know who is legally authorized to make medical decisions on your behalf.

Now you can relax, knowing that this important step is taken care of. Congratulate yourself on completing your first step in estate planning!

DURABLE POWER OF ATTORNEY FOR FINANCIAL MATTERS

A Durable Power of Attorney ("DPA") authorizes an individual to manage financial matters on your behalf if you become incapacitated. If you have a revocable trust, the trustee will have the ability to manage the trust assets if you become incapacitated. However, for tax or other reasons, some assets, such as retirement accounts, may not be held by the trust; your agent can manage these assets. If you decide to use a will rather than a trust (see "Second Month Goals"), you most definitely need a DPA.

It should be noted that a DPA is only effective while you are alive. The DPA ends at death, at which point the administration of your assets would be handled through a will or trust.

With a DPA, your agent will have only the authority explicitly granted in the document. You determine to what extent your agent can act by specifying what powers they have. For example, you could limit your agent to a certain activity, such as closing the sale of your home. Or, you could allow your agent the full scope of powers. This would mean that your agent would "step into your shoes" and manage your various assets, write checks, file tax returns, take RMDs from your retirement accounts, and manage other financial matters to the same extent that you would.

Without this document, someone who wished to act on your behalf and in your interest would need to obtain court approval to do so (known in California as a "conservatorship"). The DPA may be effective immediately; or, for a specified period of time (say, a trip abroad); or, upon a specified event, such as your incapacity.

It may be revoked or replaced at any time that you have capacity.

SECOND-MONTH GOALS

PREPARE A DURABLE POWER OF ATTORNEY IN FOUR STEPS

1. Think about who you would like to manage your finances if you are not able to manage them. This could be a spouse or partner, a close friend, or a family member. Ask that person if they would be willing to act as your agent.
2. Discuss with them what would need to be done if you are unable to manage your finances. For example, your bills would need to be paid. Make sure that person knows what to do, where your paperwork and financial documents reside, and at what point they would need to step in.
3. Contact your financial institutions. Ask if they require a special "in-house" form—one prepared by that institution—or if they will accept one drafted by your attorney. Some states have statutory forms that can be found online.
4. Once you have your completed form (appropriately witnessed or notarized, whatever is required in your state) give a copy to your financial institution and your named agent(s).

Congratulate yourself on completing your second step in estate planning!

TESTAMENTARY DOCUMENTS: A WILL OR A TRUST?

The final step of estate planning is preparing the documents that will leave your assets to chosen beneficiaries. The transfer of your assets at your death is generally accomplished through a will or a trust.

Why would you choose a trust over a will?

In California, wills must be probated. "Probate" is the legal process of collecting assets, paying off creditors, and distributing remaining property among heirs and/or beneficiaries. Probate can be time-consuming and expensive. It is also a public process; the probate court supervises the administration of your estate, and all court documents and hearings are open to the public. Probate fees are based on the value of your assets. Fees run about $4,000 on the first $100,000 of assets, and $23,000 on the first million of assets (and on from there). The administration process can take a year—or two, or more—before assets are finally distributed.

People who want to avoid probate, or who want more control over distribution of their assets, often set up a revocable trust. With a revocable trust, you are typically the named trustee while you are alive. You can revoke or amend the trust, transfer assets, and generally continue as before with your financial matters. The trust is fully revocable until your death, at which point it becomes irrevocable. In the document, you name successor trustees, who are people you trust to administer to your estate or act on your behalf if you become incapacitated. You also name beneficiaries—those people (or charities) that you want to receive your assets when you die.

A will "speaks at death": Assets you own at the time of your death are passed, after an administration period, to your named beneficiaries. A trust has much more flexibility. For example, assets may be set aside to pay for college tuition over time. Or, assets may be used to support a spouse from a second marriage until his or her death, at which point the assets could pass to the children of a prior marriage. Post-death trust administration, in general, is a fraction of the cost of probate. It is also private.

CHOOSING A SUCCESSOR TRUSTEE

How do you decide on a successor trustee for your revocable trust? Remember, your successor trustee takes over when you are incapacitated *or* after your death.

A successor trustee is very similar to an agent under your DPA; in fact, it is often the same person. The only difference, besides the fact that a DPA ends at death, is that your agent under a DPA manages assets outside the trust, and a successor trustee manages assets "in" the trust (which is to say, the title is held in the name of the trust). For example, retirement assets in California are typically not transferred to trusts; but homes are. If you become incapacitated, your agent under a DPA would request distributions from your retirement account on your behalf, and then use trust assets to continue paying your mortgage and insurance on your home (a trust asset).

Naming a successor to step into your shoes is an important decision—one that I always spend some time discussing with my clients. A good successor trustee is someone you trust implicitly and can either manage the assets and paperwork on behalf of you and/or your family, or delegate those aspects that he or she will not perform. Your successor may decide to hire an accountant, bookkeeper, or investment advisor—just as you may do yourself.

For those with continuing trusts after their death, it is especially important to select a successor trustee carefully. A continuing trust may be set up to provide for minor children, young adults, or even older adult children. You may feel the children are not old enough to receive assets outright, or you may simply want to protect your adult children from creditors or divorce by leaving their inherited assets in trust. If so, your successor trustee will need to manage distributions and field requests for money. This is not an easy task! Your successor should ideally have an understanding of how you would make distributions, as if you were still making them yourself.

Another common use of a continuing trust is when there is a second marriage and children from a prior marriage. The surviving stepparent spouse may receive income from trust assets while they are alive. Then, at the stepparent's death, the remaining trust principal is distributed to the children of the first marriage. The successor trustee will need to walk a careful line between the current beneficiary of the trust (the stepparent spouse) and the remainder beneficiaries (the children who will eventually receive whatever is left after the stepparent dies).

Sometimes parents setting up a trust don't want to choose from among their children as successor trustees. The parents are unwilling to "play favorites" or acknowledge that there are conflicts among their children. They name all their children as co-trustees in the misguided hope that siblings with different views will "cancel each other out." I don't recommend this option, as multiple co-trustees can be a recipe for disaster. Also, you don't want to name someone a successor trustee simply to avoid hurt feelings. Name someone who is right for the job, and who has your confidence.

If there are too many potential conflicts among your choices, or simply no appropriate person available for the job, consider naming a bank or private professional fiduciary to take over. That professional or institution is trained, bonded, and paid to take the heat. I typically recommend having the option for a professional trustee in your trust, in case those you have named are not able to take over when the time comes. It's best to have options.

TITLING ASSETS

In California, the final step, once you have a trust, is to make sure that your assets are properly funded into the trust. That is, certain assets need to be "titled" in the name of the trust rather than your individual name. Your attorney will help you with this or give you instructions for titling assets in the name of the trust. This is also a good time to check beneficiary designations on assets outside the trust and update those as needed. Assets that transfer directly to a named beneficiary at your death (such as retirement accounts, annuities, some pensions, and life insurance) are not governed by your will or trust.

Whether you have a will or a trust, keep your document up-to-date. If you are no longer in contact with the person you wish to manage your affairs (executor or successor trustee), name someone else. Let your attorney know if you get divorced or married, or anytime there are other significant changes in your life.

Your named successors should know where your original estate planning documents are kept and how to access them. After your death your successor trustee or executor should contact your estate planning attorney—or any other estate planning attorney—to administer your estate. Hiring an attorney ensures that all post-death administration work is properly done, following all the laws in your state. This protects both the person you have named to administer your estate and your beneficiaries.

THIRD-MONTH GOALS

WRITE YOUR WILL OR TRUST IN FOUR STEPS

NOTE: Goals this month may take longer.

1. If you don't already have an estate planning attorney, ask your CPA or a financial advisor for recommendations. You can also ask friends. Interview a few by phone and set up an appointment. Have a meeting with your attorney and discuss whether a will or trust is the right option for you in your home state.
2. Think about who you want to administer your estate (executor under a will, successor trustee under a trust). Try to think of at least two people, so that you have a backup. Ask them if they would be willing to act on your behalf.
3. Think about who you want to receive your assets at your death (beneficiaries). Is there any reason to have a continuing trust at your death? Whatever you decide, have drafts prepared, review them with the attorney, and sign.
4. In California, at least, you need to complete the process by funding your assets into the trust. Your attorney can advise you on this.

Congratulate yourself on completing your final step in estate planning!

OUR PARENTS

Many clients ask me how they can help their parents as they age. I know that it can be a complex balancing act. Often people are willing to give up some tasks, but understandably unwilling to give up complete control of assets and accounts. A parent may be comfortable delegating certain tasks, like balancing a checkbook or paying bills. Of course, whoever takes over these duties must be trustworthy and accountable.

If it is time to completely turn over management of financial assets, most trusts have a mechanism to accomplish this. Either the current trustee (the parent, in our example) resigns; or, there is a procedure in the trust that you follow to determine lack of capacity to manage trust assets. There should be a named successor trustee who is willing and able to take over the trusteeship. This can be a spouse or other trusted relative, a child, or a bank or private professional fiduciary.

If your parent does not have a trust, there should be a durable power of attorney for financial assets in place. Unfortunately, sometimes banks are reluctant to accept durable powers of attorney that are not on their own bank forms. In California, as a last resort, a conservatorship can be established, wherein a person is appointed by the court to manage an incapacitated person's health and/or finances. Due to the expense, this should only be considered if no other options are in place.

I also recommend talking to your parents about end-of-life wishes. This can be a difficult topic to bring up, but if anything, it is even more important than the discussion regarding management of financial assets.

I highly recommend Dr. Atul Gawande's 2014 book, *Being Mortal: Medicine and What Matters in the End.* In his view, the most important questions to consider before any major medical procedure are:

- What are your biggest fears and concerns?
- What goals are most important to you?
- What trade-offs are you willing to make, and what ones are you not?

Dr. Gawande encourages patients, physicians, and family members to have this discussion before major medical decisions are made.

While it may be difficult to make decisions around our own estate planning, it can be many times harder to discuss these issues with our parents. Patience, tact, and consideration are important to keep in mind. Remember, even though you may have the best intentions, your parents may not wish to discuss their plans for the future. Try to bring up the topic in a way that will work for your parents. All families are different; just do your best.

MY DAD'S DEATH

The death of a loved one is an event that remains in survivors' memories for years to come. A hospital may focus only on treating the patient, and may not have adequately trained staff for interactions with patients' families. That was my experience recently—even though my dad had every legal document in place, and had articulated his wishes in advance to his healthcare agent. He had done everything he could to prepare ahead of time.

My dad ended up in the ER because he was having trouble breathing. Sally (my dad's wife, primary healthcare agent, *and* a doctor) was told he would likely die that night unless he was put on a ventilator. She knew, from discussions with my dad, that he did not want to be kept on life support indefinitely; but she authorized the intervention with the expectation that my dad would be able to breathe on his own once what appeared to be an infection was treated. I am certain that my father would have wanted that treatment at that time if he understood what was going on.

He was moved up to the ICU, and Sally stayed at his bedside nearly round-the-clock for the next week, while other family members came and went—Sally's siblings and children; me and my two brothers; my dad's grandchildren. We watched as his ability to breathe on his own was tested over the next several days, but he was never able to breathe without the machine.

During this week in the ICU, he never regained consciousness.

On Tuesday, after five days in the ICU and numerous treatments and interventions, my dad was given a CT scan. A resident told Sally that it was good news—they didn't find anything. Yet the next day, Sally was told that there was going to be a meeting with the family on Thursday, and a hospice representative would be present.

On Wednesday night, I tried to prepare myself for what I would hear the next morning, I assumed it meant my dad was dying. (I later found out that Sally thought the suggestion of hospice made no sense, as she realized that he would die if the ventilator were removed.)

Unfortunately, when we arrived Thursday morning for the meeting, the staff on duty had not heard about it. They told us that *maybe* there could be a meeting Friday. A social worker then showed up and asked Sally why she had asked for hospice. She had not requested hospice, and from my estate planning practice, I know the social worker's question could have easily created discord between family members.

Overall, the statements and information from the hospital personnel were not well-thought-out, and just seemed very ad hoc. For nearly two hours we were in the hospital hallway, arguing back and forth with hospital staff about whether there was going to be a meeting concerning my dad's prognosis, and if so, when; who was going to be there; and who had called it.

Eventually, Sally told the staff that we absolutely needed to talk to someone that day. Finally, the head ICU doctor on duty brought us to a busy staff storeroom. We sat at a table piled with papers and supplies. It was not private in any way; medical personnel came and went throughout our meeting, opening cabinets and carrying supplies in and out.

In less than ten or fifteen minutes, the doctor told us that the CT scan showed "slow" brain waves; they had no further treatments to recommend, and they had tried everything medically possible. At this point, they could only continue to maintain him in his current condition, and he would now require a feeding tube and a tracheotomy to remain on the ventilator.

When Sally heard the results of the scan, which was different from what she had been previously told, she made the difficult decision to remove my dad from life support. As a doctor, Sally immediately knew what his condition meant. She also knew that he would not want to be maintained in this state, spending the rest of his life on a ventilator with no prospect of regaining consciousness. I, of course, had no idea what the doctor meant by "slow brain waves," and the whole conversation was so emotionally charged for me that I was having trouble processing the new information.

I learned a painful lesson about how chaotic end-of-life treatment can be in a hospital. I now discuss "medical advocates" with clients, much the same way I now recommend professional fiduciaries to administer trusts. A medical advocate is a professional, either within the hospital or hired privately, who understands the healthcare system and can advocate for patients and their families during a medical event. It's one more tool in your healthcare toolbox, and a good resource if you need help.

MY MONEY INFLUENCES

Combating women's financial insecurity with education and clear talk was the original intent of this book. I have lived with financial insecurity for most of my life. While writing my chapter, I examined my own views about money and thought about how those views have shaped my actions as an adult. My goal here is to pull away the curtain on my own financial life—in much the way we encourage you to peel away the layers and take steps for a better financial future.

I learned about saving for the future very early. My parents divorced when I was four and my brother was two. I don't remember the earlier years, but I do know that afterwards, money was very tight. There were times we went hungry. That's something you don't forget as a child. My grandparents would give me money for my birthday, or Christmas, and I started saving that money to lend back to my mom so that she could buy us food at the end of the month.

My grandparents taught me that I could follow financial markets. Every morning, my grandfather would read various stock share prices aloud to my grandmother. One day I asked him, "What does 'down an eighth' mean?" I didn't really understand his answer, but the fact that he tried to explain what the stock fluctuations meant made it seem like something I could follow too, even if I didn't understand yet. Every Friday night, my grandparents watched *Wall $treet Week* with Louis Rukeyser and I watched with them once I was a teenager. Again, I came away with the message that I was an appropriate audience for this information, too.

My uncle taught me that I could advocate for myself on the job. He was a dentist, and he offered me a summer job when I was in high school. I was to clean up after patients, sterilize instruments in the autoclave, wipe down surfaces, and prepare the tray with clean instruments for the next patient. My uncle started me at a reduced learning salary that he said would be temporary. Finally, weeks later, after quietly waiting, I said that I had learned the job; why hadn't he raised my salary? He replied that I had to learn that when I was worth more, I needed to ask for more.

My grandfather and a coworker in my first professional job taught me about saving for retirement. In my uncle's office I got my first paycheck with FICA withdrawals. Complaining to my grandfather, he explained that those withdrawals were important because I could get Social Security when I was older and no longer working. (It's interesting that he didn't mention a husband providing for me, given that he was born around World War I.) In my first professional job after college, an older colleague encouraged me to contribute to the company 401(k) to prepare for my financial future.

Unfortunately, I took a lump-sum distribution (paying the tax penalty) when I left the company three years later. I always wonder what that $3,000 would have grown to in forty years. It did mean that when my new husband started his job soon after, I was able to explain 401(k) plans to him, and he made contributions. The crazy thing is that I took a new job at the same time, but didn't contribute to my own plan, thinking his contributions would be enough! When I divorced twenty-five years later, I had only a very small IRA in my own name.

Later, I changed careers and became a lawyer. Later still, I made the decision to stay home with our children, leaving a corporate law job. Often I hear women say that it was the best decision they ever made; that may be true, but I took a huge financial hit in deciding to stay home. Not only were there many years of lost income, but when I did go back to work, it was impossible to find a job at anything close to my previous salary. These were things I had never considered in making my decision, nor had I considered the possibility of a future divorce—a statistically probable event. When I divorced at age fifty, I hadn't worked in nearly fifteen years.

I grew up in a family that emphasized the importance of home ownership. Now newly-divorced, it was important to me to buy a home and have some control over my housing costs in housing-crisis California. Because I was just starting my business, my income was low. My mom agreed to go on the mortgage and title with me so that her assets could be counted with mine. I bought the cheapest condo I could in my town. A couple years later I qualified for the mortgage on my own and refinanced in my name only. Thank you, Mom! I know that I was very fortunate to have that support in stabilizing my costs.

Even with my new home, my insecurity around money continued to haunt me. My retirement account was small, and I worried about losing what I had. It was hard to save anything from my business. I jumped between advisors and approaches, and sometimes I just kept my cash and sat out the market. Finally, I accepted that I was not the best person to manage my own retirement account. I settled on an advisor that was marginally better than a programmed approach after factoring in fees. My dad died last year and left me some money, providing more of a safety net when added to what I already had.

My early money insecurity was reactivated when I got divorced and went back to work to support myself. I questioned many of my money decisions and worried more than was healthy about making ends meet and providing for my kids. I was very frugal with myself, sticking to a tight budget so that I didn't pull money out of retirement assets. Eventually, I woke up and realized that

I hadn't had a vacation in five years! After that, I set aside a small budget for vacations—a way to let myself know that I deserved a vacation, just like everyone else.

Now that I'm approaching retirement age, I also realize that I deserve to retire, too. At this point I am monitoring my expenses, continuing to invest in the stock market (with professional advice now), and looking forward to retirement five to seven years from now. I realize that I could not have done it without help along the way. I hope to be able to pay it forward and pass something on to my children as well.

CHAPTER EIGHT

FAMILY MATTERS

Relationships and Your Finances

Joann Babiak
Family law attorney and mediator

A NEW BEGINNING FROM A VERY BAD ENDING

His note was stuffed into the side map pocket of my car; and when I left that day for the hour and a half drive down the turnpike, all seemed normal. I firmly believed I had my life under control. I was going to a statewide meeting of mediators to celebrate successes and continue my training experience. As I reached for the toll pass, the envelope with his note inside came with it—and then, forty minutes into my drive, at seventy miles per hour, my life skipped a beat.

The adventure that began so joyfully with my husband spanned almost two decades. According to the note I had just discovered, he was filing for divorce that day. My husband's decision to end our marriage sucked me into a paradigm shift for which I was totally and completely unprepared.

I am sharing the information in this chapter in hope that you will never be unprepared for a sudden shift in your life story. Whatever your age and living situation, this chapter can help you craft your own safety net in anticipation of life's unexpected changes. Taking control of your financial wellbeing prepares you to navigate challenging situations, and even life-altering circumstances like divorce.

A LITTLE CONTEXT

What makes me qualified to talk about divorce? I have been a California attorney since 1980, and I have worked with many couples seeking divorce.

When I started my career, if you had told me that law school was going to be a part of my future, I would have laughed. For the first decade of my professional life, I worked with patients experiencing head injury, stroke, and other medical conditions that adversely affected their ability to communicate with other people. I spent long hours in hospitals, rehabilitation centers, and other care settings, helping people experiencing communicative disorders to overcome barriers to communication and rebuild their independence. I was a Speech-Language Pathologist with a master's degree, and I had earned my Certificate of Clinical Competence from the American Speech-Language-Hearing Association.

In the span of my decade of practice, healthcare systems in the US underwent radical changes. Insurance companies imposed their business models on rehabilitative service providers in the places I worked. Programs that were once patient-focused pivoted to focus on metrics that, in my view, took the "care" out of patient care. Insurers developed cost structures that limited options for people who desperately required more intense and lengthier treatment than the new business models allowed. I felt sometimes that the new models prioritized profits over people.

I believed I could do more for those I served. I turned to the study of law, hopeful that I would learn advocacy skills to better help my patients. While a married mother of two children, I studied law and psychology in a joint JD/MA degree program at the University of Tulsa. Along with my JD, I earned certificates of advanced legal studies in health law and in alternative dispute resolution and a Master of Arts degree in Industrial and Organizational Psychology. (Human resources, leadership, and team-building were part of this course of study.) I became a mediator as well as an attorney. I had acquired the tools to create change!

But then, just after law school graduation came the day my husband informed me he was filing for divorce. This was the day I drove down the turnpike and discovered his note. At the time, I experienced a shocking betrayal. There were many more eye-opening revelations along the way. The divorce process brought with it much emotional turmoil. My life and the lives of my two children were suddenly drastically altered. The man I married almost twenty years ago announced he was moving away, and he quickly began a new life. I saw the irony in my situation—an attorney with a family law practice was now experiencing the same shock and trauma as many of her own clients. Worse—just like my clients, I felt totally unprepared!

After my marriage ended, I realized the divorce, as well as the marriage, held many lessons that could assist others transitioning into new and more hopeful life circumstances. As a result of my own divorce, I developed a passion for speaking about life transitions. I gained a deeper level of compassion for the circumstances of divorcing spouses and families in conflict. From both professional and personal experience, I learned that divorce can turn a family upside down in a minute; as can the end of any intimate relationship, regardless of marital status.

The content I share in this chapter concerns building protections into your intimate relationships in case they falter. You will also learn how to take decisive action to protect yourself should you believe that your relationship no longer serves you well.

NINETY-DAY TAKEAWAYS

- Know what you have, and what you owe.
- Familiarize yourself with your cash flow—your income and expenses. Track spending patterns that may mean trouble.
- Create written agreements. Read before you sign. Know what you are signing. If you have questions, don't sign; find help. Talk first, sign later—not the other way around.
- Talk about money with your significant other/spouse. Have the hard conversation.
- Know that your rights can be defined in a variety of contractual agreements, including a Cohabitation Agreement, Prenuptial Agreement, Postnuptial Agreement, and others.
- Create your own plan, and have your own money.
- Be aware of trouble before trouble finds you—"An ounce of prevention is worth a pound of cure."
- Domestic violence exists. Resources to help you obtain protections also exist. Take action.
- Be kind to yourself. You deserve the best.

- You can do this. Baby steps will get you there. Choose a goal to accomplish within your ninety days; complete that task; then, target your next objective.

This list broadly sets out some points covered in this discussion. Review the chapter and identify one or two content areas that may help you. Begin creating your own ninety-day action plan. Take a small step to protect those you love—including yourself!

Being aware of the risks of relationships may motivate you to seek legal protections. Whether you are in a relationship or not, you can plan ahead. If you are negotiating a relationship with a partner or spouse, put your promises to each other in writing. Your protections will differ depending on your situation. If you are looking to create a better roadmap for yourself, read on. The legal protections I describe can make a difference in your own quality of life and for the life experiences of your children, too.

AS YOU BEGIN

How can you become the author of your own story when you don't know how to begin? You learn to think about your legal and financial matters differently. With a small investment of your time and armed with a plan, you begin to find your way.

No matter where you are on life's timeline, and whatever your circumstances, you have the capacity to take control of your finances—to learn about legal matters that add to your toolkit, and to formulate a plan where you are in control. Control matters. Control means you are making your own choices.

You are motivated to read this book because you desire to change your circumstances. Knowing you have the ability to change empowers you to take another step forward, and to navigate your own journey. You can gain control of your life by gathering information, thinking about how the information applies to you, and making a plan.

First, know your legal rights. Refer to the legal rights and processes governing marriage and relationships—for example, the process for dissolving a marriage; the process for unmarried couples to put protections in place; or the process of obtaining restraining orders if domestic violence becomes an issue.

Please understand that this chapter provides you with legal *information,* not legal *advice.* Advising requires an understanding of your personal story and your goals and objectives. Understanding the protections that the law offers is only one part of the equation. Sharing your own facts with an attorney may be a critical component of your planning. Consult with an attorney who is licensed to practice law in your location if you need legal advice. You can often find an attorney by contacting a lawyer referral service administered through either your State Bar Association or your County Bar Association. Many lawyer referral services provide their clients with a low-cost or reduced-cost initial consultation session.

Once you understand the legal protections that may be available to you, you are able to make them a part of your ninety-day "shape-up" plan. Understanding leads to action!

DO YOU KNOW WHAT YOU HAVE? START TAKING CONTROL

Be brave and get started. Find out your cash flow and your net worth. Know what you have and what you owe—you, personally; as well as both of you as a couple. Know the cost of your present lifestyle and the effects of related circumstances on your bottom line. Many times, life gets so busy that we fail to stop and take stock of which assets will serve our needs and which need to be repurposed or discarded. The assets you have acquired and the obligations that you shoulder require your active attention. While married: pay attention to who owns what, and understand what is yours alone. Property you acquired before you married is your own separate property; your spouse's property acquired before marriage is their separate property. You can acquire separate property during marriage through gifts made to you *alone*, not to you and your spouse; or through inheritance gifted to you *alone*, not to you and your spouse.

Community property is yours together as a couple. Property acquired after the date of marriage, up to the date you and your spouse decide to separate with the intent to end your marriage, is community property. This can include retirement savings, 401(k) plans, pension plans, and Individual Retirement Accounts (IRAs), if they are assets acquired during marriage. Identify your separate property and your community property assets and debts. The process of identifying your assets and debts is a great point of entry into your short-term plan to protect yourself in your relationship or marriage.

You may be asking, "Where do I begin?" Here is one straightforward way to organize what you have and what you owe.

First, grab a notebook. Walk into any room in your house and get in there. Make an inventory of what you see. For example, your dining room might have a table and several chairs; a lamp; a china cabinet; some art on the walls; and so on.

Next, open the drawers in that room and note the contents. If your dining room has a closet, open the closet door and write down what's inside. Walk through your home room-by-room, including the garage and the yard, so you can add to the inventory of all the "things" that you have accumulated. Assign values to each. The assigned values should reflect prices you would find for similar items at a local used goods store. If you are married, you should include your spouse's assets in your inventory, too. If you and your spouse have made a prenuptial agreement, find it and review it carefully; the prenuptial agreement should document who owns what as separate property.

Follow up on this visual inventory of assets with an analysis of your cash flow. Inventory other important documents, such as statements from your bank and institutional investments. Also, tally up the bills you owe: phone, heat, trash, cable, and so forth—individually, or as a couple. Review your mail over the course of a few weeks and create a log of the bills you receive, the amount of payment due, and any outstanding account balances. Access any online accounts and make a similar record. Examine all your account statements. Include your pension and retirement account statements, savings accounts, credit union member holdings, and communications from accounts holding stocks, bonds, and other securities and investments.

If you are married, include all of your spouse's assets and debts as well as your own. Also, identify the type and amount of your regularly recurring debts. You might start with credit card statements so you can examine itemized expenditures, which allow you to look beyond the total monthly disbursement of any single payment to your credit card company. Keep this process simple: Begin with a short list, and keep adding to it. When bills arrive in the mail, or when your email contains an invoice, add the information to your inventory.

As you develop this inventory of assets and debts, add other details. For example, find out more about the real estate you own, including any income producing rental properties, "flat land" (unimproved acreage or lot), and any mortgage obligations. Everyone lives somewhere, and some people have property in more than one location. Identify what you own. Identify the mortgage payment and the amount of taxes paid on any real property you own. Most of us pay for having a roof overhead. You and your spouse or partner may own a home and have a mortgage, plus an obligation to pay the property tax and insurance payments that are associated with the property. Some homeowners pay additional fees to a neighborhood or homeowner's association. Find out the dollar amount of these costs. Are you on the title deed to your (and your spouse's) real property? If you don't know, find out! The county has records that you can access at the land records office or at the county assessor's office. Staff at these local government offices can be very helpful in your search for information.

After you have obtained information about your assets and debts, consider what kind of a legal safety net you might negotiate with your spouse or your significant other. If you are preparing to discuss your findings with your spouse or partner, know your objective. In a marriage, you might want to negotiate a postnuptial agreement regarding separately held assets or an inheritance. You might want to equalize an imbalance in financial control, perhaps to offset money you provided to your significant other or spouse earlier in your relationship. Arranging a consultation and advice session with an attorney practicing family law can help you to understand what these kinds of agreements can do to protect you. Discuss the negotiation process with the attorney, and get their input about the conversation you will have with your spouse or partner in advance of your planned discussion.

If you are preparing for divorce, organize your newfound knowledge and keep your information in a *secure location*. One client thought that keeping important documents in the car trunk would be secure—after all, the car was locked. Unfortunately, the spouse had a second set of keys to the vehicle, and all the documents that were locked away in the car trunk mysteriously disappeared! Think about getting your own safe deposit box at a different financial institution than the one you used during your marriage.

You will need the information you have gathered to complete some of the family law forms that provide information to the court during your divorce. For example, the California Judicial Council has developed Family Law Form FL-142, called a "Schedule of Assets and Debts." The form may help you easily identify what you have and what you owe. (You can find this form through an online search.) Even if you are not living in California, and regardless of whether you plan to go to court, this form can help you organize and identify your assets and your debts. If you happen to live outside of California, your state may have similar forms available. You might check online to view your local court's family law resources, or call your County Bar Association to ask about a comparable form.

When preparing for negotiation with your spouse or significant other, knowing your monthly take-home income from all sources, and understanding what you as a couple pay to keep your household afloat each month, provides you with two important baselines. First, you will be able to identify the dollar amount needed to meet your basic living expenses—food, clothing, shelter, transportation, healthcare, mortgage, taxes, and insurance. Second, you will be able to identify the amount of money you control after you pay for basic living expenses. The cash available after payment of your basic living expenses represents the amount of discretionary income in your monthly budget.

In California, if you are preparing for divorce, you will complete forms that capture your cash flow information based upon your own situation, not that of your spouse. Your spouse will complete a set of forms based upon their own income and expenses. Each spouse will have the opportunity to present information to the judge based on any or all of the following:

1. Your projected financial needs
2. Your current income and expenditures
3. Your estimated expenses

You have the opportunity to discuss different scenarios with the judge. You may choose to talk about one or more of the three identified above. I believe that talking about more than one of the options paints a more complete picture of your situation, and allows you to advocate by explaining more fully about the kind of financial support you might need. Rather than simply describing the situation based on income you alone take home, why not additionally prepare a realistic model reflecting your projected expenses? If you are ending your marriage, your needs will change. Tell the judge about those changes.

Whether you plan to work through the challenges in your marriage or prepare for life as a single woman, learn to allocate some of your discretionary dollars toward your long-term goals. Manage your discretionary income and tighten up your outlay for basic living expenses. Change your spending patterns: start saving more, and regularly invest discretionary income with an eye towards creating a better future.

The following list captures valuable information that can help you understand your cash flow. Enter dollar amounts beside applicable items and pay attention to where you are spending your hard-earned money. After all, you work for it; now make it work for you. Building your knowledge about your financial foundation will make you more resilient and better able to protect those you love. You will also be on a firmer footing when discussing important financial decisions, be it with a financial advisor, spouse, or significant other.

INCOME	RECURRING EXPENSES
• Employment	• Home expenses
• Self-employment business—develop a profit-and-loss statement for each business	• Repairs
• Inheritance or regularly-occurring gifts—for example, trust fund payments	• Rent or mortgage
• Investments	• Homeowner's Association dues
• Military benefits	• Property taxes
• Retirement benefits	• Landscape services
• Spousal support payments	• Gas
• Other government benefits	• Electricity
• Social Security	• Water
• Disability	• Trash collection
• Worker's Compensation	• Internet
• Other income	• Phone—landline and/or mobile phone
	• Cable service
	• Healthcare payments
	• Medical insurance
	• Dental insurance
	• Vision insurance
	• Hospital bills
	• Automobile payments, maintenance, and insurance

INCOME	RECURRING EXPENSES
	• Credit cards • Childcare and child-related expenses • Daycare • Babysitting • Tutoring • After-school programs • Summer camp • Enrichment classes (sports, art, dance, music, etc.) • Pets and related expenses—grooming, vet bills, pet food • Miscellaneous general expenses—food, clothing • Personal loans—family member as lender • Charitable causes—donations and other contributions • Payments for leisure and travel activities • Memberships, club dues • Miscellaneous personal expenses—dry cleaning, hairdresser, nail salon

This list is not extensive and is only limited by your imagination and, of course, by your ability to be fully honest with yourself about your spending.

The process of a ninety-day "shape-up" presents an opportunity to learn new skills that will better position you to face life's challenges. Knowing what you have and what you owe is an important part of designing a better future.

YOUR FINANCIAL PROFILE IS KEY

If you do not know the balance sheet for your own situation, how can you even begin to protect what you have worked so hard to acquire? What happens if you do not know what you have? In the worst-case scenario, you allow your share of wealth to be taken from you. In the best-case scenario, you plan in advance to secure a better version of your future. When you take steps to become informed about your assets and your debts, you can monitor and protect your finances.

IF YOU ARE SINGLE

If you are a single woman and have no life partner, seek out an attorney working in the area of estates and trusts, and a financial advisor. The financial advisor can discuss wealth management, and an attorney working in the area of law addressing estates and trusts can discuss legal protections available to you. This book contains a variety of chapters that will provide additional information about legal protections. When you live single and alone and do not have minor children, you may not need guidance from a family law attorney to protect your assets; however, there is one notable exception: If you experience domestic violence, the family court can help you put protections in place. A later part of this chapter shares more information about domestic violence.

If you are a single woman who enjoys a committed relationship with a loving partner, you are most certainly able to protect your assets. Why is putting protections in place important? Here's an example of a single woman who has yet to plan for her future.

Sally and her partner live in the same household. Sally owns the home. Sally and her partner agree to share the day-to-day costs; but so far, Sally has put off making any other agreements with her partner about money and property—and nothing agreed-upon has been put in a written document. Things have been going fine, but what happens if Sally's circumstances suddenly change? There are a range of unanticipated incidents that could turn life upside-down: job loss, illness, accidents, or family-related events can all create cash flow difficulties. This is a list no one wants to discuss. However, it is important that Sally and her partner do discuss the options and have the hard conversations. If you are single and in a committed relationship, so should you!

If you take away one concept from reading this chapter, it is this: *plan ahead.* An ounce of prevention is worth far more than a pound of cure. Create a plan that captures your expectations around money and property well in advance of a life-changing event. Put your agreements in writing. Assuming that you are of sound mind and over the age of majority, you and your partner can put protections in place by making a contract. Apart from common decency, if you do not have a written agreement, there are no express or implied expectations about how you and a significant other behave towards one another if you are not legally married to one another.

IF YOU DON'T WANT TO, YOU DON'T HAVE TO:

- share property
- share earnings during the relationship (or after)
- support your partner if you are not married
- provide for your partner in your will, trust, or retirement plan

WHAT HAPPENS IF WE DECIDE TO LIVE TOGETHER AS A COUPLE AND DON'T WANT TO MAKE A CONTRACT?

As two single people, each of you have the right to your own earnings, to manage your own property, and to do whatever you want to do with your own money—just as you would if you were living alone. However, life with another person in the household can get complicated and messy. Sometimes, breakups happen. Without a plan, what will be the result?

SINGLE BY DESIGN: PUTTING LEGAL PROTECTIONS IN PLACE TO SAFEGUARD YOUR ASSETS

If you want to live with the person you love, but do not want to marry, how do you protect yourself and be a couple at the same time? What you need to know depends on where you are in your life story right now, and which direction you want to head in a future that you are just beginning to envision.

Single; married; young, or not so young; in a relationship with another person, or getting out of a relationship—your state has laws that can guide you as you put legal protections in place. If you are married, the family code offers legal protections to spouses and their children.

Unmarried couples in committed relationships can reference their state's civil code, which provides opportunities to create protections through written agreements to almost everyone who is of sound mind, and who has attained the age of majority. Whether your agreement addresses who does the laundry, or walks the family dog; or how household expenses are managed—putting your agreements in writing allows you and your spouse or significant other, to create a written record of your mutually-agreed-upon expectations.

When creating written agreements, you have the opportunity to reflect on what you and the other person want, to discuss and negotiate your understandings, and to identify what happens if one or another person fails to keep their promises.

Contracts are one way to document the arrangements you negotiate as a couple, married or unmarried. Contracts are everywhere! They come into our lives in many forms. For example, when we acquire a credit card and as part of the contractual agreement that allows us credit, we promise the credit card company that we will repay the monthly charges. We are contractually obligated to pay when we hire people to perform services for us; and we get paid when we are hired by others to perform certain tasks. The point is, we all have a certain familiarity with written contracts. Contracts protect our own interests and the interests of others who have agreed to abide by the terms of the agreement.

If you choose not to marry, you can formalize the understandings between you and your life partner in a cohabitation agreement while sharing life together. If you decide to marry, prenuptial and postnuptial agreements offer protections to couples before and during marriage.

Whether you are married or sharing life in a committed relationship, as you age, you may acquire significant assets. You may wish to manage these assets so they are well-protected, particularly in circumstances where children and former spouses may be part of your lives. You may wish to protect your wealth to pass along to your children (of any age), and you may wish to safeguard your current sweetheart from having to interact with your former spouse. Put protections in place before life's more challenging moments arise!

CONTRACTS FOR RELATIONSHIPS

A contract can be defined as an exchange of valuable promises that are made between people who have the capacity to consent and a clear understanding of what they have promised.

The authoritative source, Black's Law Dictionary, defines a contract in many ways—which stands to reason, as there are multiple meanings associated with the word "contract." One Black's Law dictionary definition that is pretty straightforward describes a contract as "loosely, an enforceable agreement between two or more parties to do or not to do a thing or set of things; a compact."

A contract can be as simple as an IOU, or as complicated as a purchase agreement for real estate; but the exchange of promises to do—or not to do—something are the foundation, along with the intention that these promises are legally enforceable.

Learn a few basics about contracts to avoid unfortunate outcomes. If you have the financial resources, you might choose to seek guidance from an attorney who is experienced in creating the kind of agreement you require. You might seek out legal resources from your county bar association. Many counties have lawyer referral services, and some offer low-fee or reduced-fee services. Even if you choose to make your agreement without attorney input as you begin the process, you may want to consult with an attorney to review your draft document before signing the agreement you made.

Generally, a contract has to contain certain information to be enforceable by a court. Every contract (whether written or oral) must meet some basic requirements. If you are thinking about making a first draft and before going to see an attorney, here are a few basic requirements for contracts:

1. **Consideration.** The exchange of valuable promises. Each party has to promise to do—or *not* to do—some act. In making this promise, each party is providing something of value to the other party to the contract. Without this exchange of promises, there is no contract.
2. **Offer and acceptance.** There must be a clear or definite offer to make a contract. For example, here's an offer: "Want to buy this?" And here is an unqualified acceptance: "Yes!" Of course, the language in a written agreement might state the offer and the acceptance a bit more formally, which is why you might go see your friendly neighborhood attorney for help drafting your agreement.
3. **Legal purpose.** The purpose of the agreement must not violate the law. For example, you will not be able to enforce a loan agreement that charges interest in excess of the legal interest rate; nor can a contract for services have an unlawful objective—for example, a contract that contemplates criminal behavior.
4. **Capable parties.** Every party to a contract must have capacity to agree to the terms of the contract. To be "capable" of making a contract, each of the parties must understand their agreement. For example, there is a presumption that minors and insane people usually do not know what they are doing. For that reason, the contracts they enter into generally will not be enforced.
5. **Mutual assent.** This is also sometimes referred to as a "meeting of the minds." Each of the contracting parties must intend to be bound by their agreements, and must agree on the key terms.

TIPS FOR MAKING YOUR RELATIONSHIP CONTRACT

1. Write down your promises. Put the terms into a written document. You may wish to title the agreement—for example, if you are not married, you might be drafting a cohabitation agreement to address how you will handle financial matters and property ownership when you live together. If you are contemplating marriage, you may want to create a prenuptial agreement. If you are married, you may want to put together a postnuptial agreement to arrange how you and your spouse want to hold title to real property you plan to acquire, and address how that property would be divided between the two of you if your marriage ever were to end.
2. Identify each of the parties to the agreement by their full legal name.
3. Include the agreements made. Get specific. For example, if Sweetie is going to maintain the rental unit, identify the tasks associated with maintenance and the frequency with which they will be performed; how records of financial transactions will be kept (and where they will be located); and the timelines for sharing the financial information (for example, financial information will be shared on the first day of the month at the parties' monthly meeting).
4. Make sure you both agree on the wording of the agreements. For example, you might want to discuss a payment arrangement associated with the task of maintaining the rental unit. Include the amount of the payment; the source of the payment (rents, for example); who is receiving the payment; the date and place the payment will be made. For example, "On the last day of every

month that the unit is rented, Sweetie shall receive the first $200.00 from rental fees for the maintenance services he provided during the month. The remainder of the rental fees will be deposited in the parties' joint account at XYZ bank in (identify location of the bank)."

5. Provide a period of time for each of the parties to review the wording of the agreements.
6. Provide each party with the opportunity to seek advice from an attorney; or, if there is a self-help center at your local courthouse, ask if the staff there is willing to review the agreement *before* you sign.
7. Sign, date, and notarize each signature.
8. Make copies for everyone who signs the agreement. Each person receives a signed, dated, and notarized original of your agreement. Keep your original in a safe place so you are saved from the difficult challenge of proving the signatures on the agreement are valid.

No matter who creates the contract terms, *read every word of a contract before you sign.* If you have questions about a contract, *ask before you sign.* Hire an attorney to review and to suggest revisions and additions to the agreement before you sign.

Here is an example of what can happen (and actually did) when someone did not read a contract before signing!

The young woman was in a panic. She had just received a huge bill from a popular high-end lakeside estate for her large and spectacular wedding. Her groom had changed his mind at the last minute, leaving his fiancée with little more than broken dreams and a boatload of bills related to her booking the wedding venue.

The woman urgently needed to know whether she was stuck paying the venue thousands of dollars in rental fees despite the groom's last-minute no-show at the wedding. Months earlier, she alone had signed the contract, and put a sizeable deposit down to secure the wedding venue. Now, the venue wanted payment. Their position was that the young woman had signed the contract, and was obligated to pay.

She asked me who was responsible for payment. Didn't the "no-show" fiancé have to pay? After all, *he* stood her up!

Unfortunately, despite her righteous indignation, she was still liable. *Only the young woman and the service provider had signed the contract.* The young woman had not carefully read the terms of the agreement, but she had signed anyway. After the wedding that never was, the young woman learned that the contract had a cancellation clause. The cancellation clause clearly passed on all of the costs to the responsible party—*significant* costs! She had signed that contract; and because she had signed, she was the responsible party. Worse, she was stunned to find out that the correct answer about who had to pay was . . . "I do!" For sure, this kind of "I do" was not the response the young woman wanted to hear.

Before you sign any legal document, you might best seek expert legal advice. Hire a good attorney, if only for a single advice and consultation session. Go over the contract together *before anyone signs.* It could be the best money you spend.

If you are not clear on the meaning of a word that appears in a contract, ask an attorney before you sign.

The same goes for asking an attorney about "what-if" scenarios. Take a lesson from the wedding story. Think about potential risks *before* you sign a contract. Negotiate insurance and other protections into your contract so you have safeguards in the event the unthinkable materializes.

Form an understanding so each of you knows who does what,

and when each person is supposed to do what is promised. Make sure you know the consequences, if any, should one person or the other not live up to their promises.

Attorneys are supposed to be good at forecasting the positives and the pitfalls. Many of us in the legal profession have come to see the "dark clouds" that come before the storm, rather than the rainbows that can arrive afterwards. We are good at carrying an umbrella. See one of us so you do not have to carry a backpack filled with foul weather gear—or walk through a gully washer of a storm because you could not tell which way the wind was blowing!

SIGNING ON THE DOTTED LINE CAN HAVE MAJOR CONSEQUENCES

CAUTION: Once you sign an agreement, you are bound by its terms unless you can prove things like these:

COERCION: Someone held a gun to your head or threatened you, so you signed.

DURESS: Someone put you in a spot "between a rock and a hard place" and pressured you so you felt you had no choice but to take the deal.

FRAUD: You signed because someone intentionally misled you to get you to sign.

MISREPRESENTATION: You signed because someone made a statement before checking to see whether it was true or not, intending that you would rely on the statement and sign off on the agreement.

MUTUAL MISTAKE: Both parties to the agreement were mistaken about the meaning of a central concept (otherwise known as "material fact").

ILLEGAL PURPOSE: The agreement is for an unlawful purpose.

LACK OF CAPACITY: A person who experiences a disability that significantly affects global decision-making ability may be unable to sign a legally binding agreement.

Be careful! Do not be quick to sign a contract. Read first, sign later—not the other way around. *Read every sentence* of any document you are thinking about signing. Think of all the "what-ifs" that might happen and make a list of those possibilities. Then, go talk about these possibilities with an attorney. Do not go it alone.

CONSIDERING COHABITATION? – TAKE A LESSON FROM VINTAGE HOLLYWOOD DRAMA

After six years of unmarried bliss, the epic breakup of actor and movie star Lee Marvin and his live-in girlfriend, Michelle Triola Marvin, made the news—as well as the tabloids—with their sensational breakup story. Their subsequent courtroom battle made "palimony" a household word.

Lee Marvin earned millions as a Hollywood star during the 1950s and beyond. In 1964, while working as a cast member on the film *Ship of Fools*, Lee met Michelle Triola, a singer and actress who had a bit part in the film. Sparks flew, and Lee left his wife to move in with Michelle, initially living at Michelle's apartment. Later, the lovers moved to a home Lee purchased in Malibu—an upscale beachfront community, where many high-earners of the silver screen live in in luxury and relative seclusion.

In 1970, Lee left Michelle.

Michelle sued Lee, and hired attorney-to-the-stars Marvin Mitchelson. In the court battle, Michelle asked for one half of the value of the property Lee had acquired during the time the couple lived together; and, in addition, sought a palimony award—in other words, support payments—for the rest of her life.

Michelle's claim for palimony was based on her allegation that Lee breached the promises that the couple made to each other. Michelle claimed that she gave up her career at Lee's request in order to stay home and take care of him. In exchange, Michelle alleged that Lee promised to pay her life-long support.[1] Lee claimed he never promised to support Michelle for her entire life!

In the wake of what Michelle believed were broken promises, property rights became the flashpoint. The dispute for the court to decide was all about rights to property—whether the left-behind partner in a relationship *that was not a marriage* had legal rights to receive support payments, and half the value of all property acquired during the time the couple lived together, just as would a married couple. Would the court treat property rights of unmarried partners the same way as rights of married couples?

The Marvin case was the first ever to address whether there are legal rights to income and assets when unmarried couples split. Palimony rights are all about promises made, and promises broken. The court's analysis in a palimony lawsuit is different from how division of property happens if a marriage ends in divorce.

Unless the *married couple* has a prenup, their rights to property and to spousal support are defined by the provisions of the family code. The family code's provisions for property division do not apply to *unmarried couples*; but the judges handling the Marvin case realized that there were many unmarried couples who lived together, and court guidance was needed to define unmarried couples' legal rights when this kind of relationship ended.

California's highest court addressed the issue, characterizing it as a contract dispute. To win a palimony case, one must prove that there were promises made, either in verbal agreement or in a written contract; that the disputed terms of the agreement were actually a part of the agreement or written contract; and that the terms were never performed. "Promises made, promises broken" gave the person wronged by the broken promise the legal right to ask the court for help. Although the *Marvin v. Marvin* case made history, it was because the California Supreme Court established the right to sue for palimony—but not because Michelle Triola Marvin proved her case.

Does a palimony case give the parties the right to equally divide property acquired during their relationship? The answer in the Marvin case was a resounding "no." The court determined that Michelle Triola Marvin did not prove that the couple entered into a contractual agreement. Ultimately, the court denied Michelle's request to receive palimony, and she did not receive any significant payment at all.

The hard lesson in the Marvin case is that there was insufficient evidence of the existence of a contract. Without proof, the case went away—and with it went Michelle's hope of receiving lifetime support and a lucrative property settlement. This discussion raises an ugly issue: Make certain your state courts will consider palimony matters. In more than a few states, there is no legal basis for bringing a palimony suit.

The easy lesson that one can take away from this Hollywood story is to put agreements into written form so there is evidence your agreements exist. If you are an unmarried woman living in a committed relationship, you are free to develop contractual agreements with your life partner to address many aspects of your living situation. Just because you and your partner choose not to marry doesn't mean you are without the protections offered by a well-written contract. As with many life situations, an ounce of prevention is worth a pound of cure. Put a cohabitation agreement in place and gain the security of knowing a court will enforce your agreements.

COHABITATION AGREEMENTS

A cohabitation agreement is a contract that allows you and your partner to protect your personal assets, and to address details about how to handle debt; who carries life and health insurance; your respective wishes and agreements relating to healthcare decision-making; whether, and for how long, one of you will pay the other funds for support if you are no longer living together; the way title to real property is held; issues around personal property that you might acquire while living together; and many other provisions that could guide you during the time you live together and after, should your relationship end.

The understandings in a cohabitation agreement can be enforced in court—*if you have a written agreement in place.* Oral agreements present difficulties with proof, though if an oral agreement is part of your situation, a court will consider your facts and circumstances to determine whether an oral agreement was made and the terms of the agreement.

The terms in a written cohabitation agreement can protect your legal rights to property, allocate expenses between you and your partner, and establish guidelines about property division, as well as other logistics in the event of a future breakup. When you choose to define your responsibilities to each other in great detail, you create and shape the expectations of how you share your lives through the terms of your agreements. You have the opportunity to define your legal rights, and you can feel secure in knowing you have given structure to understandings that can be enforced in court.

A CAUTION ABOUT HOME IMPROVEMENTS IF YOU ALONE OWN YOUR HOME

Do you live with your significant other in a home that you alone own? If you are a single woman and you are the only person on the title deed to your home, be aware that your partner's help as a "Mr. or Ms. Fix-It" may add value to your home! Your partner's labor of love may actually cost you money if your partner's time, skill, and effort contribute to an increase in property value. Reimburse your partner for the value of the contribution made so you are protected from owing the amount of added value your partner has contributed to home improvements later, if your relationship becomes rocky. Consider whether your partner's efforts were offered as a gift to you. If so, document that gift!

Maintain records of payments you make for time and labor provided by your partner. Have your partner sign for payments received. If your partner made a gift of the labor, make that a part of your records.

Address how you handle home improvements in your cohabitation agreement!

THINKING ABOUT MARRIAGE?

If you are thinking of marriage, prenuptial and postnuptial agreement may offer you helpful protections.

IS A PRENUP FOR YOU?

Prenuptial agreements—known more commonly in the real world as "prenups"—are a type of contract often called a "premarital agreement" in the legal world. They can go by other names, too: for example, "ante-nuptial contracts." For convenience, we will identify this type of contract as a "prenup."

A prenup can protect your assets, particularly if you have accumulated significant wealth and would like to preserve your separate property. Regardless of what they are called, these contracts deal primarily with financial matters and contain agreements that may affect your property rights, both during marriage and, potentially, in instances where couples divorce. A prenup only becomes effective if the couple ties the knot.

California law allows a couple contemplating marriage the right to define their agreements about property, assets, and debts in a prenup. A prenup is made before marriage, and takes effect after a couple marries. This kind of contract allows a couple to opt out of the legal protections offered in the family code; instead controlling income, earnings, real estate, and personal property according to the terms of the prenup. California law imposes certain requirements on people who seek the protections of a prenup. In addition, you and your beloved can include a variety of other protections. The following list provides some available requirements.

PRENUPS . . .

- **MUST** be in writing.
- **MUST** be signed in the presence of a notary by both spouses.
- **MUST** be provided to each party for review at least seven days before marriage. Each party has a right to have their own attorney review and explain the agreement and interpret the possible consequences.
- **MUST** be fair to each party, including full and fair disclosure of both parties' assets and debts.
- **MAY** include agreements about real estate and personal property; the right to manage, control, buy, or sell property; and various other rights for either one or both of the parties.
- **MAY** include agreements about what happens to property if spouses decide to divorce or separate, if one spouse dies, or after a particular event occurs.
- **MAY** provide for the creation of other legal documents, such as a will or trust, to advance the objective of the prenup.
- **MAY** provide for the purchase of insurance, and may address ownership rights to the policy and the disposition of an associated death benefit.
- **MAY** include any other agreement regarding personal rights or obligations, other than an agreement to do illegal acts or an agreement that violates public policy.
- **MAY** address understandings regarding child support so long as the right to child support is not adversely affected by the terms of the agreement.
- **MAY** include provisions for spousal support, but the enforcement of certain agreements for spousal support may require further steps at the time the agreement is enforced.

MUST-HAVES AND OPTIONAL CHOICES FOR YOUR PRENUP

If you do not reside in California, check with a local attorney about requirements in your home state. The point of the prenup is this: in a prenup, you and your spouse can make agreements about money and asset management in ways a judge can't. Judges must follow the law as set out in the family code. If you choose to make a prenup, you do not have to follow the same rules as a judge. Instead, by formalizing your agreements in the prenup, you and your spouse-to-be control how you will manage your earnings, assets, and debts during marriage, and how you will divide property in the event your marriage ends in divorce. Be aware that the objective of the prenup is protection. The question is, do the agreements proposed protect your assets, or are they more protective of your soon-to-be-spouse? Only you are in a position to evaluate the "what-ifs." Seek out the advice of a good attorney as you negotiate the terms of your prenup.

The terms of the prenup must be fair; but keep in mind, "fair" is a relative term. If there is a dispute later about what is "fair" or "unfair," you can ask a family law judge to decide. If one or both of you choose not to retain the services of an attorney before the prenup is signed, the person without an attorney must be fully informed in writing, in a language in which they are proficient, of the terms and basic effects of the agreement; and they must acknowledge receipt of this information *in writing*. It is best if each of you—separately from the other person—retain the services of an attorney to review the prenup before signing, so you are informed how each and every one of the agreements that you make can affect your bottom line.

Prenups are not a one-size-fits-all kind of agreement. For example, you may create a prenup with agreements that keep each spouse's property separate after marriage, and provide direction to the court on how to divide property if the marriage ends. Alternatively, your prenup can identify the assets and debts that belong exclusively to each of you before marriage as separate property, and then define each person's rights and responsibilities in managing the assets and debts you acquire during marriage.

Apart from property you have identified as separate, you may agree on how you will treat later-acquired property and debt. For example, a prenup might specify that both of you share rights to certain personal property or real estate acquired during marriage, and that other acquisitions—such as the rights to work-related stock options, bonuses, and raises earned during your marriage—belong exclusively to the person who earned these assets. This example shows a prenup that provides for the division of property acquired during marriage *differently* from the provisions in the family code.

One benefit of a carefully-crafted prenup is that you and your soon-to-be-spouse can agree in advance about how property will be managed during marriage, and divided should the marriage end. Your prenup may address spousal support. Be aware that judges look very closely at spousal support provisions in a prenup to make certain the terms do not leave one spouse walking away with treasure, while the other spouse is heading out the door with nothing at all.

If the marriage ends in divorce, and one of the spouses believes that the terms of spousal support negotiated in the prenup are unfair, they can ask the judge to establish a fair spousal support award considering their current circumstances. They must ask for a hearing to obtain a spousal support order. At the hearing, the judge will consider evidence and weigh facts and circumstances, along with hearing any legal arguments presented, to determine the fair amount of spousal support. Remember to mention every issue that you would like the judge to hear.

Prenuptial agreements can provide valuable protections for one or both of you if you want to retain separate control and ownership over various assets. For example, you can decide in advance how real estate, stock options, legal settlements, retirement funds, and gifts made to you and your soon-to-be-spouse will be managed—both during marriage, and if your marriage ends. A prenuptial agreement can also address management and division of debt—both during marriage, and in the event of divorce. Your prenup can identify your plan for items of value that could, without the protections of a prenup, become subject to the division of assets mandated by the family code if divorce occurs.

Unless spouses agree that the understandings in a prenup will remain in force for only a certain number of years, your prenup exists indefinitely. The point of having a prenup is to provide the court with a different guideline than the fifty-fifty division of assets and debts acquired during marriage that the family code mandates. If the prenup is valid, the judge will divide the assets and debts according to your agreements, not the provisions of the family code.

POSTNUPTIAL AGREEMENTS

Postnuptial agreements are contracts between spouses made during marriage. As with any agreement dealing with financial matters, there may be tax consequences. Be sure to review the terms of your postnuptial agreement with a tax advisor before you formalize any of the understandings. That said, you and your spouse may wish to further develop or modify the understandings in your prenup. You might also wish to create additional understandings about money and property, as time brings many life changes that can affect how you choose to protect yourself during marriage.

There are any number of reasons you might make postnuptial agreements. Generally, couples with substantial assets create postnuptial agreements during their marriage to protect and manage assets of one spouse as separate property, especially when the value of that spouse's assets escalates significantly over the course of the marriage. It is possible one spouse has developed a business that generates a great deal of income and wishes to treat the business and related holdings as their separate property. Or perhaps one spouse receives a significant inheritance, invests successfully in various holdings, and wants to preserve all the income that flows from that inheritance as separate property. Remember, too, that postnuptial agreements can be made in contemplation of divorce, expressly directing how property and debts will be divided should the marriage end.

In California, couples cannot address child support in postnuptial agreements and are not permitted to arrange child custody in ways that would work a hardship on the minor children.

For example, a postnuptial agreement that establishes child support at a very low dollar amount might be acceptable if both parents are high-income earners, and are each willing and able to fully meet all child-related expenses without contribution from the other spouse after the marriage ends; however, what happens if only one parent makes a substantial income?

The parent with the more modest income and assets may seek a support contribution from the parent with greater income and assets, so the parent who does not generate significant earnings can provide the children of the marriage with a standard of living similar to the one the children enjoyed before their parents' relationship ended.

California courts do not favor agreements that give up child support or limit the amount of a child support payment. Similarly, California courts do not favorably view postnuptial agreements that limit the amount and duration of spousal support in a marriage that has continued for at least ten years. Keep in mind that a postnuptial agreement must be fair. If you reside in a state other than California, you would be wise to consult with an attorney before signing a postnuptial agreement—especially one that involves child support or child custody agreements.

Agreements about child custody generally must allow each parent frequent and continuing contact with their children, taking into account the children's needs and each parent's circumstances. Crafting a fair parent-share agreement is not a trivial undertaking. Children's needs change over time, and sometimes envisioning the future is difficult.

In California, a postnuptial agreement requires judicial validation before taking effect. That means you need to submit your postnuptial agreement to the court for the judge to review, approve, and sign before it is legally enforceable. If you live outside of California, check with a local attorney to learn of any requirements particular to your state.

Here are some basics that California courts look for in postnuptial agreements:

- Agreements must be set out in a written document, signed by each of the spouses and by a judge.
- Signed agreements are filed with the family court.
- Spouses' signatures in a postnuptial agreement must be notarized.
- Each spouse must understand the contents of the agreement.

- Each spouse must enter into the agreement voluntarily, of their own free will.
- The agreement must be fair to both spouses.
- Limiting child support or child custody is disfavored and may invalidate the agreement.
- Spousal support arrangements must be fair; a judge will consider the parties' circumstances when evaluating the amount of spousal support and the duration of support payments.
- The terms of the agreement must be based on true and complete information(no hiding assets, no concealing information about the existence of debt to "get" the other spouse to sign).
- The usual contract defenses will apply; meaning, the court will set aside the contract if the other party proves there was fraud, coercion, duress, or terms that are unfair.

The bottom line is that you *can* make contractual agreements, either before you marry or during your marriage, to address money and property matters the way you wish. In the event your marriage fails or your personal circumstances change, you have the ability to put protections in place far in advance of an adverse event.

FIDUCIARY DUTIES

Along with promises you made to love and honor your spouse, marriage imposes a fiduciary duty on spouses. This duty obligates each spouse to exercise the highest level of care and transparency when dealing with each other during marriage. You must be fair to one another. You must not hide assets in secret accounts, and you must not scheme to conceal assets or debts. The fiduciary duty also applies to partners in business relationships, implying that marriage is a special kind of business relationship that requires special consideration between spouses. In California, Sections 1101 and 721 of the Family Code impose the gold standard of behavior on you and your spouse, guiding you both in all financial dealings in the marriage.

As fiduciaries, you and your spouse owe one another a duty to *fully disclose* all of the assets and debts acquired during marriage; to manage the financial aspects of your marriage responsibly; to care for your assets; and to address your obligations to creditors.

The fiduciary duty even extends to a spouse's management of an asset that belongs only to the other spouse. For example, if you inherited a property, and your spouse becomes the property manager, your spouse has a duty to provide you with all financial information associated with the task of managing your inherited asset. You have a right to know all about the rental income; the costs of maintaining the property; payments of insurance, mortgage, taxes, and interest; and all of the accounts in which the property management money is housed. Your spouse is duty-bound to be transparent when keeping the books, and to share all of the financials with you. You have a right to inspect the accounts and not just take your spouse's word that all is in order. The fiduciary duty continues through the marriage and through divorce proceedings until the final division of all marital assets and debts has been accomplished.

Short story: When it comes to managing the assets and debts of your marriage, spouses must deal openly and honestly with each other throughout the entire marriage. *No* secrets. *No* hidden accounts. *No* sham loans to family or friends that are made for the purpose of shielding your money if the marriage comes apart.

Here is a real-life example of what can happen if you do not fully and fairly disclose assets acquired during marriage. In this California case, the spouses did not sign a prenup or make any postnuptial agreements. The wife and a few of her officemates had big dreams. They thought they'd form a little office pool and contribute money to buy California lottery tickets. The wife was in a troubled marriage, but she tolerated her present life circumstances and remained in the same household as her husband. Her married life was often challenging.

The women at work thought maybe they would be able to win something from the California lottery, but they never imagined how things would turn out: The office pool hit it big, sharing what was an almost $7 million dollar jackpot. The wife's share of the winnings totaled over a million dollars! The wife did not tell her husband about the win, but now that she hit the big-time, she thought she'd bail out of the marriage, take her lottery winnings, and move on. The wife filed for divorce very soon after learning of her good fortune.

Divorcing spouses have a duty to fully and fairly disclose all of their assets and debts—whether separate property, or the property of both spouses. The wife concealed the lottery winnings from her husband during the entire divorce. She never disclosed the lottery winnings in her divorce paperwork or in any courtroom discussions with her soon-to-be-ex-husband. She never shared any information about the winnings payments that the State Lottery sent to her (at her mother's home address), which began the year she filed for divorce. She moved out of the family home and went on her merry way, leaving her ex-husband completely unaware of the lottery winnings.

Meanwhile, her ex-husband remained at the home that was once the marital residence. He was in financially desperate straits and had filed for bankruptcy. True to form, even in the time after divorce, his ex-wife said nothing about the winnings she was receiving each year from the California Lottery in installment payouts. The ex-wife would have gotten away with her deception, except for one little unexpected thing: About a year after the divorce was final, a letter arrived at the former marital residence—now, the ex-husband's home. That letter asked whether the ex-wife wanted to accept a one-time lump sum payment of her lottery winnings.

The ex-husband quickly got in touch with the State Lottery Commission and confirmed his ex-wife indeed had lottery winnings. He next retained an attorney and filed suit against his former wife. The court had to decide what happens when one spouse hides assets from the other spouse before the marriage ends.

Remember, the wife and her attorney omitted any mention of the lottery winnings in the paperwork submitted to the court. Remember, too, that the wife participated in the office pool during her marriage, raising the issue of whether that winning lottery ticket was actually community property. Remember, the wife and her spouse had fiduciary duties to one another.

Ignoring a duty of the highest order did not sit well with the Court. Wife had an obligation to fully and fairly disclose *all* of her property at the time she filed for divorce. She failed to disclose the lottery winnings—a significant asset.

The aftermath of deception is never good—especially when the trial judge deciding the case had plenty of evidence that the ex-wife had concealed the lottery winnings from her husband, and that the ex-wife purchased the winning ticket during their marriage.

The court takes fiduciary duties between spouses quite seriously. The judge at the trial court level intended to undo the harm wife had caused by failing to fairly disclose her winnings. In the case of the concealed lottery prize, the court awarded every penny of the money to the ex-husband. The ex-wife appealed the trial court judge's decision. Do not be surprised when you learn that a panel of three appeals court judges upheld the decision of the trial court.[2]

Because you are reading this chapter, you are already aware that in California, the family code defines many of your rights as a married couple, including your duties to each other. If you reside outside of California, your state's protections may differ. Having read this far, you are also aware of legal protections offered by a prenup and by postnuptial agreements. Spouses always need to deal fairly with one another. You know that you can opt out of the legal protections offered in the California Family Code by making a prenup; and you can also enter into postnuptial agreements that may divide property differently than the mandated fifty-fifty division of assets and debts provided in the California Family Code.

The question is, *should you opt out of the family California Family Code's method of allocating assets and debts equally between spouses?* In some marriages, a fifty-fifty division of all of the assets and debts acquired during marriage may serve your needs better than a situation where you arrange a different division of assets and debts through a prenup or postnuptial agreement. Seek out an attorney who is skilled in creating the protections that you wish to implement during your marriage, and pay for an hour of their time. Be sure to ask the attorney to explain not just the language of the agreement you are thinking about making, but the potential consequences of signing a postnuptial agreement that may actually leave you with less than would a division under your state's laws. It is wise for each spouse to seek separate counsel so you can privately explore and discuss in confidence every aspect of these important considerations. These considerations may affect your taxes, your income, and the quality of life you want to lead.

As you can see, money matters. The old saying "knowledge is power" rings true if you understand what you have, and what you owe. Once you understand your cash flow and get a handle on your assets and debts, you are ready to have meaningful discussions with your spouse or partner.

MONEY TALK

An article was published in *Psychology Today* in January 1999 addressing the topic of "Men, Women, and Money," authored by Olivia Mellan and Karina Piscaldo.[3] Authors Mellan and Piskaldo called the woman who raised the topic of money "bold." The authors also presumed that partners were of different genders.

Boundaries have expanded in this century. It seems that in the not-so-distant past, a woman who sought financial information violated traditional societal boundaries simply by inquiring about financial affairs. The articles' authors noted that, "In these liberated times, couples discuss many things before marriage, but the meaning of money is not one of them. Money is still a taboo topic."

Lately, the conversation has evolved. Money related conversations are no longer "taboo." Relationships have changed, as have societal attitudes.

Women need to know the naked truth about how money is a gateway to freedom and independence. Financial management is a critical component of understanding how to operate in this world. Independence evolves incrementally.

PROTECT YOURSELF: CREATE YOUR LEGAL SAFETY NET

Now that you are informed about your relative net worth—your assets and your debts—you can work with professionals to protect what you have. By identifying your assets and your debts, you create a paperwork foundation that allows you to plan for saving, giving, expanding the boundaries of your roadmap to further advancement, and putting protections in place. The information you gather about your assets and debts may prompt you to seek out professional guidance. When you assess your finances and identify your dreams, you have a framework for creating a more promising future.

Take that concrete information about what you own, what you owe, and your monthly cash flow into a conversation with a financial advisor or a CPA. Decide what to plan for yourself and what you and your spouse would like to do as a couple. Make small-step adjustments to protect and conserve what you have. Learn about additional methods for income generation and budgeting. You must personally determine how to enrich your knowledge, build skills, and advance your education so you can live the life you want and take the path you choose—not the path someone else dictates you take.

If divorce is on your mind, schedule an hour-long consultation with an attorney to explore your options. Perhaps the way forward will be better informed than the path you traveled before. Knowing what you are dealing with in terms of what you have free and clear, and what you owe, will help you to define your current reality and may allow you the insight to develop and refine your goals, both for the immediate future and for the long term.

DO NOT BE AN OSTRICH

Some people unwittingly embrace a life path that embodies the expression, "ignorance is bliss." Not knowing is excusable. *Wanting not to know* is another story. Don't make the mistake of hiding your head in the sand like an ostrich. Here is what happened to one woman who chose to ignore her changing life circumstances.

Donna was a married woman who decided to live unaware. She married Will when she was nineteen years old, and had the first of their three children when she was twenty. Over time, Donna and Will purchased a home. Donna was devoted to Will and spent many hours "doing for" him so he had more time to rise up the ladder in his profession. At the time they married, Will was one step above junior-level associate in a mid-sized firm of accountants. Will was regularly invited to join more senior members of the firm to "wine and dine" clients and to attend business networking events. He remained with the firm, working hard and building a solid career for years.

Donna never really knew what compensation Will earned, and she didn't care. Will kept a separate bank account and transferred money into a shared joint account so Donna had money for everyday expenses. Donna was able to run the household with the money she accessed through the joint account. She never opened Will's mail, and he alone paid the bills—mostly on time. Will arranged to get Donna her own credit card. He managed his own credit separately. There was always enough money; but lately, there never seemed to be enough time for Donna to actually be with Will.

Donna knew Will was hard at work from morning to night. She was just as busy as he, caring for their growing family. She held a part-time job in retail to bring in money for the little luxuries she enjoyed, and for the occasional babysitter, so she and Will could have a night on the town. Donna was proud she could contribute earnings to the household economy, but her earnings were more modest than Will's.

As time passed, nights on the town became less frequent. Will spent a lot more time working late as he advanced in his position. Donna was pleased that Will's hard work was paying off. He told her that he was in line for a big promotion, but they still needed to live frugally.

Donna did live frugally—but Will now drove a luxury car and he dressed in upscale clothing. Donna joked that Will was more "suitable" for promotion now that he was dressing the part. Despite Will's expensive clothes and nice car, Donna was content to drive a "Mommobile" basic set of wheels, shop at discount stores for the kids and for her own clothes, and budget for groceries instead of impulse-buying some of the more expensive items that she really wanted. Besides, Donna was happy to follow Will's direction. He was earning enough to keep the family fed and the bills paid. She was his supportive spouse, and she did not question his decisions.

There was money now for the kids' after-school sports, enrichment, and tutoring. Donna didn't know—and didn't want to be bothered with—the complexities of financial planning, home payments, or bills. She did not even want to know anything about how to manage the future. Donna chose to have Will take total control over her financial destiny.

Life was good—until everything suddenly changed.

Will went off to work one morning and did not come home as usual. Donna heard from Will in a text message late that night. He was in a nearby town with car trouble. Donna knew that it was not a car problem. Will could have gotten a ride home. If he was out networking, a colleague could have done the driving; or, Will could have called to have Donna come and get him.

Of course, Donna discovered she was right. Will's "car trouble" had a different name: in this case, it was "Katherine."

Donna soon discovered that Will wasn't the only one in a hot mess. Over the years, she always signed off on paperwork when Will asked her to. Some of that paperwork included tax returns, which seemed to be just a jumble of numbers and a huge pile of papers that meant next to nothing to Donna. Guess what Donna discovered next? The family home was in Will's name alone! Donna had signed a Quitclaim Deed when Will asked her to "just sign a few legal things." The mortgage had been refinanced twice in the past ten years. (Donna was not a party to the mortgage because she had signed a quitclaim deed, but as a result of the refinance, there was more debt and far less equity in the home than Donna knew.) There was no money trail showing where the refinance money went.

The next month, the household bank account was underfunded because Will "forgot" to put in a part of his earnings. Tax returns revealed a different picture: Will had been making a healthy six-figure salary for years, but Donna had never learned to untangle the numbers on the taxes. She only learned these facts after Will served her with divorce paperwork.

"Unbelievable!" you say. Poor Donna sacrificed her needs and spent years scrimping and saving so Will could advance. Indeed, Will did very well; but he did not bring Donna along with him. Donna remained unaware of the real state of the household finances and, more importantly, unaware of what was going on in Will's work world. She was in for a bumpy ride once the realities came to light. As a mother and a wife, Donna never shirked her responsibility to her husband and her children; yet, when she disregarded the opportunities along the way to become financially literate, she neglected her responsibility *to herself.*

If Donna had actually read through the tax returns and taken a look at the bills that Will handled, she would have easily seen that Will was making tens of thousands of dollars more than she knew, that he had already received more than one promotion, and that he was not regularly contributing to his retirement. (All of this information is readily available if you know where to look for it.) If Donna had looked at the joint bank account, she could have seen where the money coming into that account had transferred from, and could perhaps have been in a position to find out more about expenses—or at least the source of the money feeding that joint account. More importantly, looking at financial information and finding differences in the cash flow and earnings would lead to other questions about where all the money was going. It was clear that Will had been preparing for his divorce for many years in advance of walking out on Donna.

Be aware of how money comes into your household and where it goes when it is spent. Take stock frequently of when the routine expenses are, and how the money you have is allocated. If you are sharing your life and your earnings with a significant other or a spouse, become aware of the routine patterns of income and expenses. Examine your budget and get appropriate assistance to build wealth. All kinds of experts are ready, willing, and able to offer assistance. Sometimes a little planning can make big changes in your life over a relatively short time frame.

There are many branches on the decision tree, but one thing is clear: If you *choose* not to take control of your financial affairs, and you put your head in the sand by ignoring your legal rights, you risk losing control to someone else. Better to follow the ideals of service to others, hard work, self-education, and disciplined saving than to be blind like the ostrich with its head in the sand. Ignoring the stuff you have delegated to another person is *not* productive. Choose to know. Choose to act.

SAVE, SERVE, STRIVE, AND STUDY

In 1898, my grandfather and his twin brother were born in a town just outside of Boston, Massachusetts. The twins were the youngest of six siblings, and the only children in the family born in the United States. Life was not easy, but living in a home on the outskirts of Boston held far less danger than the life the family left behind in eastern Europe. Here, with a cart filled with produce and a horse to pull the goods through the streets, my great-grandparents and their children built their future. In this family of greengrocers, the twins shaped their next steps to a better life.

The family valued financial security, service to others, striving (through hard work), and education through hours of study. Grandpa passed down that hard-learned wisdom, often speaking of "The Four S's" which became his guideposts. "Save, Serve, Strive, and Study" became my aspirations, too. "The Four S's" offer a kind of shorthand for building a good life. Let these principles guide you in creating change.

HOW TO RECALIBRATE YOUR MARITAL LIFE IN NINETY DAYS: FOCUS ON THE FINANCES WHEN MONEY IS THE ISSUE

Make a plan; change your life. Like anyone learning to master a new set of skills, small steps can help you make big changes. Base your plan on the information you gathered about your assets and debts, and the cash flow information you gather from tracking your income and expenses. You can find information online about making a household budget, both in videos and in blogs; you can consult with experts, attend programs presented by nonprofits specializing in "financial literacy," read news articles published by financial fitness coaches, and find more about the topic right here in this book!

Why would an attorney urge you to consider the importance of changing your spending and saving habits? Financial fitness is often the elephant in the room. Relationships implode over money issues. Knowing how to protect yourself involves more than identifying assets and debts; you must create a plan that serves you and those you love. Learn how to allocate funds so budgeting becomes part of your safety net. Learn how to have the hard conversation about money—first with yourself, and then with your spouse.

The internal conversations that you have around money drive your perceptions. You can uncover powerful triggers by looking back at the lifetime habits you have developed around saving and spending. Like any other relationship, the one each of us has with money has psychological overlays. Do you feel torn when making financial decisions? Are you frequently hesitant to make any decisions at all? Identifying reasons that have driven you to put off taking control of your financial decision-making may be a helpful way to move towards greater independence and confidence around legal matters. Your insights will help you to explore beyond your current perceptions and identify boundaries that may limit you. Your insights will also serve you well when you talk about money with your spouse or significant other.

HOW TO PUT YOUR INCOME AND EXPENSE INFORMATION TO WORK

- Identify total monthly income from all sources
- Identify how much you currently spend on food, clothing, and shelter (including mortgage payment, taxes, and insurance)
- Include costs for transportation, particularly gasoline and ride-share services
- Identify the cost of spending for "extras" like dining out, entertainment, travel, and gifts
- Reality check: Do the numbers make sense? If you are missing information, find it
- Prioritize:
    - Pay down existing debt
    - Increase savings
    - Create an emergency fund

NEGOTIATE YOUR BUDGET WITH YOUR SPOUSE/SIGNIFICANT OTHER

Knowledge is power. When you make choices about whether to spend or save, to splurge or scrimp, that little voice in your head saying "That's not possible!" blocks you from understanding your feelings about money. Know why you feel the way you do about your expenses and your savings. Expenditures consume your hard-earned income! Savings can build your net worth. Your spouse's money story may reveal equally critical insights.

If you are married, be alert to warning signs that can affect your budget. Always being late with mortgage payments and with credit card payments will impact your credit score. You may need to take a long, hard look at restructuring the household budget. If you are living in a committed relationship, be aware of how you as a couple share resources and handle obligations to pay debt. Married or not, it is important to become aware of money-related behaviors that can impact your life and derail your goals.

As you know, money conversations can quickly become emotionally charged. Avoid conflict, but do not avoid discussing your budget. What would happen if you and your spouse or significant other talked respectfully to each other with the objective of resolving only one single money problem?

If you have discovered several issues when reviewing your income and expenses, you may have a long "to-do" list; but tackle only a single aspect of the financial picture when you address your budget. Limit your meeting time to fifteen minutes, and focus on only one topic that is at this time the most important topic on your list—for example, "How can we make sure the mortgage is paid on time?," not "We have to manage our budget better."

Choose a different topic for your next meeting. Find a time to meet regularly, at a place that allows your conversation to unfold naturally and without interruptions. Arrange to meet when children and other family members are not present. A coffee shop or a local park might offer a calm space.

Organize your thoughts, and put your talking points on paper before you meet. You can bring documents like credit card statements and bank account transaction records to your meeting. Remember, this meeting is about only a single topic and is supposed to be short and sweet. Keep it that way. Don't get lost in details. Focus on solving the problem.

At the beginning of your meeting, identify the topic. Focus on offering a solution to the problem. Do not focus on what happened in the past. No getting lost in the weeds. Simply identify the topic, and move forward with the single issue you are meeting about.

Allow time for each of you to discuss and move forward with the *one issue* you are meeting about. Remember, this meeting is only fifteen minutes long!

Devote the last five minutes of your discussion to creating a forward-looking plan. This is often easier said than done. If the discussion triggers an argument, agree to stop the conversation for now, gather additional information, and set a time to revisit the topic. Keep all exchanges focused on resolving the topic. Give this discussion time to unfold. You can schedule another meeting if you need more time to address the issue. Keep moving the conversation forward.

Ideally, you and your beloved spouse or life partner have a level of trust and commitment that forms a strong foundation; but sometimes, you can see that something irregular is happening. If you sense a change in long-established spending patterns, consider whether the change signals that something is amiss.

RED FLAG WARNINGS IN MONEY CONVERSATIONS

- Reluctance to talk about money
- Telling you that money earned from employment is not yours
- Telling you that retirement accounts earned during marriage aren't yours
- Telling you that purchases made during marriage don't belong to you—even though in California, with only limited exception, assets earned during marriage are community property
- Refinancing a home without telling you in advance
- Taking out a loan on the basis of home equity in property you own together without telling you beforehand
- Binge spending; for example, a new car shows up in your driveway before you knew anything about this big-ticket purchase
- Hiding information and paperwork
- Not letting you review jointly filed tax returns and waiting to have you sign at the last minute

Find out what is going on sooner rather than later so you can discuss your observations and learn more before matters get out of hand.

WHEN COUPLES AMICABLY DIVORCE

Here is a story about a couple that may help you to reimagine your own. Stories about other people offer a way for you to recognize your own behaviors and allow you to deconstruct the meanings that flow from others' life experiences.

Anne is married, and works in a highly compensated corporate position . . . with some downsides: endless demands and pressures from her work, and a lack of support for her high-pressure job from Harold, her spouse.

Harold was a sole proprietor and owned his business. In Harold's work, life was either a full-out feast or a cycle of famine. Harold paid little attention to setting aside some of his earnings in advance of a rainy day. Anne did not like what she perceived was Harold's failure to plan; his cash flow was never under control. He never seemed to know what he had or what he owed. Though he made good money, much of the time, Harold did not keep track of his expenses.

Meanwhile, Anne received a hefty paycheck for her efforts, but there were trade-offs—among them, her decision to devote long hours to her job so she could reap the financial rewards. In time, Anne felt the uncertainty of Harold's finances constrained her. Granted, her life in the corporate world also had a degree of uncertainty because she had to measure up to the ever-increasing expectations of her role. She was a rising star. Anne believed that if she remained married to Harold, she would forever be subject to his financial turmoil. She came to believe she would be better off ending the marriage and going on in the corporate world.

Anne and Harold had many deep conversations about lifestyle and how they might operate if they separated. There were some difficult moments and a lot of soul-searching. Ultimately, through their discussions, they determined that the marriage was not working well.

Together, they made plans to divorce. They put together a parenting plan for their teenager. They developed a marital settlement that reflected their needs. There was emotional pain and tears along the way, but no regrets. Anne and Harold were extraordinary people. Each of them wanted the best for the other, and neither wanted to hurt their soon-to-be-ex. They worked through the difficult process of divorce with each of them feeling in control of the timing and the agreements they created.

A year after their divorce was granted, Anne had achieved exactly the life she had envisioned. The tensions and worries about how Harold handled his finances were no longer an issue. As parents, Anne and Harold worked collaboratively to provide enriching experiences for their child. Anne transitioned from married and feeling overwrought about Harold's choices, to single and embracing a new chapter in her life. Here are some common-sense lessons you might take to heart from Anne's journey, if you and your spouse are headed towards an amicable split.

PRE-DIVORCE DECISION-MAKING IN AMICABLE DIVORCE CASES

- Decide on living arrangements before papers are filed to start your legal case. Who stays in the family home, and who moves to a new place?
- Develop a schedule so each parent shares time with their minor children.
- Decide on how to cover the children's expenses.
    - Who, if anyone, pays child support?
    - Who pays for the children's healthcare expenses?
    - What after-school or childcare will your children need?

Discuss who will pay the childcare expenses, or if each parent prefers to spend time with their child(ren). Start discussions about how you handle finances from after separating to the time your divorce is granted. Discuss how to divide debt, property, vehicle use, bank accounts, brokerage accounts, and savings accounts.

These basic considerations can provide each spouse with a sense of certainty as each plans their next chapter in life. As you gain a sense of direction, you and your soon-to-be-ex may choose to hire attorneys or to work with a mediator to keep the process on track.

A WORD ABOUT DIVORCE

The process of ending a marriage is fairly straightforward. In California, you can learn the basics by accessing information provided online at the site maintained by the State of California Judicial Council (see: courts.ca.gov). This chapter is not about process; it is about protection. As you read at the start of this chapter, understanding legal protection is only one part of the equation. Sharing your own facts with an attorney may be a critical second component. Don't go it alone.

The divorce process holds some technical aspects and often a party to divorce can benefit from professional advice. The complexity of divorce is in dealing with the emotions and the issues that are particular to the spouses who wish to end their marriage. You can fill out forms, but you may not know how to present your case. The disputed issues in each case are often based on the spouses' personal situations. There is frequently no textbook answer to resolving these issues. The importance of having the right supports in place—be they legal, financial, actuarial, or psychological—are very important. Together, you and your attorney will build your team.

PRE-DIVORCE DECISION-MAKING— IF YOU ARE EXPERIENCING AN ADVERSARIAL SPLIT

What is needed to move forward in divorce if your situation is not amicable? Here are a few suggestions for you if you face conflict.

RETAIN THE SERVICES OF A GOOD ATTORNEY

Start your search for legal counsel early. You need an experienced attorney to guide you from the start when you and your spouse disagree about how to handle an impending divorce. If you have read this far into the chapter, you probably have gathered information on what you have and what you owe, as discussed in earlier sections of this chapter.

INTERVIEW SEVERAL ATTORNEYS TO FIND THE ONE *YOU* WANT

Plan to interview a number of family law attorneys who handle cases in the courthouse where your case will be heard. That's right—*you* interview *them* to see whether you are interested in doing business with the attorney and their firm.

Divorces can take time—often more than the "six months and one day" that the law defines as the minimum time that must pass to arrive at final judgment. You need to be comfortable with the personality of the attorney you choose to assist you through the process. Divorces can be stressful. Your attorney is a personal choice; find someone who is interested in sticking with you through the entire process, and who has the knowledge and skills needed to help you realize your objectives.

LOCAL REPRESENTATION MAY BE MORE AFFORDABLE, AND OFFERS OTHER ADVANTAGES

In real estate, agents and brokers often say the top three most important factors in choosing a property are "location, location, *location*!" This may also be relatively true in choosing an attorney. Each family law court has slightly different practices. An attorney familiar with the local rules of court may be quite comfortable with practices that are routine in that location. As you may already know, the devil is in the details!

For example, in certain California counties, a tentative ruling system is in place. Attorneys unaware of local practice can jeopardize a case if they are unaware of, or unfamiliar with, how to proceed when a tentative ruling system is the local practice. Choose an attorney who knows what the local judges require, is familiar with the courthouse and the staff who work there, and does not have a lengthy commute to the courthouse when appearing on your behalf in court proceedings. All the better to serve your needs and keep costs down.

CONDUCT A TARGETED SEARCH

Make a list of several attorneys who serve your geographic area. Review online information available on LinkedIn, Facebook, Yelp, Instagram, and Twitter. Get a sense of what people are saying about the attorney and the practice. Call each attorney on your list and take notes about your initial impression. Was the attorney available to take your call? Did staff or an associate answer your call? Was your call handled by an answering service? Did your call roll to voicemail, never to be answered?

Your first impression is simply one aspect of how services are provided by that attorney. Schedule a meeting. Ask questions. If you need to speak to the attorney urgently, will they be there for you after hours? You will be able to determine more when you arrange an initial meeting with the person who will handle your case. Ask the contact person at the firm—the attorney themself, or their staff—the cost of a one-hour initial meeting, and schedule a session.

Choose an attorney who you like and who wants to work with you. Both you and your spouse should retain capable, experienced counsel to help you through the divorce process. Ideally, call a few attorneys and ask the same questions of each. Start to get a feel for who you would like to help you based on the answers you receive. Apart from an attorney's knowledge of the law and how the attorney suggests your facts apply to the law, you should consider factors beyond the academic capabilities of the attorney. You might look at how the attorney treats you. Are they compassionate when you share information about your situation and your needs? Is the focus on you, or on the attorney's need for compensation? The attorney should choose to focus on you, not on the payment for services; and you should find out the costs and the billing policy up-front, so expectations around payments are clear from the start. Was sufficient time spent during the initial phone call to answer your questions? You should feel that you are in good hands, rather than experiencing a lingering sense of anxiety when you reflect on initial discussions.

PREPARE YOUR QUESTIONS AND PROVIDE YOUR FINANCIAL INFORMATION

Prepare in advance of the initial meeting. Write down some talking points that describe your case. For example, you might share how long you have been married to your spouse, and when you separated; how many children you have together, their ages, and information about their school situations, as well as how they are doing in the midst of this life change; whether you and your spouse own or rent the home you live in together; who, if anyone, has moved out of the marital residence; any unusual situations; any domestic violence or abusive behavior.

Remember, *you* are interviewing the attorney to see if they would be a good team player. Spend a little time talking about your case. The attorney may ask you questions about your situation. Take notes! Ask how the attorney plans to handle the issues, so you can assess whether the attorney's strategy is one you are comfortable with. For example, sometimes attorneys want to immediately request orders for temporary spousal support, temporary child support, and attorney's fees and costs. Would the proposed plan be appropriate for your circumstances? Discuss the attorney's proposed plan and the associated costs. Be willing to evaluate how each step will affect the divorce process.

Also, you should find out who is doing the work on your case day-to-day. Is it the paralegal, the associate, or the attorney who heads the firm? (Costs may differ significantly, and so might the experience quotient and know-how.)

Learn what you can during your phone and in-person conversations and assess whether the attorney's fees and costs, and well as their strategy roadmap, will work for your needs. Then, decide who you want to work with and retain that attorney's services.

BE AWARE OF CONFLICTS OF INTEREST AS YOU NARROW THE FIELD

After sharing details, find out whether the attorney you are speaking with has an interest in taking your case. Discuss the fees the attorney charges and find out the next steps of the onboarding process. Be aware that with each attorney you interview, you might disclose confidential information about your situation by sharing your personal facts, legal objectives, and revealing your financial matters as part of the interview process. The confidences shared with an attorney—whether hired or not—can create a conflict of interest. What if your spouse wants to hire the same firm? An attorney has a duty to protect confidential information shared by a *client*. Remember, *you are not a client until the attorney agrees to represent you*. Be careful about sharing confidential information about finances, or discussing legal strategies, with the attorney you are interviewing before choosing your legal representative.

LITIGATION OR MEDIATION? — THAT IS THE QUESTION

There is more than one way to move through divorce. Participants in divorce proceedings have a right to engage in the court process; to obtain court orders establishing each party's legal rights to personal property, spousal and child support, and a parent-share plan for their minor children; and to determine the disposition of real and personal property acquired during marriage.

Attorney preparations for court hearings and related organization of documents can be stressful for clients who must find and provide paperwork to advance their legal arguments. This is a time-consuming and expensive process that can become emotionally exhausting as well. Yet, spouses who disagree about the issues in their divorce have every right to enter the courtroom and resolve disputes through litigation.

Presenting your case to a judge is an option that engages a traditional system—one that is often quite expensive, in more ways than the financial toll exacted upon participants. The process can be taxing on participants' physical and emotional wellbeing, too. Timelines involved in litigating the issues in your case can be lengthy, particularly as life's realities in the year 2023 include societal choices around the lingering COVID pandemic. Our legal system, including operations in the state courts where divorce matters are heard, experiences significant changes to courtroom routines and delays in day-to-day operations because of the need to protect the public, as well as the need to address the volume of legal matters filed in the courts.

Keep in mind that litigation is a system that is adversarial at its core. Parties and their attorneys "argue" motions. Attorneys create legal briefs that are written expressions of advocacy that often seem—"win" or "lose." In litigation, the judge is the decision-maker; the parties seek the judge's decision, and the attorneys drive the process forward to either settlement or trial. Litigation stylizes the art of arguing a point.

However, there are options other than rulings by a judge that will allow for settlement. Another model may, in some circumstances, be helpful in preserving relationships and resolving disputed issues: mediation.

Mediation is a voluntary, out-of-court process that provides people engaging in a dispute with a private and confidential way to resolve their issues. "Voluntary" means you have a choice: You come to mediation of your own free will, and you have a right to stay, or to leave the mediation session at any time. There is no coercion. You have the freedom to decide what you want to do. It is up to you how you will participate in your mediation session. It is up to you if you want to end the session, too. However, if you want to leave, before you do, arrange to meet privately with the mediator to see whether there might be solutions that will allow you to return to productive discussions.

What does "private" mean in terms of the mediation process? There is an opportunity to engage in frank conversation and to explore openly all the topics that you want to discuss. No one is observing you, and no one is recording you. The mediator may take some notes, but those notes will ordinarily be destroyed at the end of your mediation session. Unlike the events that take place in a courtroom, mediation conversations are not open to the public.

Confidentiality is another component of the mediation process. Your work in all sessions is confidential except under very limited circumstances—commission of criminal acts, or violation of professional ethics, for example. Outside of the mediation sessions, participants, including the mediator, cannot be subpoenaed as witnesses in your court proceedings and will not testify in either your legal case nor, generally, in any arbitration proceedings. Any information that is exchanged in mediation sessions—other than a final agreement, if one is reached—remains confidential. Your mediator cannot be called into court. The mediator's role is to help you in the moment. The mediator is a facilitator, but not a decision-maker. You and your spouse are the decision-makers.

What is your role in the mediation sessions? Spouses are able to consider their options, participate fully in the mediation sessions, and develop agreements as desired. The mediator will help you engage in the process of mediation with honesty and interact in conversations with mutual respect. Speak up for your needs and what you want to accomplish. Keep an open mind. Your principles will guide you through this non-adversarial process.

The mediator's role is to facilitate your important discussions—conversations that you may not have had the opportunity to hold in other, more formal settings like a courtroom. Courts have their own rules and their own timelines that are driven by the legal system. In mediation, *you* are in control of what you want to say. You can be heard. You can speak freely about emotions as well as facts. Your solutions are not defined by case law or legal argument.

Mediation allows participants the luxury of time to explore and the ability to address goals, concerns, issues, and options in creating agreements. Should you arrive at a full settlement, terms are included in a formal settlement document. You and your spouse are the decision-makers. The mediator supports your interactions as you engage in the process of resolving your differences.

A NEW BEGINNING

Relationships are complicated and take effort to sustain. Sometimes the investment is well-worth the time and energy; other times, the challenges seem overwhelming. The information this chapter presents may be helpful in addressing the financial matters that come with relationships. This book provides you with a call to action. This chapter addresses a wide variety of facts and circumstances; yet the situations any one individual confronts in a lifetime are infinitely variable, and infinitely complex. After reading the information here, you may have discovered some protections. You may choose to explore further, evaluate your situation, make changes, and grow.

Consider the points in the "Ninety-Day Takeaways" introduced early in this chapter. The action plan offers you a starting point for change. What is important for you to take away from a chapter about relationships, legal protections, and your own financial situation? Your action plan may be defined in part by your personal history and in part by your journey into a bright and hopeful future. Perhaps now, having read about protections available to you, you will revisit the "Ninety-Day Takeaways," select a starting point, and implement the information that will help you move into your best chapter in life.

IF YOU ARE EXPERIENCING DOMESTIC VIOLENCE

There is one additional topic that may be an important consideration for some readers: Emotional and physical harm at the hands of an intimate partner. Unfortunately, domestic violence is part of many lives. It is often the hidden part of a relationship that can appear, from the outside, to be loving and fulfilled. Living in a relationship tainted by abuse can damage your emotional and physical health and harm your ability to create a strong financial foundation.

To those who endure, know that there are different choices you can make. There are people who can help. There are places where you can find safety. The process ahead may be difficult, but it is necessary. Domestic violence often extracts a financial toll that ripples out from the individual, to the family, and to society as a whole.

Maggie Germano, a contributor to the online publication *Forbes Women*, lays out the financial impact as reported by the Centers for Disease Control and Prevention as follows:

> "The financial impact of domestic violence ranges from individual to societal [. . .] the lifetime economic cost associated with medical services, lost productivity from paid work, criminal justice, and other costs, was $3.6 trillion. The cost of domestic violence over a victim's lifetime was $103,767 for women and $23,414 for men."[4]

Abusive relationships impose barriers to economic stability. Fallout from domestic violence may foreclose educational opportunities, limit career choices, and impede upward mobility over the course of a lifetime by negatively affecting a woman's ability to generate income.

Do not allow the short-term situation where violence manifests to block your forward progress to a better long-term situation. Help is available. The choices you make are entirely your own. Here are some situations where violence and abuse colored the lives of women who chose to honor themselves and to escape toxic relationships that would otherwise have robbed them of economic success.

WHEN DOMESTIC VIOLENCE IS A PART OF YOUR STORY

As part of your ninety-day plan, assess your situation. Is your spouse your abuser? Know the escalation cycle. Violence occurs in many forms. Abuse may not start with any physical contact; instead, the abuser may begin with behaviors that do not include physical contact at all. Sometimes there might be a threat to destroy your personal property, or a threat about what "might" happen; or there may be other aggressions that impact your financial or emotional wellbeing.

Make a plan. If you experience domestic violence, take notes. Describe the events you experience. Do not hesitate to seek out professional help. You need to create an action plan.

DEFINING DOMESTIC VIOLENCE

Several definitions of domestic violence follow. They are variations on a theme. You will come to recognize the themes as they repeat in the different descriptions below.

> "California's Domestic Violence Advisory Council defines domestic violence as a spectrum and often a pattern of behaviors that includes physical, sexual, verbal, emotional, and psychological abuse and/ or economic control used by adults or adolescents against their current or former intimate partners in an attempt to exercise power and authority, which has a destructive, harmful effect on individuals, the family and the community."
>
> –*California Department of Public Health Safe and Active Communities Branch*[5]

> "Domestic violence is not violence alone. Domestic violence is any behavior the purpose of which is to gain power and control over a spouse, partner, girl/boyfriend or intimate family member. Abuse is a learned behavior; it is not caused by anger, mental problems, drugs or alcohol, or other common excuses."
>
> –*Arizona Coalition to End Sexual and Domestic Violence*[6]

> "Domestic abuse is a pattern of coercive, controlling behavior that is a pervasive life-threatening crime affecting people in all our communities regardless of gender, age, sexual orientation, race, ethnicity, religion, social standing and immigration status."
>
> –*The Center for Family Justice*[7]

The law aims to protect people who are victims of certain kinds of bad behavior, commonly known as "abuse" or "domestic violence." Domestic violence and abuse are not a one-size-fits-all set of behaviors. As you can see, the definitions referenced are rich in context and nuance. When you hear the term "domestic violence," physical harm immediately comes to mind; but that kind of hurt is just the beginning of a long list of behaviors that courts and others knowledgeable in this subject area have identified as abuse. Besides physical harm, these behaviors include, but are not limited to: threats, stalking, harassment, molestation, creating fear of immediate physical harm, emotional abuse, and financial abuse.

Violent behavior is learned behavior, and it often escalates. If you live in a situation where you feel you are at risk of harm when dealing with your spouse or a member of your household—a boyfriend, girlfriend, significant other, or family member—you can file a case in the family court. Ask for a domestic violence restraining order to keep yourself and others in your household free from harm.

YOU AND YOUR CHILDREN HAVE THE RIGHT TO LIVE FREE OF PHYSICAL VIOLENCE AND ABUSIVE BEHAVIOR

If you experience physical violence, take action immediately. Put aside the ninety-day plan and *act now*. Contact the police or sheriff as soon as possible if you or any of your family members are in harm's way. File an incident report with the police, and ask to speak with an Assistant District Attorney about your situation.

The DA's office will evaluate whether they will take your case. The DA's office will advise you if a criminal case is opened. A criminal case involving domestic violence is brought by the District Attorney's office on behalf of the people of your state. While you may be called to testify in such a case, the District Attorney's objective in prosecuting criminal conduct is to serve the public good by enforcing the law. The District Attorney serves the public interest in maintaining a civil society—a different focus than legally enforcing your rights in a family court case.

It is important that you understand the difference between a family law case that *you* can file under the laws set out in the family code, and a criminal law matter that is prosecuted by the state under the laws set out in the penal code. Criminal conduct is a matter addressed by the DA's office and has different timelines and different purposes than a matter that you might file in family court; and the process of preparing and prosecuting a criminal case involving domestic violence is often lengthy.

The family code gives you rights under the law. Some legal rights, particularly as they relate to prosecuting a domestic violence case, may play out in a timeline that is longer than a ninety-day "shape-up" plan, but you can begin any time you are ready. Both the family court and the criminal court may grant domestic violence restraining orders to survivors of abuse. People and organizations in many places can guide and help you along the way. You are not alone.

You may need emotional and other types of support on your journey to freedom from abuse. Help is available from many sources. One source is the National Domestic Violence Hotline (www.thehotline.org). The telephone contact is available at 1-800-799-7233 (1-800-799 SAFE). Their website is worth exploring.

Be aware that in California, any healthcare provider employed in a health facility, clinic, physician's office, local or state public health department or clinic or other facility operated by a local or state health department is a mandatory reporter. This means a health practitioner working in the settings identified above is required to report to law enforcement that medical services were provided for a physical condition which the treater knows or reasonably suspects was sustained because of abuse or violence. Mandatory reporting to law enforcement includes special instructions that focus on preserving your privacy and safety.

RESTRAINING ORDERS

To immediately stop physical abuse or other acts inflicted on you by an intimate partner (for example, if your spouse or partner abuses you physically, emotionally, or financially), file a request for a domestic violence restraining order at your local courthouse. In California, courthouse clerks or court staff at the self-help center for family law matters will provide you with forms so you can request temporary restraining orders. A judge can issue temporary restraining orders before your court hearing. Fill out the forms and file them. There is no cost to you.

You can often get help preparing your paperwork requesting a temporary restraining order by accessing the court's self-help center. There also may be a low-fee option to obtain an attorney through your county bar association. There are also several nonprofits that work with survivors of domestic violence. Prepare your paperwork so you can properly present your case.

UNDERSTANDING THE CYCLE OF DOMESTIC VIOLENCE

Domestic violence is often characterized as an ongoing cycle of events that have the potential to worsen over time. In the late 1970s, psychotherapist Lenore Walker, Ph.D., conceptualized a four-phase social cycle theory of abuse, based upon findings from her interview of 1,500 women survivors of domestic violence.[8] Patterns emerged from information Dr. Walker gathered from interviewees about their experiences. Dr. Walker noted that discrete phases characterized the abuser's behavioral cycles, and interview information revealed overarching patterns characteristic of abusive relationships.

Dr. Walker identified an initial phase where tensions build and the abuser experiences mounting frustration, which results in increasingly negative treatment of the abused person. In this initial phase (Phase 1), the abuser fears that the abused person who is under the abuser's control (note: not affection—control) will quit the relationship. The more the abused person distances from the abuser, the more the abuser is motivated to act oppressively.

This dynamic pushes the abuser to Phase 2: a loss of control, and an exhibition of rage which explodes into physical violence.

Phase 3 is marked by the abuser's expressions of contrition for the violence inflicted. In this phase, the abuser may promise the abused the moon and the stars, including assurances that the violence will never happen again. This third phase is the "kiss and make up" phase in the aftermath of violence. Phase 3 often includes romance and all the benefits of a kind and loving relationship.

Only, this "romance" is far from kind. Recognize that it is part of the cycle of abuse. *Abuse is not romantic.* The "kiss and make up" phase is temporary. The cycle will repeat. The abuser's behavior will change to violence again. Tensions will build; the violence will escalate.

Get a restraining order (also called a protective order) if you are experiencing abuse. The protective order can keep the person who is hurting you out of your home and far away from your workplace or your school, as well. Protective orders can include your children and your pets as well as your personal property.

Ask the judge for the protections you need by completing paperwork, which the court will review. The paperwork is available at the courthouse, and California-specific forms are available online through the California Judicial Council webpage.

There is no cost to get the forms, and there is no cost to file the forms. You must only complete the forms in a way that tells the judge about the behaviors of the person who harmed you, and how you have been hurt by the other person's actions. Some courthouses in California offer help in filling out the forms. You may also be able to access supportive services through nonprofit agencies who work with people experiencing domestic violence.

If you are being harmed by an intimate partner—whether they are a significant other or spouse—the Family Court Judge can issue a protective order. The court has great discretion in whether to grant a request for protection; however, you must provide evidence of domestic violence or domestic abuse.

Evidence can include your own testimony, testimony of witnesses, testimony of experts, and testimony of law enforcement professionals. A treating physician, a police officer, an emergency responder, a mental health professional, a nurse, or a neighbor who has heard or seen an incident can testify as to what they witnessed. You can also provide the court with documents like emails, letters, photos, medical records, police incident reports, and an almost endless list of other relevant information.

To obtain legal protection in a family law domestic violence case, you must prove that you were in an intimate relationship with the person against whom you seek a protective order; and you must show that the behaviors you have experienced rise to the level of domestic violence. You must also show that you, and those you seek to protect through the order, have experienced harm or are in fear of imminent danger at the hands of the abusive person. This harm may extend to acts against people in your household, including your family pets.

The abuse or violence may be characterized as harassing; stalking; molesting; attacking; striking; threatening; sexually assaulting; battering; credibly impersonating you over the phone; harassing you by phone, including making annoying phone calls to you; destroying your personal property; contacting you directly or indirectly, by mail or online; coming within a certain distance of you; or disturbing the peace. That is a long list. You will need to tell the judge or speak out about the behaviors you have experienced. There are people available to sit next to you in court so you can feel secure in the courtroom. There is often a bailiff who will carefully monitor the behaviors of the people who are in the courtroom. If your case is handled by the DA, you will be able to access additional resources to help you feel secure while you tell your judge what has happened.

DO YOU SEE YOURSELF IN THE STORIES OF OTHER WOMEN?

Domestic violence comes in many different forms. In the following pages, I share stories that illustrate experiences and behaviors that might help you to recognize the kinds of behaviors that can create harm, not happiness, in your own life. Everyone's situation is different, and these stories may be different than your own, but these examples might awaken within you the understanding that all is not right in your world. If you are thinking, "This is kind of like my own life," you might want to contact a professional—someone who can help you break free from interactions and behaviors that can escalate and ultimately affect your wellbeing.

ARA AND ERIC—LIFE HAPPENING BADLY

Eric drove an eighteen-wheeler between stops in California's Central Valley. He was often on the road hauling goods for hundreds of miles, sleeping in the truck, and returning home, days later, exhausted. Ara felt isolated because her nearest relatives lived in a city about a hundred miles away. The newlyweds needed the money Eric brought in from trucking; Ara had no income other than her husband's earnings.

Living with Eric's family came at a price. Eric's family expected Ara to help with the cooking, cleaning, and caring for Eric's elderly grandmother in exchange for discounted rent. As a consequence of this arrangement, there was not enough time for Ara to study. Ara seemed to be on call for her mother-in-law and was constantly addressing the grandmother's care needs.

During her first year of marriage, Ara became pregnant. She put her career plans on hold, quit school, and continued to help out in the household. She and Eric became the parents of a beautiful son, Monte; but Ara did not have much time to share with her child because of the demands she experienced living and working in the home. Ara was now caring for baby Monte and Eric's grandmother day and night. She felt trapped and isolated. Eric was never around. She wondered whether she would ever have the opportunity to return to her studies and earn her degree.

When Monte was about a year old, Eric was injured on the job and had to stop working while he healed. His disability earnings were far less than his regular pay. Finances were tight, and the family was forced to cut back on basics. Eric fell into a deep depression and became increasingly bitter and angry. He often directed his anger at Ara, criticizing her in front of his parents and grandmother.

The quality of life that fueled Ara's hopes and dreams as a newlywed hardened into a poisonous existence. Ara endured the verbal badgering; but there was little, other than baby Monte, that brought her joy. One night, Eric became enraged when Ara did not respond immediately to his latest demand. He grabbed Ara's arm, yanking her toward him so he could slap her hard across the face. Her mother-in-law, observing this horrible scene, nodded her head as if in approval of her son's behavior.

For Ara, the story ended well. She had the presence of mind to scoop up baby Monte and leave the room, get behind a locked door with Monte in her arms, and call her family members to come get her. They did, and they called the local police before making the drive. Help comes in many unexpected ways, just as abuse can take many forms.

HELEN AND DAN—EMOTIONAL AND FINANCIAL ABUSE ARE DOMESTIC VIOLENCE, TOO

Here is an example of bad behavior that caused lasting psychological pain, rather than physical harm. If this reminds you of your own circumstances, get help now, before the situation escalates.

Helen and Dan lived a luxurious existence as seen from the outside. Their suburban home was spacious, meticulously decorated, and always spotless. The centerpiece of their lush garden was a gorgeous custom-designed swimming pool, with beautiful tiles and a jetted spa that had room for six people. There were, of course, the requisite two kids and a friendly medium-size dog romping in the yard. Appearances can deceive. Something was missing: Joy.

Dan was constantly putting Helen down. He would make snide comments about Helen, seemingly in a way that was meant to be helpful, but always with a clever barb in the comments he shared.

Summer weekends were filled with parties, beer, and barbeque.

Helen did not work outside the home because Dan wanted her to stay out of the workforce. His status as a good provider telegraphed a message of affluence to his friends. As a result, Helen lived on Dan's terms and had no earnings of her own. Dan provided Helen with money, but even the process of requesting a few bucks from Dan made Helen feel anxious. From the outside, the marriage looked rock solid. From Helen's perspective, the marriage was just plain rocky.

Dan never had a good word to say about Helen. At the parties Dan hosted most weekends, he would joke about Helen with his guy friends, telling unkind stories to belittle and demean Helen. If Helen protested, the conversation would go from bad to worse. Dan often drank quite a bit too much, which made his behavior aggressive. Helen had learned to keep a smile on her face and say nothing.

Dan would often leave Helen to clean up the mess after the guests went home. He would lie awake in the bed he and Helen shared, waiting to berate Helen for anything that he believed she had done—any comment that Dan thought was out of line, or any perceived failure to be the perfect hostess.

Eventually, Helen and Dan had a full-on confrontation, and Helen chose to leave the marriage. She had the feeling that life should not be lived in misery, and that she would be much better off without Dan's put-downs. Helen's experiences might remind you of a bird trapped in a golden cage. Everything looked beautiful, picture-perfect; but in fact, when examined below the surface, the glaring truth was that Helen depended entirely on Dan for her every penny.

Dan controlled Helen by confining her to a life of *his making.* Helen could have anything she wanted—as long as Dan wanted it, too. Helen had to rely completely on Dan's willingness to provide her with money for groceries, the children's needs, and her own healthcare. In short, if Dan felt like giving Helen a few dollars, it was a good day for Helen. Escaping the home with manicured lawns and every outward image of the good life well-lived became Helen's obsession.

Leaving Dan was not easy. He had financial security, and Helen initially had none. She had to create a new life from the ground up. She had to fight for her rights in a difficult divorce where Dan delayed, time and again, to finalize any agreements about either spousal support or property division. Helen was forced to move away from her home of many years. She had to create her own income stream. Fortunately, she and the children relocated to a safe location, and Dan paid a modest amount of support.

Helen was a resourceful, determined woman who had the drive to move past tough circumstances. She knew there was opportunity for her out in the bigger world, and that she was employable. Helen found support in her community and discovered a way to reinvent her life. She took a position as an administrative assistant and learned workplace skills. She was helpful to her colleagues and began to study and expand her career options. Three years post-divorce, Helen is employed in a position that offers her opportunities to develop professionally and, quite unexpectedly, she found a love-filled relationship that brings her the joy that was so markedly absent during her years with Dan.

ELIZABETH'S EXPERIENCE SAYING "NO" WHEN A FINANCIAL RELATIONSHIP BECAME PERSONAL

Finally, here is a story about a woman who took back control over her situation before things got further out of hand. When agreements are made, be sure to fully negotiate the specific terms of any financial relationship. Do not be casual about the expectations of either party when making agreements that involve financial matters. Spell out each party's expectations clearly.

Elizabeth was a third-year college student who interned at a nonprofit and studied psychology at a well-known East Coast school. She wanted her skills to change the lives of people who had little money and less hope.

Elizabeth had developed an interest in psychology partly because of her own life circumstances. She was raised in a small town by her mother, a widow who fled her homeland while pregnant. Elizabeth's mother escaped from her homeland, but her beloved husband was killed during the dangerous journey to freedom. The stories of her mother's ordcal were woven into Elizabeth's earliest memories. Sadly, Elizabeth's mother could not fully free herself from her traumatic past. As a result, Elizabeth knew all the history of her mother's difficult path to a new life.

Elizabeth also knew from an early age that a college education would provide her with the opportunity to create her own pathway to something better. As part of her studies, she landed the perfect paid internship at a nonprofit. There, she could help other students in the college community who were dealing with domestic violence, bullying, and emotional abuse.

At the start of her junior year, Elizabeth found an ideal living arrangement: a family living in a big old house offered her a room in exchange for part-time work as a nanny for their three school-aged children. All seemed well. Elizabeth was able to devote many hours to her internship experience, and she could study in the evenings after the children were asleep. As a bonus, she felt she had a great living situation and a fabulous connection with the children she cared for, as well as with the children's parents.

At times, though, Elizabeth found the husband a little too friendly . . . but she brushed off his peculiarities. In the evening, while Elizabeth was studying, the husband would often walk up the three flights of stairs to Elizabeth's room at the very top of the house to "check up" on Elizabeth as she studied. Inevitably, the husband would start a conversation with Elizabeth. Elizabeth's study time was precious, and the husband's "check-ups" ate away at time set aside for study. Elizabeth felt she had to be pleasant to her employer. After all, he provided her with a great place to live, and working as a nanny paid for food and other expenses.

Life was good—until, of course, it wasn't. The shock happened during spring break, when the children and their mother went to visit relatives. Elizabeth planned to hole up in her room and study for upcoming exams, work her internship hours at the nonprofit, and save money by staying at her employer's home until she finished her end-of-semester exams. Elizabeth got permission from her employers to remain in their home until after her exams ended. Her plan was fine with her employers, and perfect for Elizabeth—until the husband walked into her room late at night, when everyone else in the house was gone. The husband did not speak at first. He simply opened the door to Elizabeth's room, walked over, and stood next to her bed.

Elizabeth was terrified. Her first thought was of stories her mother had told of suffering at the hands of strangers on her long-ago journey to freedom. The husband broke the silence with a totally shocking proposition—one that he expected Elizabeth to accept. She had the presence of mind to look the man in the eyes and tell him where he needed to go.

Elizabeth left for good the next day, thankful that her experiences at the nonprofit had educated her sufficiently to know that remaining in her situation, even if it offered her the appearance of security, would deliver her into the hands of a sexual predator. Over the next several days, her mentors at the nonprofit helped Elizabeth find safe housing. She was able to continue her studies, and as time passed, she put the incident behind her, realizing in hindsight that the husband's frequent intrusions into her living space were signs that all was not right in what appeared to have been an ideal arrangement.

BE AWARE, STAY SAFE:
DOMESTIC VIOLENCE AND ABUSE TAKEAWAYS

- Recognize the behaviors associated with domestic violence and abuse
- Understand that abusive relationships are harmful to your physical, emotional, and financial wellbeing
- Build your safety net. Access the network of experienced helping professionals: therapists, advocates, counselors, and attorneys can help you *before* the cycle of abuse escalates
- *Do not wait.* If you experience violence or are threatened with immediate harm, *get a protective order*. The family courts can help.
- Call the sheriff or the police if you are in danger.
- Be kind to yourself. You deserve the best.
- Focus on your personal safety. When you are safe, revisit your goals for financial wellbeing.
- Discover the power of accomplishment. Choose a goal, implement it, and celebrate your achievements. Then, choose additional goals.
- You can do this.
- Never give up on yourself.

CHAPTER NINE

BE SMART ABOUT SOCIAL SECURITY

Tips for a More Secure Financial Future

Georgeana Roussos

Every person working in the United States, along with their employer, makes payroll tax contributions that fund Social Security's Retirement and Disability Insurance benefit programs. Many workers assume that because they paid FICA taxes, the Social Security Administration (SSA) will pay them a monthly income in old age or poor health. Unfortunately, that is not always the case, as many factors determine the type and amount of retirement or disability benefits you are due.

You may not realize it, but this chapter is not just about you. Besides providing you with financial support (in old age or due to a disability), your Social Security benefits may contribute towards the financial support of your children, surviving spouse, and potentially even your divorced spouse. For many, Social Security is the only old-age pension they receive. For others, it is an essential supplement to other sources of retirement income.

This chapter discusses different factors and situations that determine one's eligibility for retirement benefits, as well as strategies to legitimately maximize your Social Security benefits—with the goal being to enhance your financial security in retirement for the benefit of not only yourself, but also of those in your life. It is intended as a general overview only. To fully assess your personal situation, you should consult with a professional before acting.

INTRODUCTION

Having worked as a Social Security disability attorney for years, I have met a wide variety of wonderful people living under strikingly diverse circumstances. Some worked in the trades; many served in the military; others were civil servants, warehouse workers, nurses, hairdressers, or former pro athletes. I have met circus performers, playwrights, air traffic controllers, neon sign artists, and a rocket scientist—you name it. Bad things happen to good people from all walks of life, every day. I've seen it all too often. While some are well-prepared for such challenging circumstances, most are not.

Despite the different life trajectories that led them to my office, nearly all had three factors in common: first, they did not expect to find themselves unable to continue working so early in their lives; second, they expected that their Social Security benefits would provide more money; and third, they expected that after having paid into Social Security for so many years, the Agency would assist them right away, and they would have to do very little. This, however, is not how the Social Security system works currently.

This book is intended only to open your eyes to potential issues, not to solve them. For solutions to your particular situation, I strongly recommend that you confer with an attorney(s) before acting.[1] The government has no interest in making this easy for you, so I recommend that you get whatever help you can.[2]

So how does one prepare for the slings and arrows of outrageous misfortune? How do you stay calm and carry on? I wish I had the answer to that universal question. Unfortunately, I don't. Personally, I have struggled with financial anxiety, and that anxiety about the future has cost me more than a few well-lived moments in the present. I would like to say that it's the result of being raised by a Depression-era mother, but my mom is not about to let me get away with that.

The point is that most of us have financial insecurity. My hope is that this chapter will give you enough information to help you prepare for life's vicissitudes and relieve a bit of the anxiety that they bring.

It is important to remember that while the Social Security system is a safety net, it is an incomplete one that requires your thoughtful participation.

The Social Security Administration (SSA) changes its procedures, standards, and (alas) acronyms all too frequently. Before you file for retirement benefits, you need to consult an expert and verify that you are acting on current and correct information. Keep in mind that while I have attempted to organize the eligibility criteria and more commonly recognized exceptions for each type of benefit, the list is not exhaustive and is subject to change at any time. In fact, it's "sure odds" that the SSA will change its rules and conventions with annoying regularity.

Social Security has written explanatory articles and brochures discussing retirement benefits, which are quite useful and can be found on the Social Security website as well as in print. I have included links to pertinent information on the www.ssa.gov website, where possible, so that you can access up to date information whenever you wish. (If the link has expired, search the website's "Program Rules" and "Frequently Asked Question" sections for current information.) AARP has a particularly instructive website, too.

SOCIAL SECURITY MILESTONES

- **1935:** In the midst of the Great Depression, President Franklin D. Roosevelt signs the Social Security Act into law, saving many from destitution. Initially, Social Security checks are one-time payments made to retired workers.
- **1939:** The program expands to provide one-time payments to the dependents of retired, disabled, or deceased workers.
- **1940:** Social Security begins issuing monthly checks to retired workers aged sixty-five and over, as well as to their surviving spouse and dependents.
- **1956:** Social Security expands to cover disabled workers aged fifty to sixty-four years old, as well as the disabled adult children of workers collecting Social Security benefits.
- **1960:** Social Security expands to cover disabled workers under the age of fifty.
- **1961:** A provision for universal early retirement at age sixty-two is added.
- **1965:** Medicare and Medicaid are signed into law.

- **1972:** Congress establishes Supplementary Social Income, a program providing monthly checks to older, blind, and disabled people who have not worked enough to qualify for Social Security retirement and disability benefits and who have limited income and resources.
- **1997:** Medicare Advantage plans enter the common marketplace.
- **2010:** Under the Affordable Care Act, certain preventative care medical services must be provided to Medicare recipients at no cost.

JUST WHAT IS SOCIAL SECURITY, REALLY?

POP QUIZ:

Social Security is a federal program that provides the following benefits:

- Retirement benefits
- Life insurance
- Long-term disability insurance
- Medical insurance
- Vocational retraining
- Small payment for burial expenses
- Financial support for a dependent parent

CHOOSE ALL THAT APPLY.
YOUR ANSWER: ________________

Believe it or not, "all of the above" is the correct answer. That represents quite a variety of benefits. Recognized commonly as a retirement program, Social Security is so much more. It pays monthly benefits to eligible members of a worker's family, potentially including the worker's spouse; ex-spouse; widow/widower; minor children; disabled minor and adult children; and dependent parents. Its various programs also provide medical insurance, vocational retraining, and a small sum for burial expenses. Even though it is expansive in scope, you need to remember that Social Security retirement benefits were never intended to be anything more than a stipend, and not everyone is eligible for these benefits.

Social Security remains a significant part of any financial survival plan, and it only makes sense to understand what it can offer and what it cannot.

THE NAME AND ACRONYM GAME

Social Security can drive you mad with all its abbreviations, multiple names for the same thing, acronyms that apply to more than one thing, and brain-numbing verbiage. Below are some names, acronyms, and concepts that you need to know before we take a closer look at the various benefits and strategies to enhance your financial security.

Auxiliary benefits: The various types of benefits that can be paid off your own retirement to qualifying spouses, ex-spouses, children, dependent parents, etc.

Average Indexed Monthly Earnings (AIME): the basis for determining how much you get paid. Your AIME is the measure of your past earnings from which your monthly retirement benefit is calculated primarily. In general, Social Security adds up your highest thirty-five years[3] of indexed earnings and then runs that number through a special algorithm to arrive at your monthly retirement benefit amount (a.k.a. PIA).[4]

Child-In-Care Spousal Benefits: A special form of spousal benefits intended to provide financial assistance to families with a young or disabled child(ren) at home. It behooves you to know about this particular spousal benefit because you can collect child-in-care benefits at any age, unlike spousal benefits which require that you be at least sixty-two to collect.

To qualify for child-in-care spousal benefits, you must meet the following requirements: 1) your spouse must already be collecting retirement benefits based on their own earnings record; 2) your marriage must already have lasted at least one year, or you and your spouse are the natural parents of the child; *and* 3) your child is under sixteen years old or is disabled (regardless of age) and receiving child benefits based on your spouse's earnings record. Grandkids, too—a dependent grandchild or step-grandchild of the worker or spouse may also qualify for benefits as a "child."[5]

When the child in your care turns sixteen, you may continue to receive benefits if the child is disabled and you meet the legal requirements for having a disabled child in care.[6] *See* the Social Security Handbook for more information.[7]

Bonus: Child-in-care spousal benefits are not subject to the deemed filing rule, nor is there any penalty for early collection.[8] If you are divorced and have a child in your care during your first month of entitlement, your child-in-care benefits will not be reduced for any month in which the child remains in your care.[9]

If you are caring for an eligible child, your benefit would be 50 percent of your current or divorced spouse's "primary insurance amount," just like with regular or standard spousal benefits.

Deemed Filing Rule = Unrestricted Application = "The One-and-Done Rule" = "The One Equals Two" Rule: Everyone born after January 1, 1954, needs to understand this tricky rule because it could cost you a lot of money if you do not.

Under the deemed filing rule, Social Security has the power to require that you apply for all the potential benefits that you can. Whether or not you want to do that is of no concern to Social Security. The result? You can no longer limit your application to one type of retirement benefit because Social Security will process your paperwork ***as if*** you were applying for ***all*** the retirement benefits for which you potentially qualify. This is why it is called "deemed" filing.[10]

What is the real-world significance of the deemed filing rule? It prevents you from switching to a higher-paying type of retirement benefit later, which is why I call it the "One-and-Done" or "One Equals Two" rule because you may believe that you are filing an application for one kind of benefit, when you are really filing for two benefits.

The net effect: Absent an exception, you get only one chance to choose your retirement benefit start date, and determining when to file for your retirement benefits is one of the most important financial decisions you will make in life.[11]

Under the deemed filing rule, Social Security calculates the monthly retirement benefit for everyone born after January 1, 1954 the same way—it totals different benefit amounts to arrive at your primary insured amount, or base monthly retirement benefit. Social Security follows a specific order when calculating your benefit. First, it starts with your individual retirement benefit amount, then it looks at what you would be paid as a spouse. If you would receive more money as a spouse, Social Security subtracts the amount of your individual retirement benefit from your spousal benefit amount and adds that difference (or "excess") to your individual retirement benefit to arrive at your overall monthly benefit amount. For most people, this means that they are receiving a combination of individual and spousal retirement benefits. Conversely, if your retirement benefit amount is more than you would receive in spousal benefits, it may look like you applied only for your retirement benefits, when, in fact, you applied for your spousal benefits, too. In other words, even if you don't receive a penny in spousal benefits, you are deemed to have applied for them as of the day you applied for your individual retirement benefits; the clock is stopped for both types of benefit.

Upshot: By taking your spousal benefits early, you forfeit any increase in your spousal ***and*** retirement benefit amount, i.e., it stops the clock and permanently limits the amount of one or both benefits as of the date you first applied. This decision cannot be undone unless you meet an exception, some of which are discussed below.

The deemed filing rules apply to worker benefits, spousal benefits, and ex-spousal benefits.

Exceptions: The deemed filing rule does not apply under the following circumstances:

1. The deemed filing rule does not apply to survivor, children, child-in-care, and disabled children benefits.
2. When you apply for your individual retirement benefits, your spouse is not yet collecting individual retirement benefits. Because they are not collecting retirement benefits off their own record, you are blocked from filing for spousal benefits and are limited to collecting benefits off your own record only. The good news is that as soon as

your spouse applies for their own retirement benefits, you would be eligible at that time to collect a spousal benefit equal to one half of your spouse's retirement benefit (provided it is larger than your individual retirement benefit).

Limited Do-Over Option for Those Bitten by the Deeming Clause: If you realize that you made a mistake in claiming benefits when you did, or for any reason actually, you are allowed to correct your mistake for a limited period of time. To do this, you need to withdraw your application(s) and will be able to reverse your action *provided* that a) you change your mind within one year of filing for retirement benefits *and* b) you reimburse Social Security for any retirement benefits, tax withholding, and Medicare benefits that you received during the time before you withdrew your application(s).[12]

Delayed Retirement Credit: When Social Security retirement benefits are increased by a certain percentage for each month you delay starting your benefits beyond full retirement age, those increases are called "delayed retirement credits." For anyone born after 1943, for each month you delay collecting your individual retirement benefit, your primary insured amount increases by two thirds of 1 percent.[13]

Family Maximum Rule: Does not mean the largest number of family members whom you find annoying and can tolerate at family gatherings! Rather, it is a limit on the total amount of money that Social Security can pay to you and your family. Social Security typically caps all family benefit based benefits paid to your family at approximately 150 to 180 percent of your full retirement benefit (depending upon the type of benefit you receive and your earnings history).[14]

Because the total amount of auxiliary (or family) benefits paid on your record is capped, the more family members who collect on your record, the smaller each of their checks will be. Benefits paid to an ex-spouse are not included in the family maximum calculations and won't affect the benefits payable to you or any other family member. Different family maximum rules apply to retirement and survivor benefits than to disability benefits. The rules for calculating family maximum benefits are complicated. [15]

FICA: "The Federal Insurance Contributions Act." Under FICA, you are required to pay taxes based on your gross earned income (FICA taxes). These taxes are also called "payroll taxes" and fund Social Security, disability insurance, Medicare, and other programs. When you earn above a certain amount of income, which changes annually, you receive "quarters of coverage" and it is these quarters of coverage that determine your eligibility for benefits under Social Security's different programs.

File and Suspend: NO LONGER VALID—a defunct strategy that couples and families used to maximize their retirement benefits before it was disallowed in 2016 and replaced with the Deemed Filing Rule. The expired "File and Suspend" maneuver was a two-step strategy that worked like this:

1. upon attaining full retirement age or older, once you applied for your retirement benefits, family members could file for spousal or auxiliary benefits based on your earnings record;

2. you then quickly suspend collecting your retirement benefits until later (so that they could continue to grow until age seventy).

Under the old rule, even though you had suspended your benefit, your beneficiaries would continue to receive their Social Security benefits. (Not so today under general circumstances.)

FRA: "Full Retirement Age"—the age at which you can collect your retirement benefits without any penalty for early withdrawal. Also known as "normal retirement age." Also known as the "Finally, I can breathe!" or the "Aloha!" phase of life.[16]

Medicare: A health insurance plan run by Social Security for people who are sixty-five or older; are disabled; or have ALS or end-stage renal disease.[17]

Mother's and Father's Benefits (Surviving Spouses and Surviving Divorced Spouses): Like child-in-care benefits, but for surviving spouses (widow/widower) and surviving ex-spouses. Like child-in-care spousal benefits, mother's and father's benefits are not subject to the deemed filing rule and there is no early collection penalty and no minimum age requirement to qualify. [18]

As a widow(er), you are entitled to father's or mother's insurance benefits when caring for a child, provided: 1) your late spouse died either fully or currently insured; 2) your retirement insurance benefit is smaller than what you would receive in father's or mother's insurance benefits; 3) you are not married; 4) you are caring for a child of your late spouse who is under age sixteen or who has a disability (at any age); 5) you do not qualify for standard survivor benefits (a.k.a. widow/widower retirement benefits) ***and*** 6) you meet ***one*** of the following conditions: a) you and your late spouse were married for at least the nine months just before they died; or b) you and your late spouse had a child together; or c) you and your late spouse were married when you both legally adopted a child under age eighteen; or d) Your late spouse adopted your son or daughter during your marriage and before the child reached age eighteen; or e) you legally adopted your late spouse's child during your marriage and before the child reached age eighteen; or f) in the month before the month you married your late spouse or ex-spouse, you were entitled or potentially entitled to certain benefits based on the record of a fully insured individual under the Social Security Act or a parent's insurance annuity under the Railroad Retirement Act.[19]

You must file an application for mother's and father's benefits (unless you were entitled to spouse's benefits for the month before the month the insured worker died). As a surviving spouse, you will receive 75 percent of your late spouse's benefit, subject to the family maximum.

If you are a surviving *divorced* parent, you also may be entitled to father's or mother's insurance benefits—the eligibility for father's or mother's benefits for surviving divorced parents are similar to those for non-divorced widows/widowers, with some small differences. To learn more about the specific eligibility criteria for surviving divorced parents, check out https://www.ssa.gov/OP_Home/handbook/handbook.04/handbook-0416.html.

With these benefits, there is no duration of marriage requirement as there is for "standard" survivor benefits. Again, it is good to keep these benefits in mind in case you do not qualify for standard survivor benefits.[20]

PIA = "Primary Insured Amount": The monthly amount of Social Security retirement benefits you would collect at full retirement age (FRA).[21]

Quarter of Coverage = Social Security credit = Work Credit = Credit: The basic unit, based on a worker's earnings, for determining whether that worker is eligible to collect benefits under Social Security programs (also referred to as being "insured" under Social Security).[22]

Special Earnings Test = Retirement Earning Test: This rule applies only to those claiming early retirement benefits. During early retirement, SSA reduces the monthly amount of your early retirement benefits whenever you earn over a certain amount of annual income. Each year, the SSA determines what the reduction threshold is. Once you hit full retirement age, the earnings test does not apply to you, so the SSA will no longer withhold or reduce your earnings on this basis.[23]

Spousal Benefits: Retirement benefits paid to you based on your spouse or ex-spouse's record. You may collect up to 50 percent of the benefit amount that your spouse qualifies for at full retirement age, provided your spouse has already filed for Social Security benefits, and you are at least sixty-two years old. (You do not need to be sixty-two years old to collect spousal benefits if you care for a child who is under age sixteen or is disabled and entitled to receive benefits based on your spouse's record.) Spousal benefits provide financial assistance when you do not have enough quarters of coverage to qualify for retirement benefits on your own record. Spousal benefits are an important source of income, in particular to women, many of whom work in a family business but are not paid a salary.[24]

Spouse: Person you are married to, *or* deemed to be married to, under your state's laws. A divorced spouse is someone to whom you were once married, *or* once legally deemed to be married.

Survivor Benefits: Benefits which, in the event of a worker's death, are paid to members of their family who outlive them—such as widowers and widows (including divorced widows and widowers), children, and possibly dependent parents. How much you receive will depend upon your age, the amount of benefits you qualify for based on your own record, and whether you have dependent children.[25]

Widow and widower benefits: Sometimes referred to as "survivor benefits," even though they are only one kind of survivor benefit. Generally, survivor benefits are subject to the early retirement penalty and deeming. If you are caring for the child of your deceased spouse, there is a more lenient standard.

Bonus: for any month in which you receive a reduced widow(er) survivor benefit ***and*** have a child in care, Social Security will not reduce your widow(er) survivor benefit below the amount that the mother's and father's benefit would pay. If this is your situation, take heart in knowing that your reduced widow(er) benefit will be raised for all months that the child is in your care to the mother's/father's parent benefit amount.

"It takes as much energy to wish as it does to plan."
—Eleanor Roosevelt

Few things go to plan. Death and taxes are the only certainties, although I would add bad hair days and unexpected traffic jams to the list, but that's just me.

SOCIAL SECURITY ADMINISTERS TWO RETIREMENT PROGRAMS

When making retirement plans, remember that Social Security administers two separate retirement programs:

1. **Social Security retirement benefits** are what most people typically think of as "old-age" or retirement benefits. They are funded through the FICA (Federal Insurance Contributions Act) or payroll taxes that you paid while working. Your benefit amount is determined by your pre-retirement earnings. To qualify for Social Security Retirement benefits, you must have paid a threshold or minimum amount of FICA (a.k.a. payroll) taxes in order to qualify for work credits or quarters of coverage. (This is discussed more below.)
2. **Supplemental Security Income benefits** (**SSI**) are financial-need-based retirement benefits. Unlike Social Security Retirement benefits, you do not need work credits to qualify for SSI retirement payments. Rather, you need only show that you are age sixty-five or older and have limited family income and resources which total less than the SSI income and resource limits.

"Can I get both SSI and Social Security retirement benefits?"
Umm, maybe.

If your Social Security retirement benefits are less than what SSI retirement recipients receive, you might qualify for the difference between two benefit amounts (plus the twenty-dollar SSI overlook) if you meet SSI's age, family income, and resource limits.[26]

Say goodbye to SSI—the rest of this chapter concerns only Social Security retirement benefits.

GENERAL INFORMATION ABOUT SOCIAL SECURITY RETIREMENT BENEFITS

Social Security benefits are an essential lifeline to most Americans and their importance cannot be understated, especially for women. Women face greater financial long-term risks than men due to several factors: women earn less than men and tend to live longer, which means they are more likely to incur higher medical expenses over a greater number of years and have less money to pay their bills. Divorce and/or losing a spouse may result in a sudden loss of relied-upon income and insurance, all too often leaving women (and men, too) with insufficient money to run the household or maintain housing and accustomed lifestyle. (A husband's salary is typically greater than that of his wife, who may have been counting on his already higher retirement benefit growing over the years and providing her with greater financial support. His death locks in a lower benefit than had he lived and worked longer.) Additionally, women tend to be the custodial parent in divorce and often assume more expenses than child support covers. It is not unheard of that mothers do not receive all the child support monies to which they are entitled. Younger women are more likely to be single and never married than in the past and may have a more difficult time acquiring wealth as generally they are paid lower wages and may lack a partner with whom they can share expenses and invest in real estate holdings, a stock portfolio, and/or savings, etc.

Caring for children, parents, and spouses means some women spend years out of the job market—nine years on average—and those years of zero income are factored into their benefit calculation, which means smaller retirement benefits for them. Women are also twice as likely to work part-time to accommodate family needs, usually in jobs with lower salaries and that don't offer income-generating retirement plans where they work. All of these factors, besides a continued and very real gender-based pay gap, leave most women with lower Social Security benefits, less money in savings, and in a more precarious financial situation than their male counterparts.

In December 2023, 50.1 million retired workers collected retirement benefits averaging $1,905 a month; 2.6 million of their dependents also received benefits, and 5.8 million people collected survivor benefits averaging $1,501 a month. In 2024, almost 68 million Americans will receive a monthly a Social Security benefit (retirement, survivor's, or disability).[27] Social Security payments benefit individuals and the national economy.

HOW IS MY RETIREMENT BENEFIT AMOUNT DETERMINED?

On average, Social Security pays retirement beneficiaries approximately 40 percent of their pre-retirement income.[28] Just how much depends upon a number of factors personal to you.

A PRIMER ON CREDITS OR QUARTERS OF COVERAGE

You must have a certain number of work credits (a.k.a., "quarters of coverage") to be eligible for Social Security retirement (and Social Security disability insurance, too). When you pay a certain amount of Social Security taxes, you earn "credits" or "quarters of coverage" towards Social Security benefits for that year. Earning sufficient credits makes one eligible for disability and retirement benefits.[29] The amount of money needed to earn a credit/quarter of coverage changes periodically. In 2024, you will need $1,730 in earned income to obtain one credit or quarter of coverage.[30] Unfortunately, there is no carry-over for excess earned income—you can only earn a maximum of four credits in a year, so when you pay FICA taxes impacts your eligibility. For most people, you need to have paid enough taxes to have earned forty quarters (over your lifetime) to be eligible for retirement benefits. [31]

TIMING IS EVERYTHING[32]—CAUTIONARY TALE NO. 1

You had three years of ridiculously high salaries and bonuses before the tech bubble burst, taking your job down with it. Fortunately, you had savings. You paid bills and lived off those earnings until they dried up in early 2024. With tech rebounding, you return to work to resuscitate your bank account. After earning $100,000 in 2024, you wrongly assume that you will have more than enough quarters to collect retirement benefits as you think you just earned fifty-seven quarters of coverage ($100,000.00 ÷ $1,730.00 = 57.80). Believing yourself to be eligible for retirement benefits, you decide to stop working at fifty-two so that you can travel the world. Fast forward ten years, you are ready to retire for good. You apply for early Social Security retirement benefits. You are shocked (and not in a good way) when the claims representative informs you that you are ineligible for Social Security retirement benefits because you don't have enough credits.

"What? How can that be?" you ask. "I have at least fifty-seven credits/quarters of earnings from my work in 2024 alone, and probably a lot more, since I earned a ton for three years before the tech bubble burst."

The claims representative explains that Social Security limits the number of credits you can earn each year to a maximum of four credits/quarters of coverage, which means that you earned only four credits/quarters in 2024, and not fifty-seven as you had assumed. You earned twelve more from your earlier three years working in tech. Because of the cap, you have only sixteen credits/quarters of earnings, falling far short of the forty credits needed to collect early retirement. What to do?

You can work to earn additional credits needed for future eligibility. In this example, you need twenty-four more credits or quarters to become eligible. You are not looking forward to more years of work, but are comforted to learn that you won't need to work full time. SSA averages your earnings over twelve months when determining your number of credits earned, which means you only *need* to earn an additional $6,920[33] each year for six years (plus any annual increases in the cost of a credit). Depending upon your salary or wage and your work schedule, you might need to work as little as one week (I wish!) or two months; or, as long as a year. You reconcile yourself to working part-time for the next six years before you can apply for individual Social Security retirement benefits.

BEWARE! NOT ALL INCOME COUNTS TOWARDS SOCIAL SECURITY RETIREMENT CREDITS—CAUTIONARY TALE NO. 2

It's important to make sure you're earning enough of the "right kind" of income in order to acquire more credits of coverage each year. For example, let's say you've quit your $50,000-per-year job at the bank so that you could day-trade from home. You're incredibly successful. In five years of day-trading, you made more money than you earned in ten years at the bank. You have been living off the interest and dividends and socking away lots of money in your bank account. You're proud of yourself, and you have a newfound sense of fiscal competence.

Fast forward ten years. After reading this book, you're curious and check your PIA to see how much it has grown since you left the bank. You are shocked to learn that your projected individual retirement benefit has not grown at all—not one penny! "How can that be?" you ask, confused and angry. The reason is simple. You cannot earn "credits" through investment income or capital gains; you can only earn them through FICA tax contributions paid upon your employment earnings, which is why your decade of day-trading did not earn you a single quarter of coverage for Social Security.

But wait, there's more bad news! By not paying payroll taxes for a minimum of thirty-five years, your retirement benefit has actually *shrunk*. This is because Social Security averages the highest annual you have earned over thirty-five years. If you have fewer than thirty-five years of credits, Social Security will fill in zeros for each year in which you did not earn enough for credits of coverage. The "zeros"[34] that Social Security added really dragged your PIA down.

What to do? You might consider getting a job that pays you wages, or try self-employment and report your earnings. You can do this while you continue or give up day-trading—your choice.

HOW MUCH WILL I GET?

Social Security calculates the amount of your retirement benefits based on your thirty-five highest years of indexed earnings; how many years you earned income; and whether you collect your retirement benefits early, at full retirement age, or afterwards. Your monthly retirement payment is called your primary insurance amount, or "PIA."

WHO ELSE MIGHT QUALIFY FOR BENEFITS ON YOUR RECORD WHEN YOU COLLECT SOCIAL SECURITY RETIREMENT?

Remember, other people may qualify for benefits on your record—your collection of retirement benefits (and, in some cases, your mere eligibility for them) may permit others to qualify for benefits on your record, including:

- Your spouse, provided they are sixty-two years old or more.
- Your spouse, at any age, providing that he or she is caring for a child of yours under the age of sixteen who is entitled to collect on your record *or* has a qualifying disability.
- Your surviving spouse, who is age fifty to sixty-two, provided they have a qualifying disability.
- Your surviving spouse, at age sixty-two or older, regardless of whether they are disabled.
- Your unmarried child, including adopted children or, in some cases, a stepchild or grandchild under the age of eighteen (or nineteen, if still in high school).
- Your unmarried child, who is eighteen or older, provided they met the SSA's definition of disability for adults before the age of twenty-two and have remained disabled.[35]

***Be Aware*:** If you voluntarily suspend your benefits, other people receiving benefits based on your record (i.e., children, spouse) will have their benefits suspended, too.

THE THREE TYPES OF SOCIAL SECURITY RETIREMENT BENEFITS (EARLY, FULL, AND DELAYED)

Deciding when to retire depends upon how hard it is to get out of bed in the morning . . . and many other factors! It is a very personal decision with major financial consequences.

There are three subcategories of Social Security retirement benefits: early, full, and delayed. Each option has distinct advantages and disadvantages, depending upon your situation. Before applying for any type of retirement benefits, talk to a lawyer or benefits expert first! (I believe I may have mentioned that already.) Social Security will not pay you the sum of your retirement and spousal benefits; you'll get a payment equal to the higher of the two benefits.

WHEN YOU RETIRE, MAKE SURE TO UNDERSTAND THE DEEMED FILING RULE BEFORE YOU APPLY FOR *ANY* SOCIAL SECURITY RETIREMENT BENEFIT.

A quick recap about the deemed filing rule: Under this rule, Social Security considers or "deems" you to be applying for individual retirement—as well as any spousal benefits to which you are entitled—when you first apply for retirement benefits. It will pay you a combination of benefits that equal the bigger benefit of the two at that time. Absent an exception, you are stuck with that benefit choice for the rest of your life.

Why is this important? Your choice could inadvertently prevent you from collecting a higher monthly benefit down the road. For example, let's assume that when you turn sixty-two, Social Security informs you that your early individual retirement benefit pays $2,000, while your spousal benefit pays $2,010. The SSA tells you that you will receive a $2,010 monthly benefit. You think you are getting spousal benefits because it matches the spousal benefit amount. You think, "great!" and plan to switch from early spousal retirement benefits to your individual retirement benefit once you turn sixty-seven, at your full retirement age.[36] You're aware of the special earnings test and know that it will apply to you because you are collecting benefits early off your spouse's earnings record. Even so, you assume that it makes sense for you to continue working because you have only thirty-three years of earnings on your individual record and you want to acquire two more years of earnings so that your individual retirement benefit (or PIA) is calculated based on thirty-five years of income, not thirty-three years. (You know that in order to collect the most in individual monthly retirement benefits, you need thirty-five years of earnings or else your benefit is dragged down by the years in which you had no earned income. Remember? We talked about this.)

Sounds like a good plan, right? *No!* It is not a good plan, thanks to the deemed filing rule. By electing to take early spousal retirement benefits, you ended up applying early for your individual retirement benefit at the same time under the deemed filing rule, which made you permanently ineligible to collect an unreduced benefit at full retirement age or a maximized benefit (delayed) after full retirement age. Ouch! Ironically, you decided to wait to retire because you wanted to maximize your monthly individual retirement check. This is a worthy goal; however, it requires a good understanding of Social Security's many rules and associated pitfalls.

WHO IS EXEMPT FROM THE DEEMING RULE?

Anyone receiving Survivor or Disability benefits.

ARE THERE OTHER EXCEPTIONS TO THE DEEMING RULE?

Yes. Learn them.

1. Restricted Application: Provided that your spouse is not yet collecting their individual retirement benefit, you can file a "restricted application" beginning at age sixty-two

and limit your application to only your own individual retirement benefit. Later, when your spouse files for their own retirement benefit, you can switch to spousal benefits. In order to use this strategy, you must *explicitly*[37] tell SSA that you are filing a "restricted application" when applying for your individual retirement benefits. Doing so lets you switch to higher paying spousal benefits once your spouse applies for their individual retirement benefits; *or*

2. You were born on or before January 2, 1954; *or*
3. You are caring for a child who is under sixteen or disabled; *or*
4. You are eligible for Social Security disability benefits.

ANOTHER SLICK STRATEGY: "FILE AND SUSPEND" – ONLY FOR THOSE BORN BEFORE JANUARY 2, 1954

This strategy allows Spouse A to claim benefits off Spouse B's earning record, even though Spouse B had stopped (or suspended) their individual retirement benefits. "File and Suspend" is just as it sounds—one spouse first files for their retirement benefits, then *immediately* suspends collecting them, thereby permitting their spouse to collect spousal benefits while the working spouse's PIA grows with each year of delayed collection.

WILL I HAVE TO PAY TAXES ON MY RETIREMENT BENEFITS?

Maybe. It all depends upon what other income you receive in any one year.[38]

Tip: If you are worried about being hit with a tax bill, you can ask Social Security to withhold money from your retirement checks. Simply file an IRS Form W-4v.

Now that you understand the basics, let's take a closer look at the three different categories of individual retirement benefits.

I. RETIREMENT BENEFITS BASED ON YOUR EARNINGS RECORD

A. EARLY RETIREMENT—COLLECT EARLY, BUT GET A SMALLER CHECK

Most Americans choose to collect retirement benefits before reaching their full retirement age. For every month in which you collect benefits before attaining your full retirement age, the SSA reduces your monthly retirement benefits by a small amount. The reduction is permanent unless you meet an exception to the rule. Otherwise, no take-backs, no do-overs.

Why Is My Early Retirement Benefit Less Than What I Would Get at Full Retirement Age?

When you retire, you will have paid a finite amount of money into your account. The Social Security Administration assumes that you will live to your statistical life expectancy and reduces your early retirement benefits accordingly, so that it will have enough money to pay you benefits over a longer period of time. Never mind that many of us will not live to standard life expectancies. Some of us will die young and pretty, while others may remain fabulous when they turn one hundred. When you choose to retire can greatly impact not only how much money you'll have, but also your quality of life.

How Does the Early Retirement Reduction Work?

If your full retirement age is sixty-seven and you begin collecting retirement benefits at age sixty-two, your monthly benefit will be only 70 percent of what it would have been if you had waited to full retirement age. For example, if your PIA is $2,000 at your full retirement age (sixty-seven years old), your early retirement benefits would be only $1,400 each month. Do the math. Over twenty to twenty-five years, that adds up to a significant chunk of change.

When Might It Make Sense to Collect Retirement Benefits Early?

It may make sense to collect your Social Security retirement benefits early in a number of situations, such as:

1. You need the money now. Maybe money has been tight, or maybe you support your parents. Collecting early may enable you to avoid debt and stay current on your mortgage.
2. You have children who would qualify for auxiliary benefits as the minor or disabled adult children of a retiree. You must apply for your own retirement first before seeking benefits for your children.
3. You have parents who depend upon you for at least 50 percent of their support, and who qualify for a dependent parent auxiliary benefit.
4. Your spouse is older and has earned much less than you. Their benefit may be small, and it might make sense for you to take early retirement so that your spouse can claim a larger spousal benefit based on your record. Even with

the benefit reduction for your taking early retirement, your household may come out ahead.

5. Your spouse has a short life expectancy and has earned much more than you. When your spouse dies, your survivor benefits would be more than your retirement benefits, so you might as well collect early retirement benefits on your own record during the months or years prior to your spouse's death.
6. You have a short life expectancy.
7. Your salary pushes you into a higher tax bracket.
8. You are ready to retire and plan on living overseas in a country where your Title II benefits will afford you a good standard of living, even when docked for early collection.
9. It's time to kick back. There may be people (or pets, if you're a misanthrope) with whom you wish to spend more time; or perhaps you may choose to go back to school, enter a monastery, take up surfing, or check a few items off the proverbial bucket list while you still can.
10. A unique and time-limited business, housing, educational, or social opportunity, etc., presents itself. You want to take advantage of it but cannot do so unless you can live off the income that early retirement benefits provide you.
11. You lose your job suddenly and are hard-pressed to find a new one. Seniors face greater workplace discrimination than younger workers and are more likely to have health problems that cause them to stop working. They often tend to the health needs of others—all of which may necessitate that you take your retirement benefits early. Several years ago, a nationwide survey revealed that one quarter of all respondents—*25 percent*— retired earlier than expected due to sudden job loss.

12. You've reconciled yourself to the fact that you are sixty-two or older, and if you continue to subject yourself to the nine-to-five grind, things might go south very fast. Seriously though, your mental and physical health should always be a consideration.

Special Earnings Test When You Work While Collecting Early Retirement

You can collect early retirement benefits and continue working, but know that your earnings may be reduced if you do so. Under the earnings test, you can only earn a certain amount of money annually before Social Security reduces your early retirement benefits under the retirement earnings test (a.k.a. "special earnings test"). The earnings test is applied on a monthly basis once you begin collecting early retirement benefits. Fortunately, the special earnings test does not apply once you reach your full retirement age (FRA).

What Earnings Do I Need to Report?

It is important to inform Social Security of all your earnings in any given year because if you do not, you may be slapped with an overpayment; you must tell Social Security about any bonuses, commissions, vacation pay, or other money that your employer gave you. For more information about what income must be considered when applying the special earnings test, see https://www.govexec.com/pay-benefits/2024/01/what-you-need-know-about-social-security- earnings-test/393399/.

If you are self-employed, it is more complicated to determine what is considered income under the retirement earnings test.

See https://ww.ssa.gov/benefits/retirement/planner/whileworking.html for more information.

How Much Will My Early Retirement Benefits Be Cut Under the Special Earnings Test?

Social Security will reduce your early retirement benefits whenever you earn more than the retirement earnings test exempt amount,[39] which is based on the national average wage index and recalculated annually. In 2024, the retirement earnings test exempt amount is $22,320 unless you are going attain full retirement age in 2024, in which case the annual exempt amount is calculated differently. In the year in which you reach full retirement age, there is a higher exempt amount which is prorated for the earnings that you accrued in the months before you reached full retirement age. In 2024, the higher exempt amount is $59,520.[40]

Not only will your benefits be reduced by 25 percent or more because you filed for early retirement benefits when you were first eligible at sixty-two; under the earnings test, you will also temporarily forfeit some or all of your Social Security benefits if you have too much earned income. Also keep in mind that your earned income may cause your benefits to be taxed and/or push you into a higher tax bracket.

Watch Out: If you earn too much, you risk forfeiting some or all of your early retirement benefits. *So what?*, you think. You are pulling down a handsome salary and will have enough to cover your expenses without relying on any Social Security benefits. Ah, yes, but it is precisely this high salary which could reduce your early retirement benefit to $0 and because you would no longer qualify for a retirement benefit due to your high salary, your beneficiaries would have their benefits interrupted. *So, before you commit to a job, consider the impact your wages could have on benefit payments to your spouse, dependent children or anyone else collecting auxiliary benefits based on your individual earnings record.*

The Earnings Test Reduces Benefits at Different Rates Depending Upon Your Age

- Before the year in which you hit full retirement age, the SSA will deduct one dollar in benefits for each two dollars you earn above the annual limit.
- In the year you reach your full retirement age—and up until the month you hit full retirement age—the SSA will deduct one dollar in benefits for every three dollars you earn over the annual limit up. There is a special rule for when you retire during the year in which you attain full retirement age and work afterwards in the year.[41]
- Once you hit full retirement age, you're home free and can earn as much as you like without it affecting your Social Security retirement benefits.

Important Fact: the SSA does not reduce each monthly check by a small amount when collecting the special earnings penalty. Rather, it recoups the amount to be paid off all at one time, once. - meaning that Social Security will withhold your entire retirement benefit check(s) until the penalty is paid off. This could result in several months of Social Security sending you absolutely no money, potentially wreaking havoc with mortgage payments, household bills, sanity, etc.[42]

B. FULL RETIREMENT BENEFITS— TAKEN AT FRA: WAIT AND COLLECT YOUR FULL PIA

Full retirement age is the age at which you can collect your retirement benefits without any penalty for early withdrawal. It varies based on birth year. If you were born in or after 1960, your full retirement age is sixty-seven.[43] Full retirement age is also the age when you become freed from the special earnings test.

What's My Full Retirement Age?

If you were born in:	Your full retirement age is:
1943–1954	66
1955	66 and 2 months
1956	66 and 4 months
1957	66 and 6 months
1958	66 and 8 months
1959	66 and 10 months
1960 and later	67

Special rule if you are born on the first day of the month: If you were born on January 1 of any year, or on the first day of any other month, the SSA calculates your full retirement age as if you were born in the previous month. For example, if you were born on January 1, 1956, you luck out and get to take early retirement as if you were born in 1955 at the age of sixty-six years and two months—a full two months earlier than everyone else born in 1956.[44] Happy birthday to you!

MEDICARE TIP: It's a good idea to sign up for Medicare starting three months before your sixty-fifth birthday—*regardless of whether or not you have retired*—because in some circumstances, if you wait longer than the seven-month "initial enrollment period," you will be hit with a permanent surcharge, resulting in higher premiums for Medicare medical insurance (Part B) and prescription drug coverage (Part D). You can enroll online by calling 800-772-1213, or by visiting your local SSA office.

Exception to Penalty for Delayed Medicare Enrollment: If you are still working at age sixty-five and have group health insurance through your or your spouse's job, you may be able to delay Medicare enrollment without penalty. Contact the SSA regarding your eligibility to delay.

Exceptions to Age Requirement of Sixty-Five Years Old: You can enroll in Medicare before age sixty-five if you meet at least one of these exceptions:

1. You suffer from permanent kidney failure treated with dialysis or a transplant (end-stage renal disease). (Social Security Act § 226A, 42 U.S.C. § 426-1; Id. § 1881, 42 U.S.C. § 1395rr)
2. You have ALS (amyotrophic lateral sclerosis). Id. § 226(h), 42 U.S.C. § 426(h)
3. You have received Social Security Disability Insurance (SSDI) benefits for at least twenty-four months. Id. § 226(b)(2)(A), 42. U.S.C. § 426(b)(2)(A)
4. C. D

C. DELAYED RETIREMENT—GROW YOUR PIA BY DELAYING RETIREMENT UP TO AGE SEVENTY

When Might It Make Sense to Delay Collecting Retirement Benefits?

It may make sense to delay collecting your Social Security retirement benefits in several situations, such as:

- You are not ready to retire, financially and/or emotionally.
- You come from a long line of centenarians and expect to live a long life too.
- You want to have a comfortable retirement lifestyle. By waiting to retire, the money you saved for retirement will be spread out over fewer years, giving you a higher monthly benefit than if you took your benefits at FRA.
- You won't be getting much of a pension and/or you haven't saved enough, which means that you will be relying primarily on Social Security benefits during retirement, and you want to maximize your benefit.
- You want to max out retirement contributions. If you are fortunate enough to have a 401(k) plan through your job, once you turn fifty, you can contribute extra money to it. Some companies match contributions too, so by retiring before seventy, you may be leaving money on the table.
- You want to leave larger spousal and survivor benefits for your family members.
- It's a bear market, and your investments are not paying the interest and dividends you counted on to supplement your Social Security retirement pay. Time to shore up your bank account!

- You are too young to qualify for Medicare (i.e. under sixty-five years old), have costly health problems, and must rely upon your employer sponsored insurance coverage. Or, possibly, your spouse or child needs it.
- You grew close to the people at work and do not want to lose that camaraderie.
- If have a job you enjoy, are able to keep working, and can afford to delay collecting your Social Security retirement benefits until after your full retirement age, you will not have to contend with the earnings test (as you would have had to do if you had retired early).
- If your later years of earnings turns out to be among your highest thirty-five years, Social Security will automatically recalculate your benefit amount and pay you any increase due. You can get additional estimates based on what you think your future earnings will be with the Security Retirement Calculator at myaccount.ssa.gov.
- It can improve your health and longevity—or so some say.

To get an overall perspective, read Social Security's fact sheet on retirement planning at https:// www.ssa.gov/myaccount/assets/ materials/workers-61-69.pdf.

Remember: Be sure to sign up for Medicare three months before you turn sixty-five, regardless of whether or not you delay retirement benefits.

How Much Will My Benefits Increase If I Delay Collecting My Retirement?

The SSA's website provides a handy chart setting forth the different percentages of increase based on one's birth year.[45] For most individuals, i.e. those born in 1943 or later, the monthly rate of increase is two thirds of 1 percent (0.066%).

Note: Delayed Retirement Credits Do Not Post to Your Account Immediately. So what? You know you'll eventually receive all the individual retirement benefits due you. The problem, however, is that if you retire before age seventy, you may have to wait until the following January for the SSA to post any delayed retirement credits from the year in which you retired. It's best to check with the SSA about this when planning your budget so you don't count on receiving funds prematurely.

II. RETIREMENT BENEFITS BASED ON SOMEONE ELSE'S EARNINGS RECORD

There are two types of benefits one can collect based on a spouse's or former spouse's earnings record primarily—spousal benefits, and survivor's benefits.

A. SPOUSAL RETIREMENT BENEFITS

Generally speaking, if you are sixty-two years old and your current or former spouse is receiving retirement or disability benefits, then you are eligible for spousal retirement benefits. At full retirement age, your spousal retirement benefit will be one-half of your spouse's PIA (as calculated at their full retirement age), regardless of whether your spouse claimed Social Security benefits before, at, or after their FRA.[46]

If you collect spousal retirement benefits early, i.e., before your full retirement age, your benefits will be reduced depending upon how many months you collected them before attaining full retirement age. Remember: this is a *permanent* reduction! When applying for benefits, remember the dreaded deemed filing rule . . . and keep in mind that spousal benefits are subject to the family maximum rule. Or you could talk with a professional.

Tip: You are married and things have gotten tight moneywise. It is painfully clear that one of you needs to collect retirement benefits early in order to continue to meet expenses. In this scenario, it is smart for the lower-earning spouse to collect their retirement benefits first, while the higher-earning spouse continues to work and lets their retirement benefit grow. Once the higher-earning spouse claims their retirement benefits, the lower-earning spouse could apply for spousal benefits on their higher-earning partner's record (assuming that their spousal benefit is more than their individual retirement benefit would be).

Or, you could just talk to a benefits specialist. Just sayin'.

Eligibility Criteria for Spousal Benefits

You should qualify for spousal benefits, provided that:

1. Your spouse is already receiving retirement benefits; *and*
2. You and your spouse have been married at least twelve months; *and*
3. You are at least sixty-two years old.[47]

Exceptions to the Age Requirement

1. You are caring for your child, who is not yet sixteen years old. Once your child turns sixteen, you are no longer eligible for benefits and must wait until you turn sixty-two for your benefits to resume or you are eligible for retirement benefits on another basis; *or,*

2. You are caring for your disabled child, regardless of the child's age. The child must meet the SSA's definition of disability.

Who Else Is Eligible for Benefits When You Receive Spousal Benefits?

Unmarried minor, and dependent children are eligible to receive one half of their retired parent's full retirement amount subject to the family maximum limit. The children's benefits usually stop when they turn eighteen, with the following exception:

Exception to Child Benefit Cessation at Age Eighteen

If the unmarried and dependent children are still attending high school, benefits continue until they graduate or up until two months after they turn age nineteen, whichever comes first.[48]

Remember: If Your Spouse Is Not Receiving Individual Retirement Benefits, You Cannot Apply for Spousal Benefits.

Exception: If you are an independently-entitled divorced spouse, you may collect spousal benefits whether or not your spouse is collecting their retirement benefits.

B. D-I-V-O-R-C-E: WHEN YOU'RE NO LONGER WED TO THE ONE YOU [MIGHT HAVE] LOVED A LONG TIME AGO

Few people enter into marriage expecting it to fail—except my friend Lola, who refers to current crushes as "potential former husbands." The divorce rate in the US is dropping, thanks to security-minded Millennials getting hitched later in life (assumedly with greater wisdom than those younger).[49] Even so, there is at least a 42 percent chance that any marriage will end in divorce.[50] (It's intimidating for the newly engaged to ponder, but someone files for divorce every thirteen seconds.)

Currently, the average first marriage lasts approximately eight years. This is important to remember because you cannot collect Social Security "divorced spousal benefits" unless your marriage lasted at least ten years. So, should you find yourself in a less-than-satisfactory marriage, when pondering, "should I stay, or should I go?" remember the duration requirement—you just might wish to delay your departure until after your tenth wedding anniversary so that you can qualify for benefits off your ex's record. On the scale of potentially awkward conversations, this is a solid ten, but still something worthy of consideration.

Collecting Retirement Benefits on a Living Ex-Spouse's Record

Provided that you were legitimately married, and then divorced, and can prove both of these facts, you may be eligible to collect retirement benefits as a divorced spouse.

Eligibility Criteria for Divorced Spousal Benefits

1. You were married to your ex-spouse at least ten years; *and*
2. You have been divorced from your ex-spouse at least two years; *and*
3. You are currently unmarried; *and*
4. You are sixty-two years or older; *and*
5. Your ex-spouse is eligible to collect individual retirement benefits or is already receiving them; *and*
6. Your individual retirement benefit is less than the benefit you would receive as a Divorced Spouse.

Note: Per the SSA, the law of the state in which you were married usually determines your marriage's validity. Your state may recognize deemed marriages (e.g., a marriage which would have been valid except for a legal impediment) and "common law marriages," so you may still be eligible for benefits even if you do not have a valid marriage license. [51]

Exceptions to the Requirement of Being Divorced Two Years

1. Your ex-spouse is receiving retirement benefits, or they filed and suspended their benefits before or on April 30, 2016; *or*
2. You claimed benefits on your ex's record while you were married; *and*
3. You are currently single; *and*
4. Both you and your ex are sixty-two or older.

So, should you find yourself in the throes of love again and tie the knot with someone new, but then find yourself out of love and (soon) out of the marriage, all is not lost. Remember, you can collect divorced spousal benefits off the record of your highest-earning ex-spouse once you are single for two years after your divorce from them (even if your ex has remarried).

How Much Would I Get as a Divorced Spouse?

If your ex is alive, and you are not married to somebody, your retirement benefit as a divorced spouse would equal one-half of what your ex's individual retirement benefit amount would be at their full retirement age, provided you waited until your own full retirement age before applying for divorced spousal benefits. Divorced spousal benefits are capped at your ex's FRA and thus will not take into account any delayed retirement credits your ex-spouse may receive.

What Happens if I Collect Spousal Benefits before My Full Retirement Age?

The amount of monthly spousal benefits you receive depends upon the age at which you choose to receive them. They would be reduced as follows:

- Age sixty-two—you will collect 32.5 percent of the amount your spouse would collect at their full retirement age
- Age sixty-three—about 35 percent
- Age sixty-four—about 37.5 percent
- Age sixty-five—about 41.7 percent
- Age sixty-six—about 45.8 percent

- Age sixty-seven—about 50 percent (the maximum benefit amount)

If you elect to collect divorced spousal benefits early, your benefits will be reduced based on the age at which you took them. [52]

Will My Spouse Be Involved?

No. Social Security will process your request without involving your ex. They won't even know.

Will My Ex Be Adversely Affected by My Collecting Benefits on His/Her Record?

Again, no. Your receiving divorced spousal benefits does not impact your ex in any way. They will collect the same amount of benefits off their own record regardless of whether or not you file a claim.

In the Divorce Decree, I Signed Away My Rights to Social Security Benefits on My Ex's Earnings Record. What now?

Most likely, the clause will not be enforced. However, consideration of these scenarios should be something that you and your divorce attorney will want to discuss before signing off on any decree.

What Happens if My Ex-Spouse Remarries?

Nothing. It does not change your eligibility as a divorced spouse.

What Happens if I Remarry? (Ever the Optimist!)

If you remarry, you will lose your divorced spousal benefits unless your later marriage ends (whether by death, divorce, or annulment). In twelve months, however, you will qualify for spousal benefits on your new spouse's earnings record.

What Happens if I Remarry, but then Divorce My Newer Spouse Before My First Ex Dies?

You have hit the reset button and can explore your eligibility for divorced spousal benefits off the earnings record of each ex, provided you meet Social Security's criteria.

What Happens if My Ex Dies? Can I Collect Surviving Divorced Spousal Benefits?

Good question. See below.

C. SURVIVOR RETIREMENT BENEFITS

Basic requirement: Should you die, your family members may be able to collect survivors benefits off your record *provided* you had earned sufficient quarters of coverage or credits while alive. Your age when you die determines the number of credits needed. The younger you are when you die, the fewer credits needed. Nobody needs more than forty credits, which is the typical number of credits required.

Special Exception to the Standard Forty-Credit Requirement for Survivor Benefits: Social Security can pay benefits to your children and your spouse caring for your children and your children themselves, even if you lack the standard forty quarters, *provided* you had earned six credits within the three years preceding your death.

Note: If you are receiving retirement or disability benefits at the time of your death, Social Security does not need to check the number of credits you earned while alive—it will pay your survivors based on your already receiving retirement or disability benefits. [53]

1. DEATH OF A CURRENT SPOUSE—SURVIVOR BENEFITS (WIDOW OR WIDOWER BENEFITS)

It is hard to imagine a more crushing psychic blow than the death of your spouse (other than the death of your child). In the midst of the ensuing emotional turmoil, the last thing you may feel like doing is engaging with the Social Security Administration, which is frustrating enough to do on a good day; yet it is one of the first things you need to do when your spouse dies, since Social Security Survivor benefits may be available to you and offer you a measure of financial relief.

FOUR THINGS TO DO RIGHT AWAY WHEN YOUR SPOUSE DIES

1. Ask if the funeral director has informed the SSA of your spouse's death. If they have not, contact the SSA, as soon as is practical, to stop payments to your spouse, or give your late spouse's Social Security number to the funeral director so they can make the report.
2. As soon as it is practical, contact the SSA to apply for two different benefits: a) a one-time death benefit, and b) monthly survivor benefits (see next section). The SSA will pay $255 as a one-time death benefit to you as

the surviving spouse, provided you were living with the deceased at the time of death. (In certain circumstances, you may still be eligible for this one-time payment even if you were living apart from your spouse.)

Re: One-Time Death Benefit: The application for this one-time death benefit must be filed within two years of your spouse's death. Contact the SSA for details. You can file for both these benefits by calling the SSA toll-free at 1-800-772-1213 to start the process. Please note that you can ask for a call-back during busy times, which is usually reliable, and beats being placed on hold for up to an hour and a half or more. If you decide against the call-back, make sure your phone is fully charged so you can browse online while you wait.

In the event that there is no surviving spouse, a child may qualify for this benefit provided they were eligible for benefits on their deceased parent's record during the month when their parent died. Other family members may be eligible, too.

3. Request ten to fifteen extra official/certified copies of the death certificate from the funeral home or mortuary. They will come in handy when applying for benefits, dealing with the bank and utilities, etc.
4. Sign up for direct deposit, if you have not already done so.

ELIGIBILITY CRITERIA FOR BENEFITS AS A SURVIVING SPOUSE

1. Your late spouse paid into Social Security and was fully insured; *and*

   Exception to the Fully Insured Requirement: Your late

spouse worked at least one and a half years during the three years preceding their death, and you are caring for you and your spouse,

2. You are at least sixty years old; *and*

   Exceptions to the Age Requirement: You are at least fifty years old, medically qualify for Social Security disability, and your disability started within seven years of your late spouse's death; *or*, regardless of your age, you take care of your late spouse's child who is not yet sixteen years old and receives survivor's benefits on your late spouse's record; *or*, you are caring for you and your spouse's disabled child, regardless of the child's age. The child must meet Social Security's definition of "disability."

3. You and your late spouse were married for more than nine months.

   Exceptions to the Nine Months of Marriage Requirement: If you weren't married for at least nine months, you could still collect survivor's benefits *if any of these situations apply to you:*

   a. You and your spouse have a child together; *or*
   b. Your spouse's death was an accident; *or*
   c. Your spouse dies in the line of active military duty; *or*
   d. You are not subject to the deeming rule.[54]

Most retirees are stuck with the choice they made when they first collected retirement benefits, thanks to the deemed filing rule. But if you are a widow, widower, or surviving divorced spouse, you are spared the deemed filing rule and can take advantage of the Restricted Application "bait-and-switch" strategy.

The Restricted "Bait-and-Switch" Strategy in action: If you receive survivor benefits already, you may also qualify for a more generous individual retirement benefit. Unlike recipients of ordinary spousal benefits, you can apply for one type of retirement benefit and then change your mind later if you are a widower, widow, or surviving divorced spouse. In this situation, you can choose to receive the survivor benefits first, and then switch to your own individual retirement benefit at age seventy or later. After all, why not let your retirement benefit grow to its max and then savor the 24 to 32 percent increase in your benefit amount thanks to delayed credits? This only makes sense if your surviving divorced spousal benefit is less than the amount of your individual retirement benefit.

In other words, there is no financial penalty for remarrying after turning sixty—you can still collect survivor benefits off the earnings record of your highest-earning deceased spouse, who was über-rich, even though you recently married your new true love, a kind circus performer with minimal earnings.

The rules are complicated, so consult with an expert before making your selection.

HOW MUCH WILL I COLLECT?

As with all Social Security retirement benefits, that depends on when and what type of benefit you collect! If you collect survivor's benefits before reaching your full retirement age, they will be reduced 0.396 percent for each full month you collect them prior to your FRA.[55] The advantage is that you collect the benefits over a longer period of time; but the disadvantage is that you receive a smaller payment each month. You can claim the survivor benefit when you want; there is no requirement that you take the survivor benefit immediately upon your spouse's death, so you can wait until the benefit reaches 100 percent at your full retirement age, if you want—and if you can swing it financially.

Per the SSA, in most typical survivor claims for benefits:

- A widow or widower, at full retirement age or older, generally gets 100 percent of the worker's basic benefit amount.
- A widow or widower, age sixty or older, but under full retirement age, gets 71 to 99 percent of the worker's basic benefit amount.
- A widow or widower, any age, with a child younger than age sixteen, gets 75 percent of the worker's benefit amount.
- A child gets 75 percent of the worker's benefit amount.

WHAT HAPPENS IF I'M ALREADY GETTING SPOUSAL BENEFITS AND MY WIFE OR HUSBAND DIES?

If you're already getting retirement benefits as a spouse based on your spouse's work, SSA should change your payments to survivor benefits when you report the death.

If you're getting benefits based on your own work, contact the SSA to see if you would receive more money as a widow or widower. SSA will pay you the higher paying benefit. Keep in mind that you must provide the SSA with your spouse's death certificate and complete an application to switch to survivor benefits.

Less than Ideal Circumstance: Working While Receiving Survivor Benefits When You Are Younger than Your full Retirement Age: Losing a partner and a possible second income stream is bad enough, but if you work while getting Social Security survivor benefits and are younger than full retirement age, Social Security will make things even harder by reducing your benefits under the earnings test. If your earnings exceed the earnings test's limits, your survivor benefits may be reduced or suspended. The cut in benefits is temporary, however, because once you reach your full retirement age, the earnings limit no longer applies to you.

Fortunately, the earnings test will reduce only your benefits, and not the benefits of other family members.[56]

WHO ELSE COULD COLLECT SURVIVOR BENEFITS WITHIN THE FAMILY UNIT?

Your unmarried children who are younger than age eighteen (or up to age nineteen, if they're attending elementary or secondary school full-time) are also eligible for survivor benefits. Under certain circumstances, Social Security also pays survivor benefits to stepchildren, grandchildren, step-grandchildren, and adopted children. Even your dependent parent may qualify for survivor benefits, provided they are at least sixty years old and receive at least half of their support from you.[57]

WHAT HAPPENS IF MY EX DIES? COLLECTING SURVIVING DIVORCED SPOUSAL BENEFITS?

As a surviving divorced spouse, you may qualify for retirement benefits based on the earnings record of your deceased ex-husband or ex-wife.

2. ELIGIBILITY CRITERIA FOR SURVIVOR BENEFITS AS A DIVORCED SPOUSE

The rules are the same for a surviving divorced spouse as they are for other survivors, i.e., you must be age sixty or older (fifty if disabled) and your marriage must have lasted at least ten years.

Exception: You do not have to meet the age or length-of-marriage requirements if you are taking care of your and your former spouse's natural or legally adopted child who is under age sixteen or disabled. Benefits paid to you as a surviving divorced spouse won't affect the benefit amounts for other survivors receiving benefits based on your deceased ex's record unless you are the surviving divorced mother or father caring for the worker's child.

WILL MY BENEFIT AMOUNT CHANGE?

Yes. Any divorced spousal benefits you were receiving will be doubled once you inform SSA of your ex's death so that it can convert your benefits to surviving divorced spousal benefits.

This is a brief introduction to the world of Social Security retirement benefits. Now, how to convert understanding into action . . .

A SIMPLE, NINETY-DAY PLAN TO MAXIMIZE BENEFITS, ENHANCE FINANCIAL SECURITY, AND GET YOU READY TO EFFICIENTLY DEAL WITH THE SSA

General Tips:

1. Talk to an attorney or benefits specialist first.

2. Make sure to document every contact with the Social Security Administration. Always have a pen and paper handy whenever you deal with the SSA. Keep track of with whom you spoke, the office(s) in which they work, the phone number(s) you called, the date(s) and time(s) you spoke with them, and what was discussed. If you go into the local office to conduct your business, *always* ask for a paper statement or receipt confirming your contact and a date-stamped copy of what was filed on your behalf.

3. When working with a spouse, make sure each of you pays sufficient FICA taxes on your respective efforts. All too often, wives work along with their husbands in a family enterprise, but they are not official employees and have not paid FICA taxes in their own name and, thus, are foreclosed from collecting Social Security benefits. What may seem like an economical decision at the time may be fraught with disappointment later on when you try to apply for your own individual retirement or disability benefits and are told that you do not qualify. Your husband is covered, but you are not, even though you put in forty-hour weeks just like he did. This becomes all the more painful if you should divorce before the marriage has lasted ten years. You get zilch (nothing), then and in the future.

4. For each of your spouses, keep a record of:
    a. Their SSN
    b. Date and place of birth
    c. Their parents' names

    d. Date and place where your marriage and divorce certificates were issued (better yet, keep a copy of each).

You will need this information in case SSA cannot locate your ex's record—trust me, such mistakes do happen.

5. Get extra "official" copies of needed paperwork. The SSA requires original documents or certified copies of birth and death certificates, marriage licenses, divorce decrees, etc., from the issuing entities. Photocopies won't work. It is best to request multiple copies of each required document so you can submit it and still have a copy at home, just in case someone—the SSA or you, or, more likely, the Feds—misplace it, or your dog eats it, or a flood carries it away, or it self-combusts. Stuff happens; be prepared.

THE NINETY-DAY PLAN

Here's what you can do within the next ninety days to ensure that Social Security is there for you when you need it.

- Check on your benefits. Are they what you expect?
- Check on benefits accruing for your children and your spouse(s), past and current. Are they what you expect?
- Determine what actions are necessary to protect or maximize your benefits, if that is your goal, and make a plan.
- Determine whether you might qualify for benefits on another person's work record. Research the facts in advance. Have marriage, divorce, and death documents ready, or obtain these if they are missing from your files.

Keep track of each spouse's Social Security number, the city or town where they were born, and their birthdates. (See below.)

HERE ARE THE STEPS NEEDED TO ACCOMPLISH YOUR GOALS

1. Set up a "My Social Security" account and check the accuracy of your earnings record. You can do this by visiting the Social Security website at socialsecurity.gov and creating a "My Social Security" account for yourself. By accessing your account, you can review the information Social Security has regarding your income over the years, get an estimate of future benefits, update your address, and manage your claim or benefits, etc. Alternatively, you can contact Social Security directly and request that Social Security send you a paper copy of your *detailed* earnings record. (Your detailed earnings record lists your annual earnings for each employer—you want this information.) Examine it carefully to make sure that the SSA has listed all of your jobs and earnings and has not made any errors or omissions. If you find earnings listed that are not yours, best to treat it as potential identity theft and alert Social Security right away. Verifying your earnings history will also clue you in to the negative effect of unemployment and/or part-time work upon your accrual of quarters.

   Now that you know how much you can expect to receive in monthly Social Security benefits, update your financial planning to reflect the percentage that Social Security would contribute to your household income once you retire . . . and plan accordingly.

2. Correct any errors on your earnings record quickly. If you find a mistake on your social security statement, the burden is on you to prove the error. You can use SSA's "Request for Correction of Earnings Record" form. Make sure to keep copies of whatever evidence and statements you submit—canceled checks, tax forms, and your explanation. If you are at your local Social Security office, ask them to date stamp your copies. If you are not dropping your Request for Correction of Earnings Record at your local Social Security office, consider sending your paperwork via the appropriate e-fax number, or send it as a certified letter with return receipt requested. (Actually, this is a good habit to use whenever you are writing to any governmental entity.)

3. Get your papers and necessary info together. It is always a good idea to keep original or notarized copies of the following documents on hand:
    - Your birth certificate.
    - Birth certificates for all your and your spouses' children (for whom you care).
    - All marriage and divorce decrees, both for you and, if married, your spouse. (You will need to prove the length of your marriage if seeking spousal benefits on your ex's record.)
    - Naturalization or citizenship certificates, or other documentation establishing legal residency.
    - Confirm the amount of your expected retirement benefit with the SSA.

Knowledge is power, and knowing what Social Security estimates your retirement benefits to be is essential info when planning for your future. For the most accurate estimate, go to your "My Social Security" account and use its Retirement Calculator, which gives personalized retirement benefits estimates based on your listed earnings. You can explore different scenarios with Social Security's Retirement Calculator, i.e., how much money you would receive if you retired at sixty-two, versus at full retirement age, versus at age seventy or somewhere in between. Very useful information.[58]

4. If you are married, have your spouse do the same—you will need to know their estimated retirement benefit amount (PIA) in order to determine who the higher earner is and develop a joint retirement strategy.

5. Don't forget to investigate your potential eligibility for retirement benefits based on each of your former or late spouse's records too! Call the SSA for an estimate of how much you would receive as a divorced spouse or survivor, based on your former spouse's earnings record. Be ready with their SSN; or, if you don't know it, their date and place of birth, and parents' names. You will need this info for each former or late spouse in question.

   Depending upon your age and marital status, you may even be eligible to claim benefits on your former spouse's record even if they haven't retired, provided you have been divorced from them for at least two years before applying for benefits.

6. If you are married, have your spouse investigate their eligibility for benefits off someone else's earnings record.

7. If you are part of a couple: Determine the best time for each of you to apply for retirement benefits.

   Generally speaking, couples can maximize their retirement income if the higher-earning spouse delays collecting retirement (so that the higher earner's benefits grow 8 percent for each year that they delay retirement from FRA up to age seventy). While the higher earner is "delaying" their collection of individual retirement benefits, the lower-earning spouse can collect retirement benefits on their own record whenever they want, starting at age sixty and afterwards. The lower-earning spouse cannot claim spousal benefits based on the higher earner's record until *after* the higher-earning spouse files for retirement benefits. Remember, the spousal benefit is half of the higher earner's retirement benefit amount if claimed at FRA (and not earlier).

8. Explore your eligibility for other Social Security benefits besides retirement.

   Disability—If you or your spouse are sick or injured and unable to work, check your eligibility for Social Security disability insurance (and state disability, too)!

   Social Security is intended to provide financial assistance to a worker and (possibly) other members of the worker's family when that person can no longer work. When a worker pays FICA taxes, they are also contributing to the Social Security disability insurance fund. In order to qualify for Social Security disability insurance, you must have sufficient quarters of coverage and be able to show that you have a medically-determinable physical or mental impairment which can be expected to result in death, or which has lasted or can be expected to last for at least twelve months in a row. [59]

Note: Many states have short-term disability programs that are funded through state payroll taxes. The states vary in whether or not they provide such protections and, if they do, what they specifically require to be eligible. In California, for example, state disability benefits "provides short-term benefits to eligible California workers who have a loss of wages when they are unable to work due to a non-work-related illness, injury, or pregnancy." Generally, those states who have short-term disability benefits for its citizens have eligibility criteria that are far more lenient than those of Social Security benefits. For some state disability benefits, you need only establish that a short-term disability prevents you from performing your usual occupation. For an example of a state's eligibility criteria for short term disability benefits, see California's requirements on State Disability Insurance, EMPLOYEE DEVELOPMENT DEPARTMENT @ https://edd.ca.gov/Disability.

TIP: If you cannot work due to a non-work-related illness or injury and are fortunate enough to live in a state that provides short-term disability benefits, you should apply for state disability benefits right away, even before you apply for Social Security disability benefits. State disability benefits are short term only and provide a useful economic cushion while you wait for your Social Security disability claim to be decided, which can take years. Generally speaking, the eligibility requirements for state disability programs are less stringent than those for Social Security disability benefits as state disability programs typically only require that you prove that illness or injury prevents you from performing your usual vocation whereas Social Security will not pay you if, despite your impairments, your disability does not prevents you from performing any single job, even if you have never done it, which exists in significant numbers within the national economy. This is a much more difficult standard to meet.

Also, state disability programs generally do not have durational requirements, whereas Social Security disability does—Social Security requires that your impairment(s) has lasted or can be expected to last for at least twelve continuous months or can be expected to result in death.

Tip: As there is no bar to applying for both state and federal disability benefits, you would be wise to apply for both as soon as possible, starting with state disability benefits.

DIFFERENT SOCIAL SECURITY PROGRAMS HAVE DIFFERENT APPLICATION PROCESSES

Certain Social Security programs, such as survivor benefits and disabled adult child benefits, still require that you apply in person at a local Social Security office. Other benefit programs such as retirement, disability, and Medicare allow you to file online at www.ssa.gov.

Call 1-800-772-1213 to start the filing process or to find out which office is nearest you (and confirm its address, direct telephone number, and e-fax number for future reference).

In sum, a little bit of investigation and strategizing now can really pay off.

MEDICARE

Having Medicare coverage can save you a lot of money and offer you expanded treatment options, so it's a good idea to sign up for Medicare starting three months before your sixty-fifth birthday, regardless of whether or not you have retired; in some circumstances, if you wait longer than the seven-month "initial enrollment period," you will be hit with a permanent surcharge, resulting in higher premiums for Medicare medical insurance (Part B) and prescription drug coverage (Part D). You can enroll online by calling 800-772-1213, or by visiting your local SSA office.

EXCEPTION TO PENALTY FOR DELAYING ENROLLMENT

If you are still working at sixty-five and have group health insurance through your or your spouse's job, you may be able to delay Medicare enrollment without penalty. Contact the SSA regarding your eligibility to delay.

EXCEPTIONS TO AGE REQUIREMENT OF SIXTY-FIVE YEARS OLD

You can enroll in Medicare before age sixty-five if you meet at least one of these exceptions:

1. You suffer from permanent kidney failure treated with dialysis or a transplant (end-stage renal disease); or
2. You have ALS (amyotrophic lateral sclerosis); or
3. You have received Social Security Disability Insurance (SSDI) benefits for at least twenty-four months.

Give yourself a pat on the back—you're done! Now you are ready to sit down an attorney or a benefits specialist to make a detailed plan your future.

MISCELLANEOUS TIPS: HAVE THE FOLLOWING INFORMATION READY WHEN FILING FOR YOUR SOCIAL SECURITY BENEFITS (IF POSSIBLE)

Information about You

- Your date, place of birth, and Social Security number;
- The name, Social Security number, and date of birth or age of your current spouse and any former spouse. You should also know the dates and places of marriage and dates of divorce or death (if appropriate);
- The names of any unmarried children under age eighteen; age eighteen to nineteen and in elementary or secondary school, or disabled before age twenty-two;
- Your bank or other financial institution's routing transit number and the account number;
- Your citizenship status;
- Whether you or anyone else has ever filed for Social Security benefits, Medicare or Supplemental Security Income on your behalf (if so, Social Security needs information on whose Social Security record you applied);
- Whether you have used any other Social Security number;
- If you are applying for retirement benefits, the month you want your benefits to begin; and
- If you are within three months of age sixty-five, whether you want to enroll in Medical Insurance (Part B of Medicare).

Information about Your Work

- The name and address of your employer(s) for this year and last year;
- The amount of money earned last year and this year. If you are filing for benefits in the months of September through December, you will also need to estimate next year's earnings;
- A copy of your Social Security Statement or a record of your earnings. If you do not have a statement, you can view your Social Security Statement online by creating an account online. If you do not have a record of your earnings or you are not sure if they are correct, Social Security claims it will help you review your earnings when you apply;
- The beginning and ending dates of any active US military service you had before 1968;
- Whether you became unable to work because of illnesses, injuries, or conditions at any time within the past fourteen months. If "Yes," be prepared to identify the date when you became unable to work;
- Whether you or your spouse have ever worked for the railroad industry;
- Whether you have earned Social Security credits under another country's Social Security system; and
- Whether you qualified for or expect to receive a pension or annuity based on your own employment with the Federal government of the United States or one of its states or local subdivisions.

Documents That Social Security Might Require When You Apply for Benefits

If you apply online, at the end of the application, Social Security will give you a list of documents that it needs, along with instructions on where to submit them.

Such documents might include:

- your original birth certificate or other proof of birth. If you do not have your original birth certificate, you may submit a copy of your birth certificate certified by the issuing agency;
- proof of US citizenship or lawful alien status;
- a copy of your US military service paper(s) (e.g., DD-214 - Certificate of Release or Discharge from Active Duty);
- a copy of your W-2 form(s) and/or your self-employment tax return for last year.

Important: Social Security accepts photocopies of W-2 forms, self-employment tax returns, or medical documents. Even though Social Security should return your documents, you may wish to make an appointment and bring them to the local office instead. Social Security requires original copies of most other documents. Do not mail foreign birth records or any documents from the Department of Homeland Security (DHS), formerly the Immigration and Naturalization Service (INS), especially those you are required to keep with you at all times. These documents are extremely difficult, time-consuming, and expensive to replace if lost, and some just can't be replaced. Instead, make an appointment and take the requested documents to your local Social Security office for verification so that you may leave with the documents in hand. Please remember to write down the Social

Security claim representative's name, the local office you visited, and the date and time you did so. Ask the claims representative to provide you written confirmation of your visit.

WHAT IF YOU DON'T HAVE ALL OF THE DOCUMENTS?

Go ahead—file and submit whatever you have. Do not wait until you have all the paperwork together. Waiting may cost you benefits down the line (unnecessarily). The sooner you apply, the longer your potential period of retroactive benefits. File as soon as you can, i.e., right after you submit your application for state disability benefits, otherwise you may lose potential benefits. If you are applying for Social Security disability insurance, file sooner versus later because it generally simplifies matters if you file before your "date last insured" expires.

The Social Security website states that Social Security may be able to assist you in getting needed documents, but I am skeptical given the agency's understaffing. Per SSA, if you need a copy of your birth certificate, your local Social Security office can help you contact the state Bureau of Vital Statistics in the state in which you were born and verify your information online (at no cost to you). You will need an appointment. If Social Security cannot verify the information it needs online, it "can still help you get the information you need." In my limited sample pool, that never happens, so don't wait for and count on it. Any time you delay in submitting an application could cost you benefits that would otherwise be due you.

WHAT SHOULD YOU DO IF SOMEONE USES YOUR SOCIAL SECURITY NUMBER?

First, alert Social Security right away.

Then, visit IdentityTheft.gov to report the theft and learn more about steps to take.

Next, notify the Internal Revenue Service (IRS) right away to prevent the thief from hijacking your tax refund (by filing a fake tax return and instructing the IRS to mail the refund to the thief's address instead of yours).

Having your identity stolen is disturbing enough, but to make matters worse, your Social Security Statement might show income from the thief's work, too. If so, it may look like you under-reported your income, putting you at risk of penalties for tax underpayment. If you have tax issues because of identity theft, go to www.irs.gov/uac/Identity-Protection or call 1-800-908-4490.

Last, but definitely not least: Report the theft to the three major credit reporting agencies—TransUnion, Equifax, and Experian—and ask each one to put a fraud alert on your credit report.

NOTES

CHAPTER 2

1 Tom Gray and Robert Scardamalia, "The Great California Exodus, A Closer Look," Manhattan Institute, September 25, 2012, https://media4.manhattan-institute.org/pdf/cr_71.pdf.

CHAPTER 3

1 Suparna Bhaskaran, "Pinklining: How Wall Street's Predatory Products Pillage Women's Wealth, Opportunities, and Futures,"A ACE Institute, https://d3n8a8pro7vhmx.cloudfront.net/acceinstitute/pages/100/attachments/original/1466121052/acce_pinklining_VIEW.pdf?1466121052.

CHAPTER 4

1 Board of Governors of the Federal Reserve System, "Compare Wealth Components across Groups," Federal Reserve, accessed May 10, 2024, https://www.federalreserve.gov/releases/z1/dataviz/dfa/compare/chart/.

2 National Association of Realtors, "2023 Profile of Home Buyers and Sellers," NAR, October 2023, https://cdn.nar.realtor/sites/default/files/documents/2023-profile-of-home-buyers-and-sellers-highlights-11-13-2023.pdf.

CHAPTER 7

1 Jessica Nutik Zitter, "First, Sex Ed. Then Death Ed," *The New York Times*, February 18, 2017, https://www.nytimes.com/2017/02/18/opinion/sunday/first-sex-ed-then-death-ed.html.

CHAPTER 8

1 Marvin v. Marvin, 18 Cal. 3d 665,666 (1976).

2 See: In re the Marriage of Denise and Thomas Rossi 90 Cal. App 4th, 35 (2001).

3 Olivia Mellan and Karina Piskaldo, "Men, Women, and Money," Psychology Today, updated June 9, 2016, https://www.psychologytoday.com/us/articles/199901/men-women-and-money.

4 Maggie Germany, "Domestic Violence Has a Financial Impact Too," *Forbes*, October 17, 2019, https://www.forbes.com/sites/maggiegermano/2019/10/17/domestic-violence-has-a-financial-impact-too/?sh=52d05e49d041.

5 California Department of Public Health, "Domestic Violence / Intimate Partner Violence," CA.gov, accessed May 26, 2024, https://www.cdph.ca.gov/Programs/CCDPHP/DCDIC/SACB/Pages/DomesticViolenceIntimatePartnerViolence.aspx.

6 Arizona Coalition to End Sexual and Domestic Violence, "Domestic Violence," acesdv.org, accessed May 26, 2024, https://acesdv.org/domestic-violence/.

7 The Center for Family Justice, "Identifying Abuse: Domestic Violence," CenterforFamilyJustice.org, accessed May 26, 2024, https://centerforfamilyjustice.org/signsofabuse/domestic/.

8 Janet K. Wilson, "Cycle of Violence," *The Encyclopedia of Women and Crime*, August 23, 2019, doi: 10.1002/9781118929803.ewac0083.

CHAPTER 9

1 Whether you choose to consult a certified financial planner, financial advisor, or lawyer, make sure to ask up front whether they have the knowledge *and* experience to advise you properly on Social Security retirement matters (as some do not).

2 In its defense, the Social Security Administration is overextended and underfunded, which has resulted in significant processing delays. Social Security assisted nearly forty million people in 1990. By 2023, that number had grown to over sixty-seven million. Congressional funding has not kept pace with the significantly increased demand for the agency's services.

3 In certain situations, such as when you did not work because you were disabled, Social Security will not count those years of no earnings against you when computing your AIME, potentially increasing your monthly benefit amount. (See https://www.ssa.gov/OP_Home/cfr20/404/404-0211.html.) Make sure that Social Security is properly taking into account years when you were disabled or caring for a child. Also, depending upon your spouse's age when they died and other factors, your AIME as a surviving spouse may be calculated differently; Social Security will pay the higher amount. Call SSA at 1-800-772-1213.

4 Social Security, "Social Security Benefit Amounts," Social Security

Administration, accessed May 26, 2024, https://www.ssa.gov/oact/cola/Benefits.html.

5 *See* https://www.ssa.gov/OP_Home/handbook/handbook.03/handbook-0325.html for more information.

6 Your eligibility for Child-In-Care Spousal Benefits is based on a number of factors, including the age of the child and the extent of services you provide and control that you exercise over them. *See* https://secure.ssa.gov/poms.nsf/lnx/0301310001.

7 Social Security, "Online Social Security Handbook," Social Security Administration, accessed May 26, 2024, https://www.ssa.gov/OP_Home/handbook/handbook.html.

8 Social Security, "Program Operations Manual System (POMS)," Social Security Administration, accessed May 26, 2024, http://policy.ssa.gov/poms.nsf/lnx/0301310001.

9 Social Security, "Program Operations Manual System (POMS)."

10 Social Security, "Filing Rules for Retirement and Spouses Benefits," Social Security Administration, accessed May 26, 2024, https://www.ssa.gov/benefits/retirement/planner/claiming.html.

11 Example: Your Spousal Benefit at age sixty-two is $400 a month, and your individual retirement benefit is $399. You go to your local Social Security office and apply for spousal benefits. You deliberately do not apply for your individual retirement benefit because you know that by deferring collection, it should grow to approximately $496 at age seventy. Spousal benefits, on the other hand, do not increase after full retirement age. On your seventieth birthday, you contact Social Security to apply for what you believe to be your now maximized individual retirement benefit. You are stunned when Social Security refuses to accept your application for individual retirement benefits – you are told that there is no application for you to submit because you had already applied for individual retirement benefits when you signed up for spousal benefits at age sixty-two. "Hold up," you say, "I've been deliberately waiting until I'm seventy before applying for my individual retirement benefit because I have always wanted to receive the maximum benefit amount. I would never have applied for individual retirement benefits back then because that would have sabotaged my long-term plan." The Social Security claims representative tells you that even though you may not have explicitly filed for your individual retirement benefits eight years earlier, Social Security required (deemed) you to have applied for both benefits. Social Security pays a combination of retirement and spousal benefits that together equal the higher benefit amount (individual or spousal retirement benefit) at the time that you first apply for retirement benefits. The sad upshot is that your individual retirement benefits will forever be capped at $399 because Social Security

considers you to have signed up for them when you filed your application for spousal benefits at early retirement age. You might not have taken your spousal benefits at that time if you had understood the deeming rule, especially if you expected to be earning significantly more money in your later years. (For more info, see https://www.ssa.gov/benefits/retirement/planner/claiming.html.)

12 Social Security, "Can I Withdraw My Social Security Retirement Claim and Reapply Later to Increase My Benefit Amount?," Social Security Administration, accessed May 26, 2024, https://faq.ssa.gov/en-us/Topic/article/KA-01993.

13 Social Security, "Delayed Retirement Credits," Social Security Administration, accessed May 26, 2024, https://www.ssa.gov/benefits/retirement/planner/delayret.html.

14 Social Security, "Is There a Limit to the Amount of Monthly Benefits My Family Can Get on My Record?", accessed June 3, 2024, https://faq.ssa.gov/en-US/Topic/article/KA-02107. Social Security, "Retirement Benefits," accessed June 3, 2024, https://www.ssa.gov/pubs/EN-05-10035.pdf.

15 *See* https://www.ssa.gov/oact/cola/familymax.html for more information.

16 Social Security, "Retirement Age Calculator," Social Security Administration, accessed May 26, 2024, https://www.ssa.gov/benefits/retirement/planner/ageincrease.html.

17 "Who's Eligible for Medicare?", U.S. Department of Health and Human Services, accessed June 3, 2024, https://www.hhs.gov/answers/medicare-and-medicaid/who-is-eligible-for-medicare/index.html. U.S. Department of Health and Human Services, "Original Medicare (Part A and B) Eligibility and Enrollment," U.S. Department of Health and Human Services, accessed June 3, 2024, https://www.hhs.gov/guidance/document/original-medicare-part-and-b-eligibility-and-enrollment-0.

18 *See* https://secure.ssa.gov/poms.nsf/lnx/0301310001; *see also* https://www.ssa.gov/benefits/retirement/planner/claiming.html.

19 *See* https://www.ssa.gov/OP_Home/handbook/handbook.04/handbook-0415.html; *see also* RS 00208.001 "Mother/Father Definitions and Requirements" at https://secure.ssa.gov/poms.nsf/lnx/0300208001.

20 Social Security, "Program Operations Manual System (POMS)."

21 *See* https://www.ssa.gov/oact/cola/piaformula.html.

22 *See* https://www.ssa.gov/oact/cola/QC.html.

23 Social Security, "Exempt Amounts under the Earnings Test," Social Security Administration, accessed May 26, 2024, https://www.ssa.gov/oact/cola/rtea.html.

24 Social Security Administration, "Do You Qualify for Social Security Spouse's Benefits?," Social Security Matters (blog), August 24, 2023, https://blog.ssa.gov/do-you-qualify-for-social-security-spouses-benefits/.

25 Social Security, "Survivors Benefits," Social Security Administration, accessed May 26, 2024, https://www.ssa.gov/benefits/survivors/.

26 Social Security, "Supplemental Social Security Income (SSI)," Social Security Administration, accessed May 26, 2024, https://www.ssa.gov/ssi.

27 Social Security, "Fact Sheet; Social Security," Social Security Administration, accessed May 26, 2024, https://www.ssa.gov/news/press/factsheets/basic-fact-alt.pdf.

28 Social Security, "Retirement Ready: Fact Sheet for Workers Ages 61–69," Social Security Administration, accessed May 26, 2024, https://www.ssa.gov/myaccount/assets/materials/workers-61-69.pdf.

29 Remember, SSI retirement benefits are available to individuals who have not accrued forty quarters or credits and meet SSI's financial eligibility criteria.

30 Social Security, "Social Security Increases—Cola and Wage-Indexed Amounts," Social Security Administration, accessed May 26, 2024, https://www.ssa.gov/oact/cola/.

31 Social Security, "Social Security Credits," Social Security Administration, accessed May 26, 2024, https://www.ssa.gov/benefits/retirement/planner/credits.html.

32 "They say, timing is everything. But then they say, there is never a perfect time for anything." —Anthony Liccione

33 The cost of a quarter varies by year.

34 This happens when you day-trade, live off rent receipts as a landlord, or otherwise generate passive income.

35 Social Security, "Retirement Benefits," Social Security Administration, accessed May 26, 2024, https://www.ssa.gov/pubs/EN-05-10035.pdf.

36 Alternatively, you could have waited until age seventy for a maximum monthly benefit of approximately $3,543. That's a lot of money in lost benefits left on the table over the next twenty-plus years. Rats! If only someone had told you to talk with a benefits specialist before applying, you might have chosen to wait and avoid this harsh result: https://www.fool.com/retirement/social-security/how-much-social-security-increase-after-62/#:.

37 Do yourself a favor and inform Social Security in writing that you are claiming only your individual retirement benefit. If nothing else, write "RESTRICTED APPLICATION" on top of your application or in the comments section that you are filing a restricted application for only the type of benefits that you have selected. If you are applying in person, bring two copies of a letter that says that you are restricting your application to only one kind of benefit and get one copy date-stamped for your records.

38 Read *Tax Guide for Seniors* (IRS Publication No. 554) and *Social Security and Equivalent Railroad Retirement Benefits* (IRS Publication No. 915) at www.irs.gov/publications, or call the Internal Revenue Service at 1-800-829-3676.

39 Try saying that ten times quickly!

40 Social Security, "Exempt Amounts."

41 See https:// www.ssa.gov/benefits/retirement/planner/rule.html for additional information on the rule and how it impacts self-employed workers performing substantial services during that year.

42 Social Security, "Social Security in Retirement," Social Security Administration, accessed May 26, 2024, https://www.ssa.gov/retirement.

43 Everyone is eligible to opt for Early Retirement benefits at age sixty-two—unlike full retirement benefits, for which one's birth year determines one's Full Retirement Age. See https://www.ssa.gov/benefits/retirement/planner/1960-delay.html for information on how much one's benefit increases with waiting to collect after full retirement age up until age seventy.

44 Social Security, "Program Operations Manual System (POMS)."

45 For more information, see: Delayed Retirement Credits, https:// www.ssa.gov/benefits/retirement/planner/delayret.html.

46 Dawn Bystry, "Do You Qualify for Social Security Spouse's Benefits?," Social Security Matters (blog), August 24, 2023, https://blog.ssa.gov/do-you-qualify-for-social-security-spouses-benefits/. See also https:// www.ssa.gov/oact/quickcalc/spouse.html for a benefit calculator.

47 Social Security, "Benefits for Your Family," Social Security Administration, accessed June 3, 2024, https://www.ssa.gov/benefits/retirement/planner/applying7.html. Social Security, "What Are the Marriage Requirements to Receive Social Security Spouse's Benefits?", accessed June 3, 2024, https://faq.ssa.gov/en-us/Topic/article/KA-01999#:~:text=What%20are%20the%20marriage%20requirements%20to%20receive%20Social%20Security%20spouse%27s%20benefits%3F&text=Generally%2C%20you%20must%20be%20married,year%20rule%20does%20not%20apply. For a quick calculation of spousal benefit amounts, use the calculator at https://www.ssa.gov/oact/quickcalc/spouse.html.

48 Social Security, "Benefits for Your Family," Social Security Administration, accessed May 26, 2024, https://www.ssa.gov/benefits/retirement/planner/applying7.html#.

49 Christy Bieber, "Revealing Divorce Statistics in 2024," Forbes, updated January 8, 2024, https://www.forbes.com/advisor/legal/divorce/divorce-statistics/.

50 Here are some other statistics about divorce in the US:

- Sixty-six percent of divorces are filed by women.
- Fifty percent of children in the US will have parents who divorce.
- Forty-one percent of first marriages end in divorce.
- Sixty percent of second marriages end in divorce.
- Seventy-three percent of third marriages end in divorce.

Divorce Lawyers for Men, "Divorce Statistics and Facts in the US," Divorce

Blog (blog), accessed May 26, 2024, https://www.divorcelawyersformen.com/blog/divorce-rate-us-2018.

51 Social Security, "Program Operations Manual System (POMS)," Social Security Administration, accessed June 3, 2024, https://secure.ssa.gov/poms.nsf/lnx/0200305055#:~:text=For%20entitlement%20to%20spouse's%2C%20divorced,valid%20except%20for%20a%20legal.

52 Social Security, "Delayed Retirement Credits," Social Security Administration, accessed May 26, 2024, https://www.ssa.gov/benefits/retirement/planner/delayret.html.

53 Social Security, "Social Security Credits," Social Security Administration, accessed May 26, 2024, https://www.ssa.gov/benefits/retirement/planner/credits.html.

54 Social Security, "Benefits," Social Security Administration, accessed May 26, 2024. See also https://www.ssa.gov/pubs/EN-05-10084.pdf.

55 Social Security, "Receiving Survivor Benefits Early," Social Security Administration, accessed May 26, 2024, https://www.ssa.gov/benefits/survivors/survivorchartred.html. See also https://secure.ssa.gov/poms.nsf/lnx/0302501021.

56 See https://secure.ssa.gov/poms.nsf/lnx/ 0302501021 and https://www.ssa.gov/pubs/EN-05-10084.pdf.

57 See https://www.ssa.gov/benefits/survivors/; https://www.ssa.gov/benefits/survivors/onyourown.html and https://www.ssa.gov/benefits/survivors/ifyou.html.

58 Social Security, "Plan for Retirement," Social Security Administration, accessed May 26, 2024, https://www.ssa.gov/prepare/plan-retirement?.

59 See 20 C.F.R. § 404.1505.

ABOUT THE AUTHORS

Ashley Card Dimas is a Bay Area native, and she has been a licensed mortgage advisor since 2005. Ashley has worked with hundreds of families to help them achieve their dream of homeownership. With her business degree, Ashley developed the skills to problem-solve and invent creative solutions to fit her clients' needs. Ashley has been a top mortgage producer since 2018 and has been in the top 1 percent of women mortgage originators in the United States.

Georgeana Roussos has represented Social Security claimants for over twenty-five years. Her practice focuses on representing underrepresented people in pursuing Social Security disability benefits. Her existential challenge has always been, and continues to be, navigating Social Security's entropic and overwhelmed bureaucracy.

Tamara Hull is a certified public accountant who loves helping people. She volunteers for many nonprofit organizations. She loves cars, racing cars, and rollercoasters.

Jennifer Cowan is an estate planning attorney with an office in San Rafael. She holds a master of laws in taxation and graduated with honors in 2008 with an emphasis in estate and gift taxation from Golden Gate University School of Law. Since opening her own practice in 2008, she has focused exclusively on trust and estate law, including estate planning, probate, and trust administration.

Joann Babiak is a member of the California State Bar and practices matrimonial law. She has earned numerous awards, recognition, and honors for community service and is involved as a member of the board of directors for several local organizations. When she is at leisure, she often hikes scenic trails near her home.

Kathleen Tedesco is a financial planner who works with people searching for solid footing to reach their financial goals. For people planning life transitions, Kathleen offers deep knowledge of retirement, divorce, and estate planning. She is affiliated with two national advisory firms. She entered the financial services industry more than nineteen years ago.

Kathryn Davis is president and CEO of Valley First Credit Union and has spent nearly thirty years working as a consumer advocate for affordable financial products, access to fair credit, and affordable housing. Ms. Davis holds a bachelor of arts degree from the University California of Riverside and a master of arts degree from Chapman University.

Letitia Hanke grew up in a small town in Lake County dreaming of a music career. In 2004, she started her own roofing company, ARS Roofing and Gutters. She was featured on two Emmy award-winning TV shows with Kelly Clarkson and Mike Rowe. Letitia also won the Most Influential Woman of the Year award by the *North Bay Business Journal*. In 2015, Letitia founded the LIME Foundation, a nonprofit that advocates for underserved youth through construction education, career pathways, and the arts.

Sandra Luna is a real estate agent and property investor in the San Francisco Bay Area. Sandra focuses on supporting the wealth goals of her clients and enjoys working with "budding" investors as well as established and savvy investors. In her free time, she enjoys spending time with her dogs and traveling to countries throughout Europe. She is a board member of Big Skills Tiny Homes and Meals of Marin.